Fundamentals of Tourism System

FUNDAMENTALS OF TOURISM SYSTEM

A.K. RAINA
R.C. LODHA

KANISHKA PUBLISHERS, DISTRIBUTORS
NEW DELHI-110 002

KANISHKA PUBLISHERS, DISTRIBUTORS
4697/5-21 A, Ansari Road, Daryaganj
New Delhi-110 002
Phones : 2327 0497, 2328 8285
Fax : 011-2328 8285
e-mail: kanishka_publishing@yahoo.co.in

First Published 2004

Second Edition 2008

ISBN 81-7391-652-7

PRINTED IN INDIA

Published by Madan Sachdeva for Kanishka Publishers, Distributors, 4697/5-21A, Ansari Road, Daryaganj, New Delhi-110 002; Typeset by Sunshine Graphics, Delhi, and Printed at Chaudhary Offset Process, Delhi.

PREFACE

Rajasthan is known for the past glory of Rajwadas (Kingdoms) which came into existence on 1st November, 1956 after consolidation and integration of local kingdoms. Areawise it is a single largest state of the country spread over 3.42 lakh sq. kms. Area of Rajasthan state is more than double of England and almost equal to Japan. Rajasthan is divided into 32 districts, 92 sub-districts, 228 tehsils. The people of Rajasthan are perhaps the most colourful in land of colour—their history, religion, music, dance, arts and crafts remain vibrantly alive and active—and presented in all their variety and ways. The landscape beauty of Rajasthan covers the expanse from forested and hilly area to pastoral and flat plain land, to shifting sand dunes, making it a tourist paradise.

Economy of this state is based on agricultural and mineral production. The total cultivable area in 275 lakh hectare and irrigated is only 20 per cent, *i.e.*, 54 lakh hectare. The principal crops are jowar, bajra, maize, wheat, grains, oil seeds, cotton and sugarcane etc. As for the industrial scenario, the state has been a land of Marwaris, the business community of Rajasthan, has had an industrial enterprise exhibited by the dwellers since times immemorial. The Birlas, Goenkas, Dalmias, Ruias, Poddars and Singhanias amongst other are the sons of the great Rajput land who advanced, diversified, and got into core sectors. Today, these very names figure in the who's who of Indian industry and economy. Having produced such business giants, it is believable that the land has immense business opportunities lying only to be explored. Rajasthan has vast potential for investment mainly in its six trust sectors, *i.e.*:

- Minerals
- Handicrafts and handloom

- Tourism
- Gems and jewellery
- Agriculture
- Industrial infrastructure

Rajasthan is much in cultural royalty but average in industrial development that's why it is called underdeveloped state of India. In terms of economic development as indicated by the level of per capita income of new domestic product. The per captia income is approx. Rs. 11,045 as compared 14,682 one of the such state, *i.e.*, Punjab. Rajasthan is one of the few states of India that shows great contrast from one or another states of India. This disparity is noticeable in respect of climate, soil, mineral resources.

From industrial development side textiles, rugged woollen goods, sugar, cement, marbles, potteries, dyes, motor parts, guar gum industries are there. Two major PSU—Hindustan Zinc and Hindustan Copper Ltd.—units are located in the Rajasthan state. There are 2.10 lakh SSI units with capital investment of Rs. 2,000 crore, giving employment to 8 lakh people in the state.

Rajasthani handicrafts are world-famous, especially marble work, woollen carpets, embroidery, articles of leather, pottery and brass embroidery and tourism industry contribute a lot in the development of the state.

As already mentioned above, Rajasthan is underdeveloped, there is a scope to tap resources of income to overcome financial difficulties of the State and the field of tourism still has great scope to add in new dimensions of income and employment for the state. Since the state is rich in its inherited heritage, its culture and glory hence, the study of social and financial implications of tourism has been undertaken for exploring new avenues and new dimensions of income and employment through domestic and foreign tourists for the state.

Authors

Contents

LIST OF TABLES

ABBREVIATIONS

A.A.I.	Airport Authority of India
A.I.E.S.T.	International Association of Scientific Experts in Tourism
A.S.S.O.C.H.A.M.	The Associated Chamber of Commerce and Industry
A.T.O.	Air Taxi Operators
B.I.P.	Bureau of Industrial Promotion
B.E.P.	Break Even Point
C.A.A.	Civil Aviation Authority
C.A.P.A.	Commission of Asia and Pacific Area
D.G.C.A.	Directorate General of Civil Aviation
D.I.T.	Domestic International Tours
D.O.T.	Department of Tourism
E.C.A.F.E.	Economic Commission for Asia and Pacific
G.A.T.T.	General Agreement of Tariffs and Trade
G.D.P.	Gross Domestic Product
G.O.I.	Government of India
H.A.I.	Hotel Association of India
H.H.A.I.	Heritage Hotel Association of India
H.R.D.	Human Resource Development
I.A.	Indian Airlines
I.A.A.I.	International Airport Authority of India
I.A.T.O.	Indian Association of Tour Operators
I.H.A.	International Hotel Association
I.H.R.A.	Indian Hotel and Restaurant Association
I.I.T.M.	Indian Institute of Tourism Management
I.T.D.C.	Indian Tourism Development Corporation
M.O.T.	Ministry of Tourism
N.A.A.I.	National Airport Authority of India
N.T.D.C.	National Tourism Development Corporation
P.A.T.A.	Pacific Asia Travel Association
R.I.T.T.M.A.N.	Rajasthan Institute of Tourism and Travel Management

R.T.A.C.	Regional Tourist Advisory Committee
R.T.D.C.	Rajasthan Tourism Development Corporation
S.A.T.T.E.	South Asian Travel and Tourism Exchange
T.A.	Travel Agent
T.A.A.I.	Travel Agent Association of India
T.T.F.	Travel and Tourism Fair
W.A.T.A.	World Association of Travel Agents
W.T.O.	World Tourism Organisation

Chapter I

TOURISM AND INDIAN ECONOMY

Introduction

> "We must welcome these friendly visitors from abroad for economic reasons for tourism brings foreign exchange, but even more so because this leads to greater understanding and mutual appreciation. There is nothing that the world needs today than this mutual understanding."
>
> —Jawaharlal Nehru

India is a land, which we see in various forms and facts. Nature is manifested in this country, with beauty and serenity. We observe sand and snow, heavy rainfall, isles, mountains, hills, rivers, ponds, glaciers, orchards, stream, pastures and deserts. We see the burning summer and shivering winter. The glamour of harvest and flowering springs. This is verily a fine composition of nature that we see from the pilgrims of north Himalayas to the coastal areas, which is surrounded by Indian Ocean and Bay of Bengal in the eastern part of India and Arabian Sea of the West. All this catches the human psyche to under the vibrant force which is behind India, where statics and dynamics of Indian environment is congenial with regards to tours and travel.

India has grand tradition with a spiritual ethics, cultural heritage bearing its focal points on the arts, architectural folk, dress and handicrafts other social economic and socio-cultural combination. The diversity which we find in Indian environment is the point if negation but of integration and interaction. We have thus, the heritage tourism, which invites the men who long for understanding the wonder, *i.e.*, INDIA. The Maharajas, Nawabs and Emperors have put their best to change the natural phenomenon of India into human resources which keep the ways open for the tourists to see for themselves the craftsmanship in big palaces, havelis, dharamsalas, temples, mosques, cathedrals and pagodas. These all religious have flourished in India, thus, tourists in India sees the application of religious flavour in the Indian architecture.

The tourist who visits India is amazed to see the human resource involved in making the tourist industry on the world map. We have the best of infrastructure, magnificent tourist policy, publicity, organisations, communication system, air-links, roadways, and railways to meet the requirements of the tourist in reference to his budget. The geographical location of the destination area in relation to the tourist generating sports is very essential to examine through tourist traffic. Its safeguards are to be made by the destination area to combat seasonality of the demands.

At the local level, tourism is encourage due to its ability to generate employment, increase standard of living and provides linkage effects with other sectors of the economy. The tourist industry is said to be highly labour-intensive, which is integrated with, direct and indirect investment related problems. The volume of employment generation, the nature of skills required and the development of absorption of the local people in tourist activities vary with state tourism development. Tourism is therefore, for job orientation in competition with other sectors of economy with respect to utilisation of both land and labour.

Studies of physical impact,[1] which are reviewed, are loosely related to mountain region, pilgrimage, heritage, cultural, traditional, architectural and other human resources. Aravali Range, for example, exhibit how it is low in mass tourism and with destruction of vegetation and wildlife with alteration in the physical structure. As Aravali is the ancient range of mountains, in the world and forts have been constructed by the then princely states exposed the historical facts which cannot be overlooked from the historical point of view.

As a pre-requisite to understanding the socio-cultural impact of tourism, a sociological clarification of the term 'tourist' as well as the nature and extent of tourist host encounter is necessary. This section, therefore, suggests a re-examination of the conceptual definition of tourism.

The physical presence of tourists creates problems of a purely socio-psychological character also. Tourists, who normally come from higher productive centre impresses upon possessing material wealth and superiority. This gives rise to feelings of relative deprivation. The hosts tend to evaluate the lifestyle of the tourists and nurture aspirations for the material standards and values of the tourists. This complicated socio-psychological effect is called the 'demonstration effect'.

The relation between domestic and international tourism is not only a close one, but of the complementary nature. Except in the areas of food and accommodation, where domestic and foreign cultures may be different, domestic and international tourism are mutually interacted. Again the foreign tourist may like the local food and accommodation and as such, these items could supplement a tour package to the mutual benefit of domestic and international tourism.

Tourism like other economic activities, flourishes best when it fits into the content in general, economic policy and programmes designed to lead to the optimum growth of the economy of a country as a whole. Not only is general national planning essential for a developing country but a vibrant national programme for a tourist industry is necessary as well. Here, it is assumed that national objectives and policies on tourism are well defined in furtherance of which a national plan is envisaged.

Indian Economy and Tourism

Today, we are on the threshold of a new area. It is an era of tourism, an era, which includes the growth of leisure travel around the world is expected to swell the dramatic proportions, an era in which people of all classes in the countries will come to regard travel as a normal part of life. Almost every country in the world is either reaping benefits from or looking hopefully at the potential of tourism. In addition to the direct revenue earned by the supply of basic tourism needs, tourism expenditures percolate down through man levelled of the economy.

India has enjoyed unprecedented growth in tourism in the last decades. Foreign arrivals passing the million mark in 1985, is expected to reach in millions by 2005.[2]

With the setting of Ministry of Tourism in 1967, tourism industry has received the necessary impetus and foreign tourists have increased from mere 7 lakh in sixties to 50 lakh in nineties.

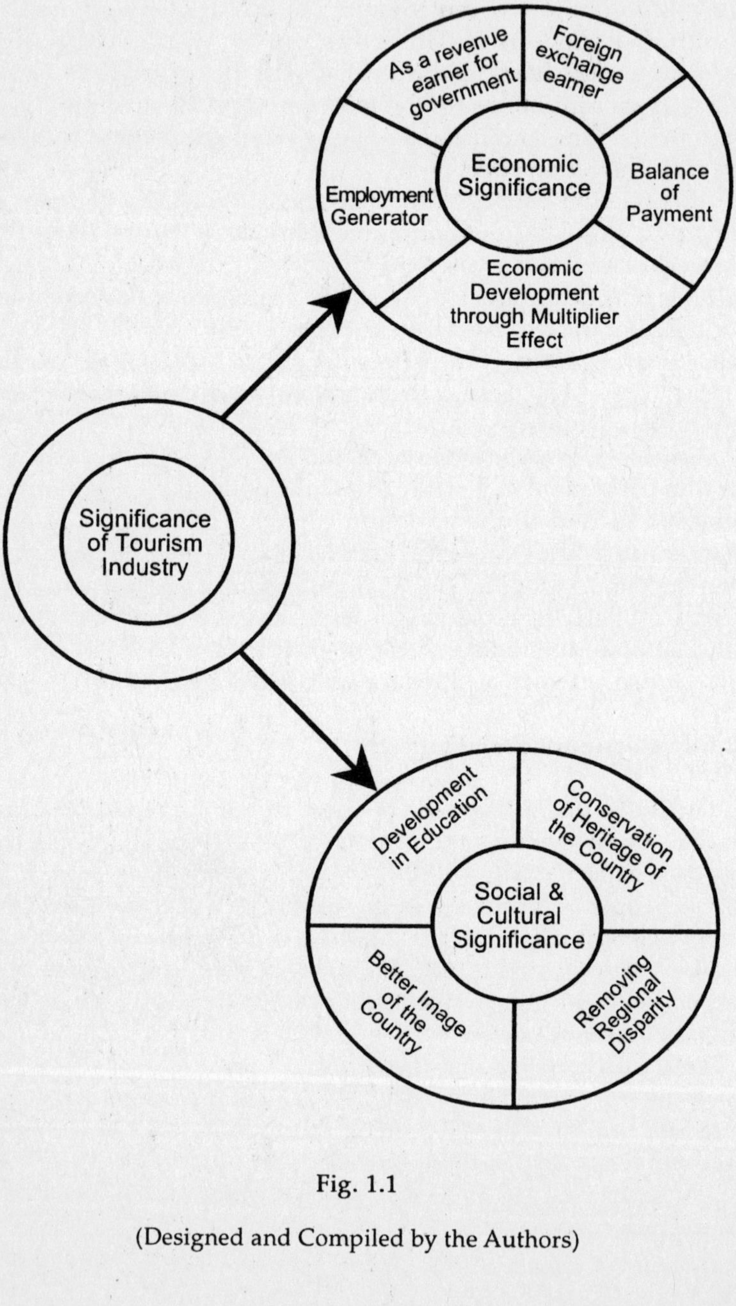

Fig. 1.1

(Designed and Compiled by the Authors)

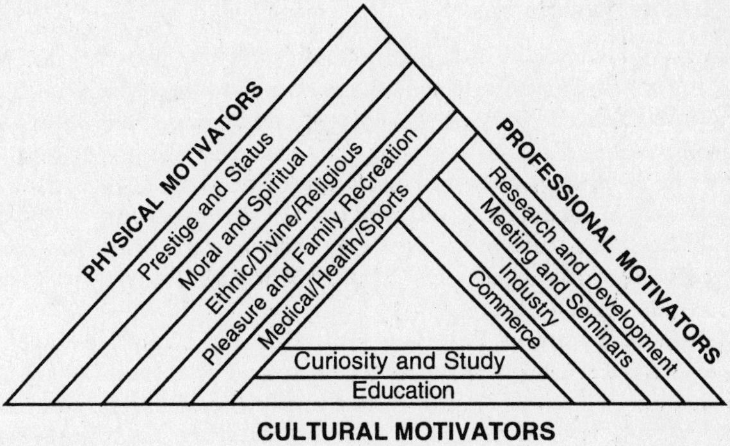

Fig. 1.2

Tourism Motivators
(Designed and Compiled by the Authors)

The increase in foreign tourist has boosted foreign exchange earning on an average from Rs. 11,726 million per annum a peak of Rs. 14,40,863 million per annum during 1999-2000. At present this tourist industry has emerged as a third highest foreign exchange earner industry as per following data:

Table 1.1: Foreign Exchange Earning from 1991-2002

(*Rs. in crores*)

1991	4,110.50	54.4
1992	5,886.95	43.2
1993	6,465.72	9.8
1994	7,281.66	12.6
1995	8,633.30	18.6
1996	9,819.96	14.9
1997	10,725.64	8.1
1998	11,950.78	11.4
1999	13,041.81	9.1
2000	14,408.63	10.5
2001	14,344.00	0.7
2002	14,195.96	–1.0

Source: Annual Report 2002-03, Ministry of Tourism, GOI.

Tourism Dimensions

Tourism, as we know, is a phenomenon of the modern times. From a simple travel of yester years, this phenomenon, today has become a very complex activity encompassing a wide range of relationship. Simply defined, tourism can be considered to be a movement of people away from their normal place of residence. According to Hermann V. Schullard,[3] "the sum total of the operators, mainly of an economic nature, which directly relates to the entry, stay and movements of foreigners inside and outside a certain country, city or region is called tourism."

Another famous Professor Hunziker and Krapf[4] stated that Tourism is the totality of the relationship and phenomenon arising from the travel and stay does not imply the establishment of a permanent residence and is not connected to a remunerated activity.

As per Dr. Zivadin Joviac,[5] it is a social movement with a view to rest, diversion and satisfaction of cultural needs.

As per McIntosh and Goldner,[6] Tourism is the sum of the phenomena and relationship arising from the interactions of tourists, business, host governments and host communities in the process of attracting and hosting these tourists and other visitors.

As per L.J. Lickorish,[7] Tourism embraces all movement of people outside their community for all purposes except migration or regular daily work. The most frequent reasons for this movement is for holidays but it will also include, for example attendance at conferences and movement on sporadic or infrequent business purpose.

As per W.T.O. recommendations,[8] Tourism comprise the activities of persons travelling to and staying in places outside their usual environment for not more than one consecutive year for leisure, business and other purposes.

Tourism is, therefore, a composite phenomenon, which embraces the incidence of a mobile population of travellers who are strangers to the places they visit. It is essentially a pleasure and recreational activity in which money earned in one's normal domicile is spent in the places visited.

Definition of a Tourist

Tourism is a product, which cannot be strictly defined under any of the accepted concepts of consumer or industrial marketing.

NEW DIMENSION OF

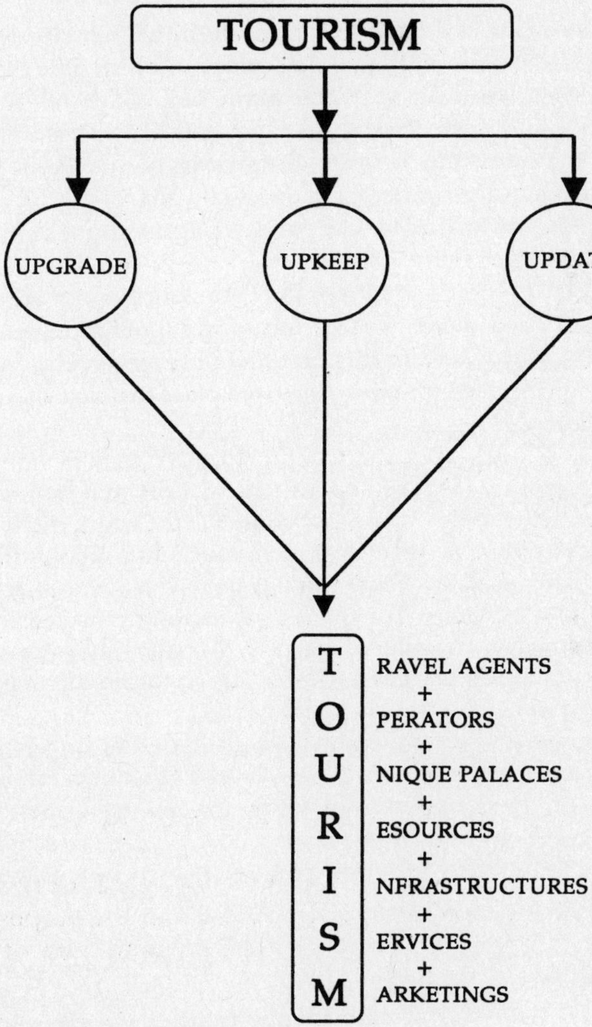

Fig. 1.3

(Designed and Compiled by the Authors)

It is the physical and the treat a physical combined together it is a package of ideas and even dreams of consumer product and of service.

Today tourism is a basic and most desirable human activity deserving the praise and encouragement of all people and all governments. The tourist is the main key character in this phenomenon and is also the basic components of its measurement. Although the tourism is very important part of our life in vedic person also. Our sages understood the great value of tourism, they made it a pious duty of all to visit various pilgrim centres situated in different parts of India.

The word 'Tourist' come from the Latin word "Tour", this is a derivation of Latin word "tornos" meaning a tool for descending a circle or turners wheel. In this first half of seventeenth century, the term was first used for travelling from place to place, a journey or an excursion.

The 19th Century Dictionary define "tourist" as a "person who travels for pleasure of travelling, out of curiosity and because he has nothing better to do". The term "tourist" the Oxford dictionary tells us; was used as early as in the year 1800. According to Dictionary Universal, the "tourist" is a person who makes a journey for the sake of curiosity. For the fun of travelling or just to tell others that he has travelled. The new Webster Encyclopaedic Dictionary of English Language (1972) defines tourist as "one who makes a tour, one who travels for pleasure".

"Any person visiting a country other than that in which he has his usual place of residence, for any reason other than following an occupation remunerated from within the country visited".

This definition covered:

1. Tourists, *i.e.,* temporary visitors staying at least twenty-four hours in the country visited and the purpose of whose journey can be classified under one of the following headings:
   (*a*) Leisure (recreation, holiday, health, study, religion and sport).
   (*b*) Business, family, missions, meeting.
2. Excursionists, *i.e.* temporary visitors staying less than twenty-four hours in the country visited (including travellers on cruises).

CHARACTERISTICS OF TOURISM

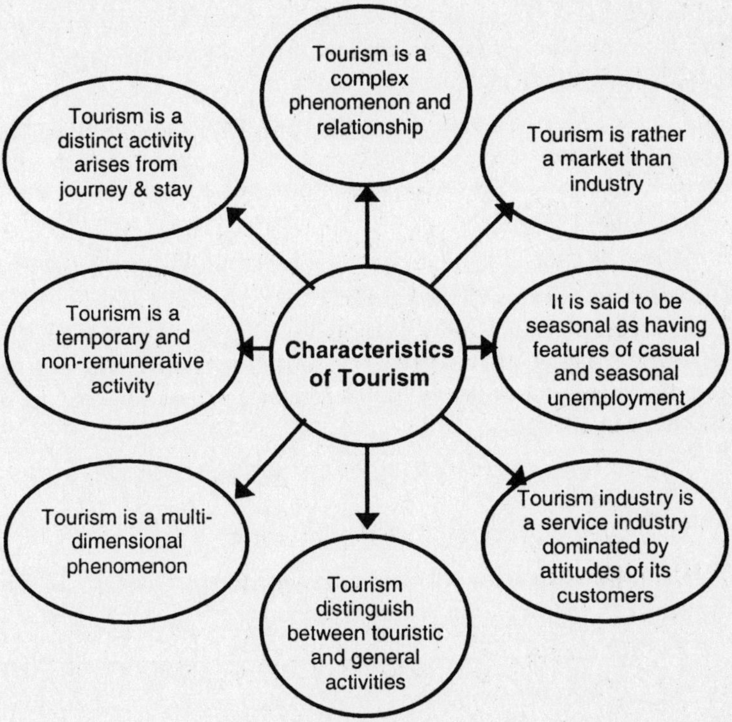

Fig. 1.4

(Designed and Compiled by the Authors)

This definition of the "tourist" does not include "travellers", who do not enter the country. It also excludes the day visitors or "excursionists from the category of the "tourist" as recommended by expert statistical group on International Travel Statistics Commission, 1967.

Lambert[9] has recorded the following three distinguishing characteristics of tourists:

1. He journeys of his free will.
2. He journeys primarily in search of enjoyment.
3. He returns finally to his original starting point.

According to Cooper C.P.,[10] "Tourism is the temporary short-term movement of people to destinations outside the places where they normally live". Ogilive[11] has laid down the following criterion, he maintains that a person is tourist when:

1. He spends his money in the place he visit without earning it there.
2. The person is away from home for a period of less than one year.

The Tourism Department of Government of India has adopted following definitions of the tourist.[12]

A foreign tourist is a person visiting India on a foreign passport, staying at least twenty-four hours in India and the purpose of whose journey can be classified under one of the following headings:

1. Leisure (recreation, holiday, health, study, religion and sport).
2. Business, family, mission, meeting.

The following categories are not regarded as Foreign Tourists:

1. Person arriving with or without a contract, to take up an occupation or engage in activities remunerated from within the country.
2. Persons coming to establish residence in the country.
3. Excursionists, *i.e.* temporary visitors staying less than twenty-four hours in the country (including travellers on cruises).

Statistics do not include the following:

1. Nationals of Pakistan and Bangladesh.
2. Nationals of Nepal entering India through land routes.
3. All foreigners entering India from Bhutan by land.

The broad spectrum of these definitions have laid greater emphasis on the "duration of stay" in defining a tourist while as motives of visiting a particular place have been relegated the secondary importance.

Concept of Tourism and Its Characteristics

Tourism means, activities of a person, who remains out of his general 'parivesh' place, at least for one year, for leisure-holiday, business or any other purpose.

Characteristics of Tourism

(*a*) Domestic tourism: involves such tourists/residents who travel within the borders of a known country.
(*b*) Internal tourism: involves such non-resident persons, who travel within the known country.
(*c*) External tourism: involves such residents/tourists who travel to another countries.

Basic Units of Tourism

Travellers involved in tourism are called tourists. Therefore, traveller word denotes the basic characteristic of tourism.

Traveller	
Excursionist	Other travellers
Tourist (stays after midnight)	Day long tourist

International Tourist

A person, who for a maximum period of 12 months travels, outside his native place and who is not involved in any profitable business activity during excursion of that particular country.

International tourists, include

Tourists (after midnight)	*Day long tourists*
Those tourists, who stay for one night in a private hotel or residence during their excursion in a country	Those tourists, who do not stay at any night in private hotel or residence during their excursion in a country. This definition includes travellers of Cruise, who return back to the cruise in night, though ships stay for several days in the port of that particular country. This group includes, those travellers, who are owners of the ships or residing in a train in-groups.

Domestic Tourist

Any person, for a maximum period of 12 months travels out of his native place on general conditions and who is not involved in any business activity.

Tourism as an Industry

Tourism is a multi-dimensional concept and implies many things to many people. For the tourist it is travel, relaxation, a holiday and an expose to other culture and traditions. Those who "sell" tourism naturally see things differently. To them it is an industry, a source of income, especially of foreign exchange.

Thus conceptually it is an amalgamation of phenomena and relationships arising from the movements of people "to" and their "stay" at the different destinations. The "journey" (a dynamic element) and "stay" (a static element) are the two necessary constituents of the mass phenomenon called tourism.

One of the earliest definitions of tourism as given in 1910 by Austrian economist Hermann, V. Schullard is "The sum total of operators, mainly of the movement of foreigners inside and outside a country, city or region". Lickorish and Kershaw,[13] considered travel industry as analogous to tourism and defined it as that part of national income, which caters for the traveller, who is visiting the place outside the locality, where he resides works.

The Swiss Professor Hunizkai[14] and Kraw, however, enunciated that tourism is an entirety of relations and facts constituted by travel and sojourn of person out of their normal place of domicile, as far as this sojourn and travel are not has been adopted by International Association of Scientific experts in tourism for international compatibility and the formation of domestic policies for the promotion of tourism. Tourism, thus, is a complex and composite phenomenon, which embraces the "incidence" of mobile population of travellers, who are strangers to the place they visit.

It is composed of heterogeneous units and has directly or indirectly widespread influence on almost every section and activity of the society. The tourism industry thus involves environmental, geographical, ecological, sociological and economic considerations with all the manifestations. However, its basic components are transport, locale and accommodation.

The transport dualism is a pronounced feature of nearly all the developing economies. Efficient and cheap transport coupled with comfortable and suitable accommodation, though are basic ingredients yet the locale with its attractions and amenities is most important constituents of tourism industry. The area of destination must offer the optimum combination of "attractions" to a tourist whose tastes vary very widely.

Details explain table of Peter's Inventory of Tourist attractions is given ahead.

Peter's Inventory of Tourist Attractions

Cultural	Sites and areas of archaeological interest, historical buildings and monuments, places of historical significance, museums, modern culture, political and educational institutions, religious institutions
Traditions	National festivals, arts and handicrafts, music, folklore, native life and customs
Scenic	National parks, wildlife, flora and fauna, beach resorts, mountain resorts
Entertainment	Participation and viewing sports, amusement and recreation parks, zoos and oceonariums, cinemas and theatres, night life, cuisine
Other attractions	Climate, health resorts or spas, unique attractions not available elsewhere

Source: International Tourism, 1969, pp. 148-49.

*Geographical Components of Tourism**

1. Accessibility and location
2. Space
3. Scenery
   - Landforms, e.g. mountains, canyons, coral reefs, cliffs, etc.
   - Water, e.g. rivers, lakes, waterfalls, geysers, glaciers, the sea.
   - Vegetation, e.g. forests, grasslands, moors, deserts, etc.
4. Climate, sunshine, clouds, temperature conditions, rain and snow.

* A Geography of Tourism, H. Robinson, 1979, p. 42.

PETER'S INVENTORY OF TOURIST ATTRACTIONS

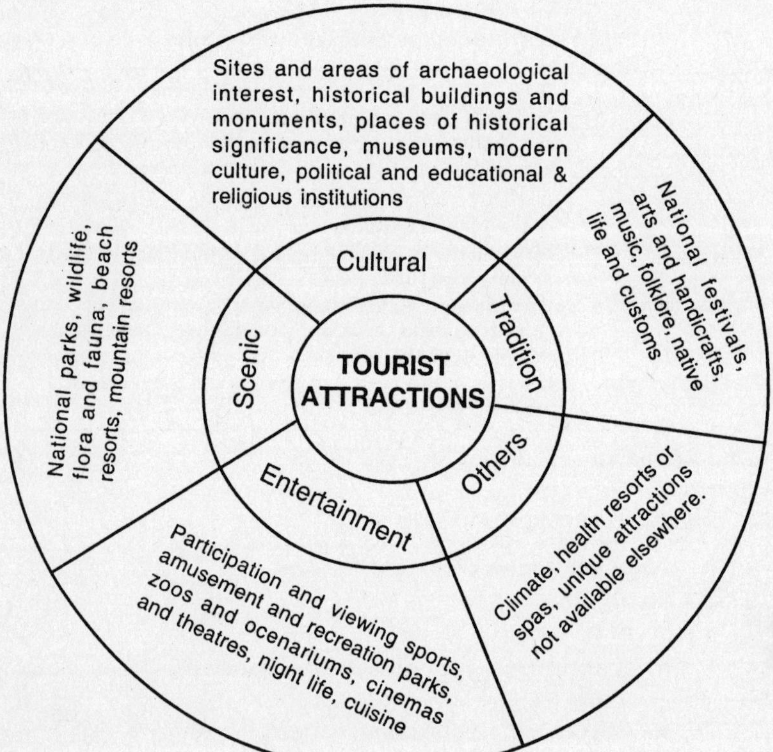

Fig. 1.5

Source: Peter Michael 'International Tourism'
(Designed and Compiled by the Authors)

MAJOR CLASSIFICATION OF TOURISTS

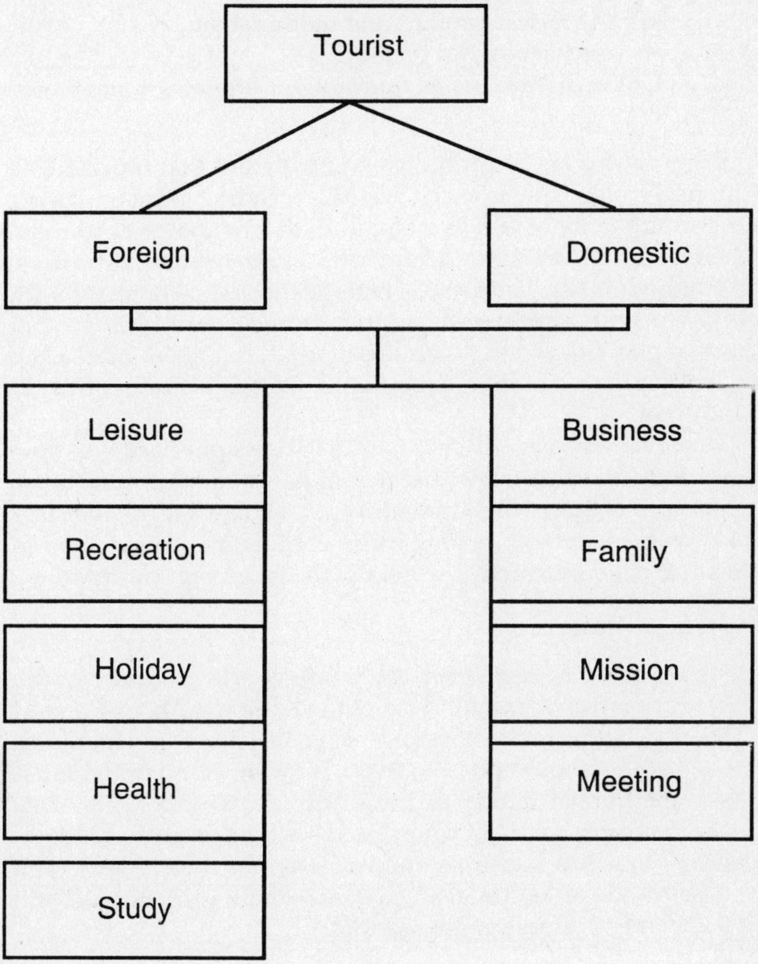

Fig. 1.6

(Designed and Compiled by the Authors)

5. Animal life
   - Wildlife, e.g. birds, game reservations, zoos
   - Hunting and fishing
6. Settlement features
   - Towns, cities, villager
   - Historical remains and monuments
   - Archaeological remains
7. Culture: Ways of life, traditions, folklore, arts and crafts, etc.

From the above illustrations, it is apparent that tourism is a multi-dimensional phenomena and all pervading industry, owing to the multiplicity of travel motivators the incidence or tourism industry is felt on related and unrelated human activities, accordingly tourism industry is heterogeneous in character with consistent and inconsistent aggregation of variables. In fact "tourism plant of region is composed of such a queer marketing mix that tourism is more often thought of a market rather than as an industry."

However, tourism, it needs hardly to be emphasised, has now been accepted as an industry because of its economic implications. And it is one of those "New Industries" that is capable of providing rapid economic growth in jobs, income, standard of living and in activating other productive sectors in the receiving country.

Tourism in India*

> "If we were to look over the whole world to find out the country most richly endowed with all the wealth, power and beauty that nature can bestow—in some parts a very paradise on earth—I should point to India. If I were asked under what sky the human mind has most fully developed some of its choicest gifts, has deeply pondered over the greatest problems of life and has found solution of some of them which well deserve the attention even of those who have studied Plato and Kant—I should point to India."
>
> **—Max Muller**

Where rest of the world is deprived of all seasons, India is the only land witnessing every season available to human kind. India

---

* Business Travel Directory, Jan.-Feb., 1985.

is a land of contrasts—from tropics to snows. It is vast, varied and strikingly beautiful. The second most populous and the seventh largest country in the world, India has the most ancient cultural heritage. More than six hundred and sixty million people diverse in many ways inhabit over 32,87,782 sq. kms. of the Indian soil. It has a land frontier of 15,200 kms. and a coastline of about 6,000 kms. The variety of its scenery, its intensive and equally varied agriculture, its extremely diversified industry, its big cities and thickly populated areas, its vast open countryside, its ports, its variety of languages and finally its manifold relations with other nations of the world all of these make India an exciting and fascinating destination.

Physically mainland comprises four well-defined regions viz., the great mountain zone, the extensive middle section of Indo-Gangetic plain together with the Brahmaputra valley of Assam, the desert region and the Southern Peninsula.[15] The Himalayas comprise three almost parallel ranges intersperse with large plateaus and valleys some of which like the Kashmir and Kullu are very fertile, extensive and extremely rich in scenic beauty. Some of the highest peaks on the world are found in these ranges.

The extensive middle section of Indo-Gangetic plain is about 2,400 kms. long and 240 to 320 kms. broad and is formed by the basin of three great river systems, the Indus, the Ganga and the Brahmaputra. These are one of the most densely populated areas on earth. The desert regions can be divided into two parts—the great desert and the little desert. The great desert extends from the edge of the Rann of Kutch to beyond the Luni river between Jaisalmer and Jodhpur in Rajasthan up to the northern wastes. Between the great and little deserts lies a zone of absolutely sterile country consisting of rocky land cut up by limestone ridges. Due to the scanty rainfall, this region is almost absolutely sterile.

The great Peninsular plateau is marked off from the Indo-Gangetic plain by a mass of mountain and hill ranges varying from 460 to 1,200 meters in height. Prominent among these are the Aravali, Vindhya, Satpura and Ajanta. The Peninsula is flanked on one side by the Eastern Ghats, where the average elevation is about 610 meters and on the other by the Western Ghats where it is generally from 915 to 1,220 meters rising in places to over 2,440 meters. Between the Western Ghats and the Arabian Sea lies a narrow coastal strip while between the Eastern Ghat and the Bay of Bengal there is a broader coastal area. The southern trip of the plateau is formed by the Nilgiri Hills where the Eastern and Western Ghats meet.

*Tourism in Ancient India**

India is a wonderland for the rest of the world from ancient period. Our country is a dreamland, a land full of mysteries, with the grand tour of this untouched nation, the majesty of its age-old monuments, colours, traditions and exodus. Many tourist from various parts of the world visited India time to time, to see this wonderland. St. Thomas, an apostle of Jesus Christ who came to the South India shore in the 1st century AD. Hieun T. Sang the devout Chinese Buddhist made the perilous journey to India around AD 633.

Before these two important pilgrims it was also recorded that during the era of Gupta's rule. The caravans of Persians visited India for commerce and trade.

There is also a mention of cultural exchanges between Persia and India deference has also been made to the influence of Persian customs in the court of Chandra Gupta Maurya.

Emperor Ashoka the Great, travelled a great deal in his eagerness to spread the doctrines of Buddha. Ashoka and his entourage first travelled to Nepal starting from Patliputra and then ventured to Lumhari gardens, the land of Buddha's birth and to Kapilvastu, the place where Buddha spent his childhood and other places *i.e.*, Sarnath, Gaya. Through his travels, Emperor Ashoka had special memorials set up in each spot and also rest homes where travellers could pause and refresh. Harsha was another Emperor who was greatly influenced by the Buddhist Scriptures. He built numerous monasteries, temples, Dharamsalas and rest houses for the pilgrims. At this time Religion played a crucial part in travel.

Some other travellers, whose names need special mention, are Alexander the great, Julius Caesar, Marcopolo, Benjamin of Tudela, Ibn Batutah, Francisco Friar, Alfanso D' Albuquer Gue and Mark Twain had visited India. Lateron in sixteenth and seventeenth centuries, many more European Monks, travellers and adventurers visited India in search of knowledge. The first great sailor to do westward circumnavigation of the world was Francis Drake who

---

* Ram Acharya, Tourism in India, 1977.

TOURISM IN INDIA FROM CLASS TO MASS

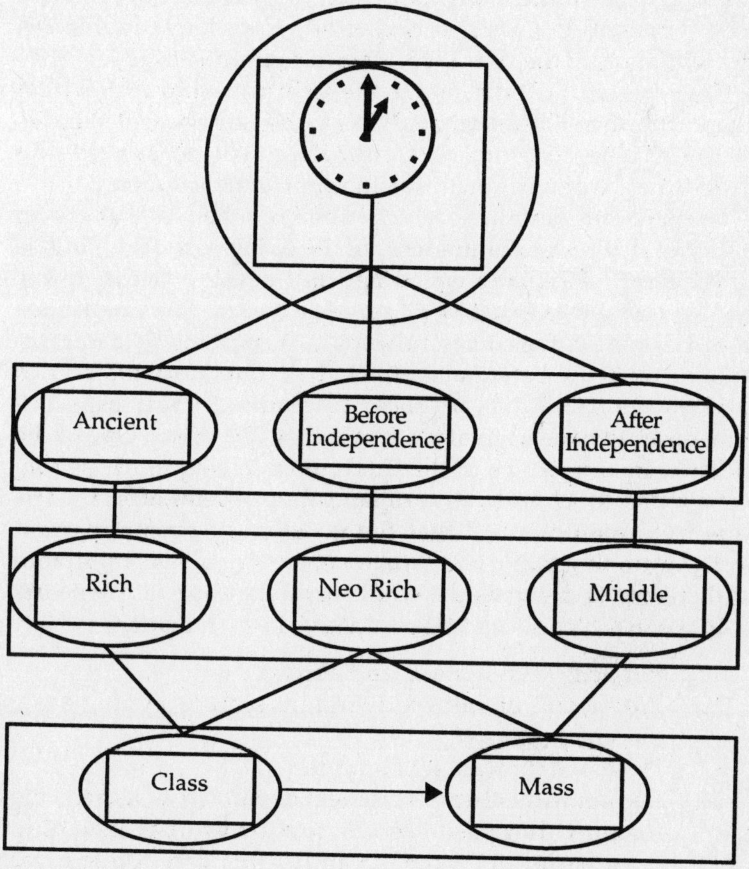

Fig. 1.7

(Designed and Compiled by the Authors)

was knighted by Queen Elizabeth I in the year 1581. From 1768 to 1779 Captain James Cook visited India through the long voyages.

Tourism before Independence

In India, the importance of tourism had been recognised even before the Second World War. The intervention of war, however, put a stop to the tourist promotion activities of the Government. The first conscious and organised efforts to promote tourism in India was made in the year 1945, when a committee was set up by the Government of India under the Chairmanship of Sir John Sargent,[16] the then Educational Adviser to the Government of India. The main objective of the Committee was to survey the potentialities of developing tourism traffic in the country.

The Sargent Committee, which submitted their interim report in October 1946, was unanimously of the opinion that it would be in the interest of India to encourage and develop tourist traffic both internal and external by all possible means. The Committee was of the opinion that successful steps in the promotion of tourism would result in a substantial addition, both direct and indirect, to India's revenue and that, if properly organised, every aspect of business could benefit greatly by an influx of tourists. One of the major recommendations of the Committee related to the setting up of a separate representative organisation of semi-officials. The committee recommended that the question of promoting and developing tourist traffic was a matter of great national importance and therefore, it deserves the whole time attention of a separate organisation which should take initiative in such matters as:

1. Publicity both in India and abroad.
2. Production of suitable literature such as guide-books, folders, posters etc.
3. Provision for training of guides.
4. Liaison with other government departments responsible for providing facilities required by tourists including information in regard to industries and commercial matters.
5. Liaison with the travel agencies which would necessarily remain responsible for the detailed arrangements of tourists.
6. Liaison with hotels and catering establishments.
7. Collection of tourist statistics.

Some of the major recommendations of the Committee were:

(*a*) Coordination with air and train services with a view to facilitate both air and train journey and to make it comfortable in India.

(*b*) Provision of chain of first class hotels of international standards for the convenience and comfort of foreign tourists.

(*c*) Starting of publicity bureaus in London and New York and in the capital of other countries from where substantial numbers of tourists might be forthcoming.

Tourism after Independence

Tourism in India developed properly only after a central tourist organisation was set up as a result of the recommendation of the Sargent Committee. It was only after the creation of a separate Tourist Traffic Branch in the year 1949 that whole-time attention was paid to the development of tourist traffic in India.

With the increase in its activities the Tourist Traffic Division expanded considerably and during the year 1955-56 the Headquarters establishment was increased from one branch to four branches, each having wide ranging duties. The four sections looking after various subject were viz., (1) Tourist Traffic Section, (2) Tourist Administration Section, (3) Tourist Publicity Section, and (4) Distribution Section.

Tourist Traffic Section was to look after a large number of travel trade subjects which included development of both internal and external tourist traffic, legislative matters, five year plans, travel agencies, hotels and rest houses, facilitation, tourist statistics and monthly reports. It also dealt with international conferences on tourism and references relating to UN and its agencies, coordination with railways, establishment of tourist bureaus in States and development of tourist centres and the training of guides.

Tourist Administration Section was to deal with administration work relating to tourist offices both in India and abroad, budget, delegation of financial powers to tourist offices, opening of new Tourist Offices in India and abroad and periodical inspection of tourist offices. Tourist Publicity Section was to deal with publication of the tourist literature such as pamphlets, guide-books and posters, issue of advertisements and participation in exhibitions and fairs. Distribution Section was to deal with the distribution of tourist publicity literature in India and abroad.

Within a short period of time there was many-fold increase in the activities of the Tourist Traffic Branch. The four branches as they developed during the years 1955-56 performed a variety of duties covering almost all the important segments of tourism. These branches were functioning under one Deputy Secretary and two Under Secretaries.

At this stage there was a proposal for the creation of a Directorate-General of Tourism. One reason advanced in favour of setting up a Directorate-General of Tourism was that the policy-making and executive functions were combined in the existing staff of the Tourist Division of the Secretariat and that these should be separated. However, this proposal did not find favour as it was felt that the subject of tourism had not developed to an extent as would justify an immediate of these two functions.

Role of Ministry of Tourism (Government of India)

It was on 1st March 1958 that a separate tourism department was created in the Ministry of Transport to deal with all matters concerning tourism. The new department was put under the charge of the Director-General who had under him one Deputy Director and four Directors each in-charge of Administration, Publicity, Travel Relations and Planning and Development.

By the Presidential order dated 14 March, 1967, the Department of Aviation and Tourism which was under the Ministry of Transport and Civil Aviation was formed into a separate Ministry designated as the Ministry of Tourism and Civil Aviation, with two constituent departments; (1) Department of Tourism and (2) Department of Civil Aviation. The Ministry was put under the charge of a full-time Minister.

The functions of the Union Ministry of Tourism and Civil Aviation in terms of specific responsibilities are:

1. Organisation of meteorological services.
2. Provision of aerodromes, regulation and organisation of air traffic, aerodromes, aircraft, and air navigation.
3. Provision for the safety of aircraft.
4. Carriage of passengers and goods by air.
5. Establishment of corporations under the Air Corporation Act, 1953.
6. Establishment of Railway Inspectorate.
7. Development and promotion of tourism.

8. Establishment of youth hostels.
9. Establishment of close contact with other ministries in respect of promotion of tourism.
10. Coordination of various activities through various committees of Parliament, and other associations.
11. Negotiations with international and bilateral agencies.
12. Planning and organisation of tourist activities throughout the country in collaboration with the State Governments and the Planning Commission.
13. Inquiries and statistics for the purpose of any of the matters specified in this list.
14. Implementation of treaties and agreements relating to any of the matters specified in this list.

Department of Tourism

The Department of Tourism has now became an attached non-participating office of the Ministry of Tourism and Civil Aviation headed by the Director General of Tourism. The Director General of Tourism carried an ex-officio status of an Additional Secretary to the Government of India. Although an attached office, the department is both a policy-making and an executive organisation and corresponds directly with the other ministries and departments of the Central Government and the State Governments. The Director-General is assisted by one Additional Director-General, one Joint Director-General, a Deputy Secretary and five Deputy Director-Generals.

The functions of the Department of Tourism are both promotional and organisational which are conducted by the following seven divisions: (1) Planning and Programming, (2) Publicity and Conference, (3) Travel Trade and Hospitality, (4) Accommodation, (5) Supplementary Accommodation and Wildlife, (6) Market Research, (7) Administration.

The activities of the Department have since increased many-fold and cover a wide range of subjects. The many-fold activities fall under the following broad heads:

1. Collection, compilation and dissemination of tourist information in India and abroad and attending enquiries from international tourists, tour operators and travel industry, such as airlines, steamship companies and hotels.

2. Cooperation with international travel and tourist organisations at government and non-government levels.
3. Development of tourist facilities of interest to international tourists.
4. Publicity at home and abroad with the object of creating an overall awareness of the importance of tourism.
5. Simplification of frontier formalities in respect of international tourists.
6. Regulation of activities of the various segments of the travel trade, such as hotels, youth hostels, travel agents, wild-life out-fitters, guides, tourist car operators and shopkeepers catering to tourist needs.
7. Compilation of statistics and market research on international tourist traffic to India and their utilisation for more effective tourist promotion.

Organisational Chart of Ministry of Tourism (G.O.I.)

Secretary

Director General and Ex-Officio Addl. Secretary	Joint Secretary and Chief Vigilance Officer	Joint Secretary and Financial Adviser
• Overseas Marketing • Hospitality • Administration • Indian Institute of Tour and Travel Management, including Goa Water Sports Projects • National Council for Hotel Management and Catering Technology and HMC Division • Official Language (Hindi Section) • Travel and Trade • Hotel and Restaurant including Hotel and Restaurant Approval and Classification Committee (HRACC) • Domestic Publicity and Promotion • FIB/PAB cases	• Policy Planning and Project Finance • International Cooperation, UN Organisation • Externally Aided Projects • Domestic and Adventure Tourism, Gulmarg Winter Sports Project • Parliament • Public Sector Undertaking (ITDC Ltd.) • Vigilance • Union Territories • Market Research Division	• Integrated Finance • Audit • Budget and Accounts

Chart

Source: Annual Report, Department of Tourism, Government of India.

Role of State Government

The department has a chain of ten Tourist Information Offices established in important cities in India. Four of these offices (Regional Offices) are located at Bombay, Delhi, Calcutta and Madras, which are the major ports of entry. Remaining sub-offices are functioning at focal points of tourist interest in Agra, Aurangabad, Cochin, Jaipur, Khajuraho and Varanasi.

The tourist offices in India furnish information to the tourists regarding travel and tourist attractions in India and also render assistance of non-financial nature. These offices help the Department in exercising some measure of control over various segments of travel trade and try to ensure that the foreign tourists get various services at reasonable cost and are not inconvenienced in any way during their period of stay in India. All these offices work in close collaboration with State governments, travel agencies excursion agencies, hoteliers, carriers, shikar out-fitters, photo safari and tourist car operators. On the same line Rajasthan Government has opened Tourist Offices in India. A list of Rajasthan Tourist Offices in Rajasthan is given below:

Alwar	Ajmer, Jaipur
Banswara	Barmer
Bharatpur	Bikaner
Bundi	Chittorgarh
Dungarpur	Jaipur
Jaisalmer	Jhalawar
Jhunjhunu	Jodhpur
Kota	Mount Abu
Ajmer	Nagaur
Nathdwara	New Delhi
Pushkar	Sawai Madhopur
Sikar	Udaipur

Impact of Tourism on Indian Economy

Tourism has been become an important segment of Indian economy contributing substance to its foreign exchange earnings. The estimated foreign exchange earnings during January to December 2000 were Rs. 14,408.63 crore as compared to Rs. 13,041.81 crore during the same period of 1999 and registered an increase of 10.50 per cent. Comparing the foreign exchange earnings financial year-wise, the estimated foreign exchange earnings during April

1999 to Dec. 1999 were Rs. 8,817.91 crore as compared to Rs. 8,333.62 crore during the same period of previous year and registered an increase of 5.8 per cent.

The potential of domestic tourism has grown substantially during the last few years due to increase in income levels and emergence of a dynamic urban middle class. As per the figures reported by the State Governments, the domestic tourist visits in the accommodation establishments during 1998 are roughly estimated to be 166.9 million.[17]

The following surveys/studies have been completed during the year 2003-04:

Techno-Economic Feasibility Study in river Brahmaputra for development of inland water transport for tourist traffic.

The following surveys/studies are in progress:

(*a*) Preparation of detailed Project Report for the construction of convention centre at Leh, Ladakh (Second Phase).

(*b*) Preparation of Master Plan for the Union Territory of Pondicherry.

(*c*) International Passenger Survey.

(*d*) Preparation of Master Plan for the development of Tourism in Bhalukpong Tawang Circuit of Arunachal Pradesh.

(*e*) Preparation of comprehensive Master Plan for Tourism Development in Goa.

(*f*) Tourist Potential Survey of Rajasthan.

As a consequence of economic restructuring and liberalisation of policies, the Tourism Industry was declared as a priority sector for foreign investment. The horizons for foreign investment in the tourism sector were widened and it is eligible for automatic approval of Foreign Direct Investment up to 51 per cent of the equity since July, 1991. Higher foreign equity participation in specific cases is also allowed on a case to case basis. Non-Resident Indian investment is allowed up to 100 per cent. Automatic approvals are given for foreign technology agreements and management contracts within specified parameters. Under these revised Guidelines, 365 proposals involving foreign investment of Rs. 42,066.34 million were approved till the end of July 1999.

The world organisation estimated a big jump in total world arrivals by the year 2000. Such big lots of tourists would spend millions of dollars on accommodation, catering, local transport and other goods and services. Receipt from international tourism in the year 1996 accounted for more than 12 per cent of world traded goods and services and gained tourism a place among the top three constituents of world trade alongside the oil and automobile industry.

According to recent statistics conducted by the Whaton Econometric Forecasting Association (WEFA Group) on behalf of the American Express Travel Service Company, "Travel and Tourism is the largest industry in the world in terms of employment in almost every country of the world (Int. Tour, Fundamental and Pract. p. 447). The study went on to say that travel and tourism employs more than 101 million people globally, *i.e.*, one out of every 16 workers.

As a matter of fact, travel and tourism employment investment output and value added together exceeds those of such major industries as steel, automobiles, textiles and electronics in virtually every country as per the above statistics.

The sum of total of the above points reveals an important fact that tourism today assumes a great economic force. Its status as a major economic activity has been well established by almost all the nations of the world both the developing and developed.

However, it is significant to note that the benefits of tourism are not to be judged in terms of economic benefits alone. Tourism as an industry has wider implications encompassing not only economic benefits but also social and cultural benefits as well. True benefits of tourism can be appreciated only on a broad basis, which includes all the above aspects.

Growth Rate of Tourism in Rajasthan

The growth rate of tourism in the State of Rajasthan has shown that tourist arrivals to the State of Rajasthan is increasingly annually leaving out year 1994. But if we look towards the percentage growth rate figures are not very impressive. In 1992 it was 21.19 per cent which had gone down to (–) 14.32 per cent in 1994 and then again risen to 12.59 per cent in 1995 but has decreased to 8.71 per cent in 1996, 1.44 per cent in 1998 and 3.48

per cent in 1999 which means more attention needs to be paid to this sector in the State Plans.

Table 1.2: Growth Rate of Tourism in Rajasthan

Year	*Total Tourist Arrivals*	*% Growth*
1991	4795007	15.46
1992	5810923	21.19
1993	5995059	3.17
1994	5136687	-14.32
1995	5783611	12.59
1996	6287387	8.71
1997	6895175	9.67
1998	6994679	1.44
1999	7238213	3.48
2000	7997491	10.48
2005* (Est.)	11000000	37.54 (for 5 years)
2010* (Est.)	15000000	36.36 (for 5 years)

Source: Actual from Annual Report 2000 D.O.T., Jaipur and estimated on the basis of trend series analysis.

Table 1.3: Growth Rate of Domestic and International Tourist in Rajasthan

Year	*Domestic Tourist*	*% Growth*	*International Tourist*	*% Growth*
1991	4300857	15.15	494150	18.32
1992	5263121	22.37	547802	10.86
1993	5454321	3.63	540738	–1.29
1994	4699886	–13.83	436801	–19.22
1995	5248862	11.68	534749	22.42
1996	5726441	9.10	560946	4.90
1997	6290115	9.84	605060	7.86
1998	6403310	1.80	591369	–2.26
1999	6675528	4.25	562685	–4.85
2000	7374391	10.46	623100	10.74
2005* (Est.)	9297431	–	862895	–

Source: Annual Report 2000, Department of Tourism, Art and Culture, Government of Rajasthan, Jaipur.

---

* Based upon forecasting technique.

IMPORTANCE OF TOURISM IN RAJASTHAN

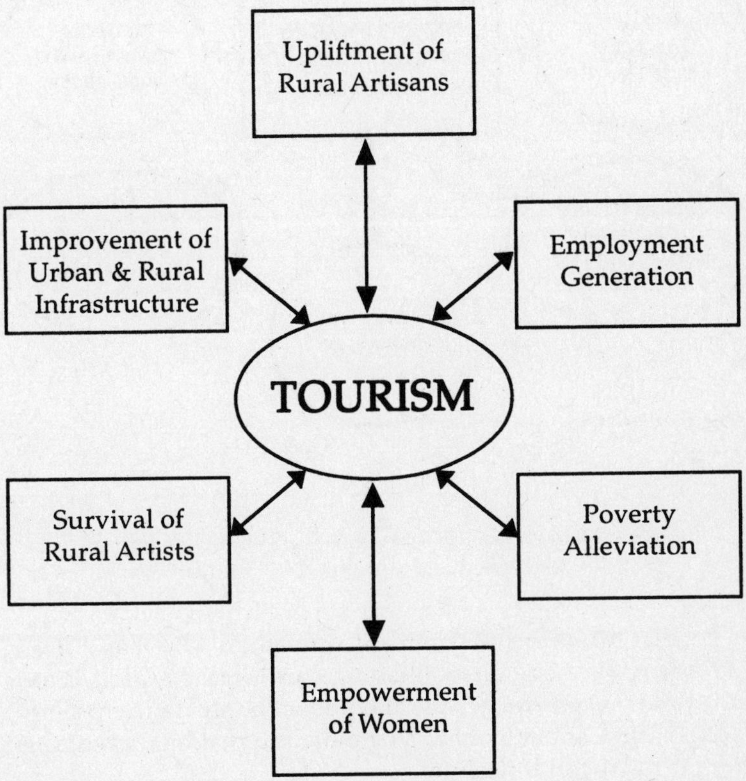

Fig. 1.8

(Designed and Compiled by the Authors)

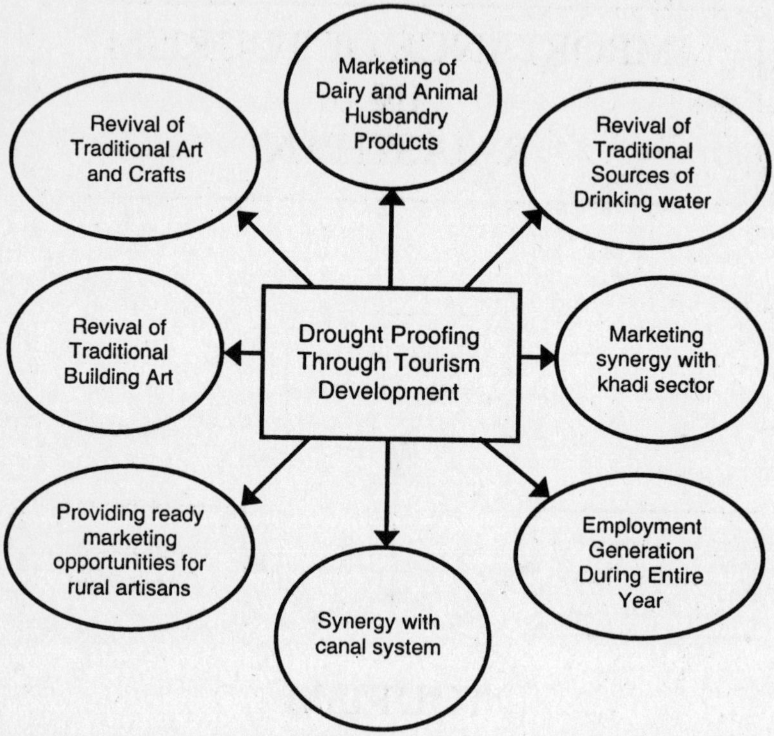

Fig. 1.9

Source: Department of Tourism Art and Culture, Jaipur (Designed and Compiled by the Authors)

Tourist spots on the map of Rajasthan whereas Jaipur, Chittorgarh, Mt. Abu, Ajmer, Bharatpur are lagging behind. Efforts need to provide greater private and public cooperation to promote tourist in these spot by organising more international events and better infrastructural facilities.

Reasons for negative growth

- Lack of infrastructure facilities
- Political instability
- Danger of external aggression

- Climatic factor
- Pokhran explosion etc.

Table 1.4: Top Ten Countries Tourist Arrivals in Rajasthan (2002)*

Sl. No.	*Country*	*Tourist Arrivals*
1.	France	78980
2.	United Kingdom	60709
3.	Germany	53731
4.	U.S.A.	32598
5.	Italy	36010
6.	Australia	19510
7.	Japan	28897
8.	Switzerland	15587
9.	Canada	12391
10.	Bangladesh	8672
11.	Others	81352
	Grand Total	**428437**

Source: Ministry of Tourism, Government of India.

It is inferred from above table that France, U.K., Germany, Italy, Australia, Japan, Switzerland and Canada constitute the main market for Rajasthan Tourism. Residence of Bangladesh and Pakistan usually visits Rajasthan for religious purposes (Pilgrimage to Dargah) at Ajmer.

REFERENCES

1. Hansuria, R.K., *A Eco Study of Rajasthan* Royal Publications, Noida, pp. 52-54.
2. Mali, R.K., *Tourism Prospectus in India* Skylark Publishes, New Delhi, p. 32.
3. Schullard, Hermann V., *International Tourism,* 1982, p. 112.
4. Hunziker, W. Grand Rises Der. Aldagenmeinen Freedmen Zurich Polygraphischerverigee A.G. 1942.
5. Zivadin, Joviac, "*Articles on Tourism and Geography*" in the International Travel and Recreation Journal, No. 3, p. 23.
6. Robert Mc.Intosh W. Charles and Goldner, 1983, "*Tourism Principles Practices Philosophies*", New York, 1991, J. Wiley & Sons Inc., pp. 3-4.
7. Loickorish, J.L., "*An Interim Study or Tourism*", Practice Press Ltd. London 1953, pp. 14-15.

8. W.T.O. Travel and Tourism Barometer, Madrid, May 1993.
9. Richard's, Lambert, *'The Fortunate Traveller'*, Andrew Melrose Ltd. London, 1950, p. 10.
10. Cooper, C.P., An article in *Tourism and Geography,* International Tourism Research Journal, No. 3, p. 38.
11. Ogilive, F.W., *Tourist Movement*, Staples Press Ltd., London, 1941.
12. Annual Report 1999-2000 Ministry of Tourism G.O.I.
13. Lickorish, L.J. and Kershaw A.G, *'The Travel Trade'*, Practical Press Ltd., London, 1958, p. 2.
14. Ramakar, J.G., *'Tourism and Transport Scientific Commissary of Alliance International 1954'*, De-Tourism, p. 8.
15. *Business Travel*, Directory, Jan.-Feb. 1985.
16. Sir John Sargent, Educational Adviser to G.O.I., 1945.
17. Annual Report 2001-02, Ministry of Tourism, G.O.I.

Chapter II

UNIQUE FEATURES OF TOURISM IN RAJASTHAN

"Rajasthan exhibits the sole example in the history of mankind of a people withstanding every outrage barbarity can inflict or human nature sustain, and bent to the earth, yet rising buoyant from the pressure and making calamity a whetstone to courage."

—Col. James Todd[1]

Rajasthan is the land of a people who are brave and chivalrous, people with a work lifestyle around whom grew the most amazing legends of romance and heroism. Everything in Rajasthan is breathtakingly beautiful, impressive and fascinating.

The tell-tales of its land and soil, its palaces,[2] its Rajput heroes and their Bhil companions, Forts, Ponds and Lakes are parts of State's glorious history. Besides this, the art and culture, religiously tolerant and laborious male and females, clad in colourful dresses, play an important role for tourist attraction.

Everything about Rajasthan fascinates from miles of golden structure of sand to the kaleidoscopes of magnificent forts, opulent palaces and marvellous havelis, each a splendid architecture creation having a legend of its own. The beautiful laid out gardens and lakes contrasting perfectly with the hilly ranges are a sight to gladden the eyes of a tourist.

The cities of State still retain the medieval flavour keeping alive the timeless traditions in their rich art and crafts, colourful market with different varieties of commodities etc. grains to fruits and vibrant people wearing multi hued costumes and a bright smile. Here we can also find the true blend of modernity and tradition like camel, oxen and elephants the common modes of transports with the new models of cars, buses and other luxurious means of transportation.

The State is also known with livid exuberant folk dances and music, ballads and spectacular festivities that are an inseparable part of Rajasthan's culture. Especially enchanting are the evenings here, when melodious tunes echoing through the solitude of shimmering sands fill the air.

Many beautiful temples dating back over centuries dot the entire State. Making it a popular pilgrim spot for people from many faiths. Even for wildlife enthusiasts the States is an excellent retreat with its arid zone of the Thar Desert and the dry deciduous forests that offer a rich variety of flora and fauna. Some of the finest national parks and sanctuaries are found here.

Rajasthan is also renowned for exquisite miniature painting and frescoes not forgetting the incredibly fabulous Rajasthan fabrics and Jewellery along with a wide range of beautiful handicrafts.

Tourist Attractions

Ministry of Tourism, Government of India is an active member of a leading international tourism organisations such as World Tourism Organisation (WTO), Pacific Asia Travel Association (PATA), Indian Ocean Tourism Organisation (IOTO), and International Congress and Convention Association (ICCA), etc. It has been the Rajasthan Government endeavour to bring international conferences and conventions to Rajasthan to give a fillip to tourism by providing adequate exposure to the foreign visitors and policy-makers attending these conferences.

No doubt, it is absolutely true that the whole Rajasthan State is the place of tourist attraction. Everything here is the thing, which magically attract the tourists from every part of world as well as from our country. Major tourist attractions in this State can be presented in the following headings.

Fort, Palaces and Heritages[2]

Rajasthan is the land of Raja-Maharaja and their nobles. The majority of Rajas are from Rajput families, these Rajput community

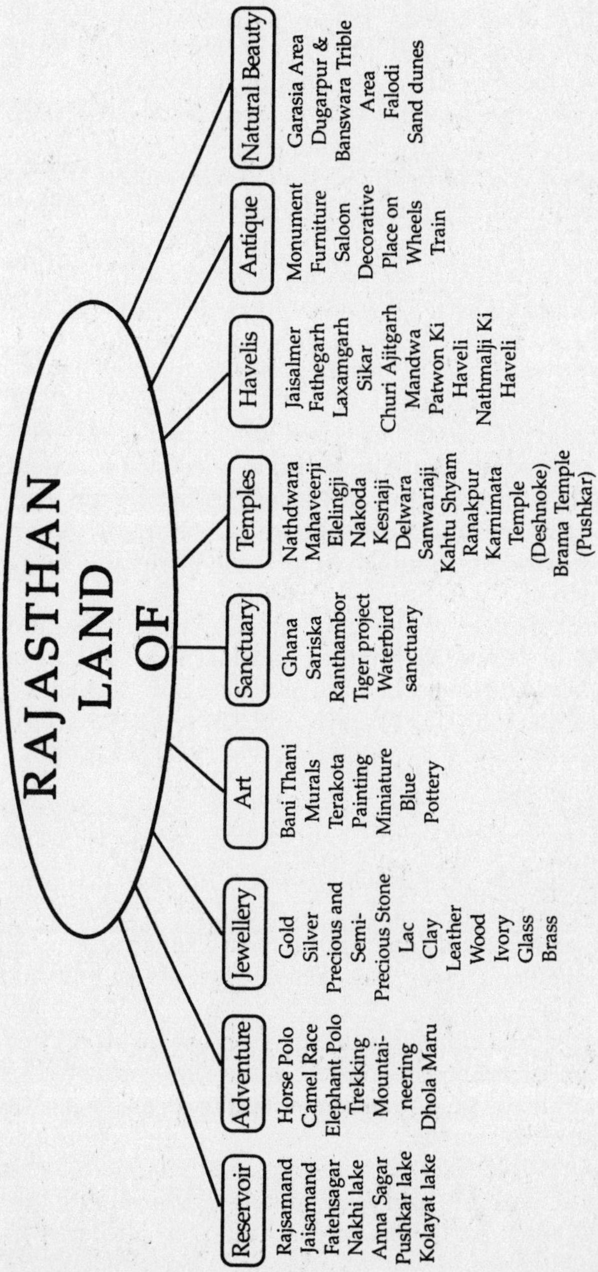

Fig. 2.1: Unique Features of Tourism in Rajasthan
(Designed and Compiled by the Authors)

were renowned for their loyalty, vigour, sacrifices, bravery and due to the specific geographical situation of the State, the State livelihood always faced the invasions of foreign invaders.

Simultaneously, the State has to face consequently or regularly drought conditions and scarcity of water due to its geographical diversities of desert and the chain of Aravali mountains. Due to scarce water resources, the State mainly depends on rains, resulting in lower agriculture production and the inhabitants are always affront to unemployment or to earn regular livelihood. This might be a reason that kings of Rajput dynasty always kept their people engaged/employed in constructing Palaces, Forts, Buildings, Ponds, Lakes to provide them job security and a regular livelihood. This farsightedness has enriched Rajasthan in its glorious and beautiful heritage of palaces and forts, buildings and temples, still capable to attract tourist round the world, to witness the ancient glory and magnificent architecture in a speechless wondrous awe.

The world fame forts of Rajasthan are Chittorgarh, Amer, Jaigarh, Jodhpur, Jaisalmer, Ranthambore, Kumbahalgarh, Bundi, Mandalgarh, Bikaner.

The beautiful palaces of the State are Chandramahal and Rambagh Palace at Jaipur, Jag Mandir and Jai Niwas Palace at Udaipur, Vijay Vilas at Alwar, Lalgarh and Junagarh at Bikaner, Rana Kumbha Palace at Chittorgarh and Ummaid Palace at Jodhpur still behold domestic as well as foreign tourists equally.

Arts and Crafts[3]

Rajasthan is amongst the richest States in the country as far as the field of arts and crafts is concerned. The people of State have creative senses, artistic skills having the most brilliant forms of stone, clay, leather, wood, ivory, lakh, glass, brass, silver, gold and textiles.

In Baroli, in the Hadoti region, presence of several sculptures proves that a regular art school existed in the 10th century. The cave painting, terracotta and other stone sculptures excavated at different sites corroborate this.

Story of Rajasthan reveals that the kings and their nobles were patrons of Arts and Crafts and they always encouraged their craftsman for excellent Arts and Crafts activities. Their desire to decorate their surroundings was very strong. Animals like regal elephant to the lowly donkey, the great palaces and the inner chambers of forbidding forts were decorated. The heroic warriors also decorated their clothing and armour with meticulously ornamented swords and shields. The horses and the elephants that took the warriors to battles also adorn with Jewelled Saddles and intricate silver Howdas.

For women there were infinite variety, tie and dye fabrics, embroidered garments enamelled Jewellery, inlayed with precious and semi-precious stones, leather Jooties. They also decorated their houses with wall painting with geometric designs or with the simple motifs. The women also displayed their talents with the needle and thread and papier-mâché. Some of popular Arts and Crafts are as under:

(a) Meenakari

This enamel art is famous for its delicacy and its use of colours. Jaipur, Nathdwara and Pratapgarh are famous centers in Rajasthan for fine quality of enamel work.

(b) Jewellery[4]

Rajasthan is rich in jewellery having different style in different parts of State. Some of traditional designs are Rakhri, Timaniyan, Bala, Bajubandh, Gajrra, Gokhru Jod etc. Tribal and rural women wear heavy simply crafted jewellery and seem to carry the weight (up to 5 kg.) without much discomforts almost all the time. Men also wear the form of Chockers and Earrings.

Ivory

The ivory bangles that most Rajasthan women wear are considered auspicious. Ivory is also inlaid and shaped into intricate items of great beauty. Miniature paintings were also executed on ivory.

Stone

Statues on religious themes are carved all over the State and in several cities like Jaipur, Sirohi, Banswara, where the stone carvers are working giving final touches to statues or each pillars.

Others

Lakh and glass work, sandal wood and wood toys, blue pottery, handbook printing, painting on camel hide, embroidery, cloth painting, carpets, durries, inlay work on brass are the other famous craft work in state.

***Rajput Painting*[5]**

It was widely believed that the miniature artists of Rajasthan were practising and perfecting their art as early as the beginning of the 16th century. Each school of painting had its distinctive features. For instance, the flowing rivers, dense forest, lush green fields of Kota, Bundi region were transferred to the painting of that region. In palaces of Kota, Bundi painting are displayed depicting hunting scenes, animal fights and figures of women with the bright colours.

The rulers of Amer-Jaipur were very close to Mughals, where the Mughal influence can be seen in the paintings of this region. The Keshavgarh school is best known for its Bani-Thani paintings with a totally different style with highly exaggerated features-long knees, large almond shaped eyes, long fingers with subdued colours.

Jodhpur has a very strong folk tradition and here the figures are mainly robust warriors and dainty women paintings of the Legendary Lovers like Dhola-Maru or camel-back hunting scenes, which included innumerable horses and elephants dominating the paintings of the Marwar region. The colours used by the miniature artists were made from minerals, vegetables, precious stones, indigo conch shell, pure gold and silver. Another important category of painting is called Phad-Scroll painting used by the Bhopas and the Pichwais-cloth hangings used behind the deity in Vaishnava temples.

***Folk Music and Dance*[6]**

The people of Rajasthan live life to the hilt. After hard work in the harsh desert sun and the rocky terrain, whenever they take time off they let themselves go in gay abandon. There is dancing, singing, drama, devotional music, and puppet shows and other community festivals which transform the hard working Rajasthani into a fun-loving and carefree individuals.

Each region has its own folk entertainment. The dance styles differ as to the songs. Interesting enough, even the musical instruments are also different. These folk music and dances have great emphasis on the religious occasions. Some of the famous and renowned of entertainment in the State are as under:

Main Folk Dances of Rajasthan

Ghoomer	Chari dance	Drum dance
Gher Ghoomer	Khachhi Ghodi	Terah Taali
Gher	Fire dance	Kathputli
Pabhu ji ki phad	Mand	

Besides these, most popular and traditional folk dances, many musical instruments of the State are very important and essential component of hard workers of State. These instruments are very simple but quite unusual. Hand crafted by the musicians themselves, they are rather unique and include instruments like the Morchang, Nad, Sarangi, Kamayacha, Rawanhattha, Algoza, Khadtal, Poongi, Bankia and Duff.

Fair and Festivals[7]

Festivals and melas have their unique place in the State of Rajasthan. The habitants of Rajasthan organise several of them round the year, out of their laborious routine for leisure and entertainment. Since people of the State regard their cattle stock and the deities equally, they arrange such festivities to give importance to them. Later on, to attract the tourists and to make them understand Rajasthani culture, some special melas and festivals are now being organised, besides traditional ones.

R.T.D.C. along with the Department of Tourism, art and culture and other organisation organises number of fairs and festivals backed with fun, frolic excitement and rituals are observed throughout the year across this sprawling State. Participants costumed in their traditional colourful finery whole heatedly partaking in these events as usual delight, colour, rhythm and melody blind the Rajasthan festivals in a unique manner providing a veritable feat. Events like turban competition, tug of war, camel race, horse race all are enchanting and delightful along with the rich music and dance forms. Below is the list of festivals going to be organised in the coming years.

Table 2.1: Fairs and Festivals of Rajasthan

Sl. No.	*Name of Fairs and Festivals*	*Place*
1.	Camel festival	Bikaner
2.	Nagaur fair	Nagaur
3.	Desert festival	Jaisalmer
4.	Elephant festival	Jaipur
5.	Gangaur fair	Jaipur
6.	Mewar festival	Udaipur
7.	Summer festival	Mt. Abu
8.	Teej fair	Jaipur
9.	Dussehra fair	Kota
10.	Marwar festival	Jodhpur
11.	Pushkar fair	Ajmer

Source: Annual Report 2003-04 of Tourism Department, Government of Rajasthan.

Details of above is given here under:

(a) Pushkar Fair[5]

This fair is well-known and marked with largest participation of all the festivals of Rajasthan. Pushkar is an important pilgrimage as well as the venue of mammoth cattle fair. Bazaars with cultural beauty, music and local sports are important highlights of this event.

(b) Baneshwar Fair[8]

A religious festival with simple and traditional rituals. This fair is the center of attraction of a large number of tribals from the neighbouring States of M.P., Gujarat, who join their brethren from Rajasthan in offering prayers to Lord Shiva.

(c) URS Ajmer Sharif—Ajmer[9]

This fair is being held in the memory of the revered Sufi Saint Khawaja Moinuddin Chisti. It is an occasion for thousands of believers to congregate at the shrine and offer their prayers. Whole of Ajmer seems to take on a festive air and several programmes are organised to mark the festivals.

(d) Desert Festivals[10]

This festival has been organised by Tourism Department at the golden city of Jaisalmer. This famous festival is celebrated in the month of Jan.-Feb. every year in the hearts of desert.

(e) Gangaur Festival[11]

This holy and traditional festival devoted to Goddess Parvati, the consort of Lord Shiva. The teenagers' girls dress up in their Finery and pray for the grooms of their choice and the married women pray for the well-being of their husbands. This is a day festival and is laced with various activities and culminates in a grand procession marking the arrival of Shiva to escort his bride home.

(f) Mewar Festivals[12]

This festival is held at Udaipur to welcome the spring season. There are songs, dances, processions, devotional music and fire work, where almost everybody participates.

(g) Summer Festivals[5]

This summer festival is organised in June every year at the only hill station of Rajasthan at Mt. Abu. This is the coldest place at this time of the year. Folk dances and a general atmosphere of gaiety prevail in this tiny hill resort and the tourists have ample time to relax and enjoy themselves.

(h) Marwar Festivals[13]

This festival is celebrated at Jodhpur in the month of October every year. This festival is devoted mainly to the music and dance of the Marwar region. This is the festival that allows the visitors to understand and enjoy the folk traditions of this part of the State.

(i) Other Festivals[5]

Besides the above important festivals, another festivals organised in the State are Elephant Festival—Jaipur, Shilp Gram Festival—Udaipur, Camel Festival—Bikaner.

National Parks and Sanctuaries[14]

Rajasthan is a heaven for a wide spectrum of wildlife. The topography of State ranges from the barren desert, scrub-thorn, arid forests, rocks and ravines to wetlands and lush green forests and each of these areas have typical type of races of large variety of animal and birds. Some of them are very rare while some are endangered.

Rajasthan is the home of the tigers, black bucks, chinkara, the rare desert fox, the endangered Caracal, the great Indian bustard, gavial, monitor lizard, wild boards, porcupines migratory birds like the common crane, ducks, pelicans, and the rare Siberian cranes, imperial sand grouse falcons, buzzards Flock etc. to this State during the winter months.

Typical areas representing each of the ecosystems have been earmarked as special areas for the protection and management of wildlife. Rajasthan boasts of two natural parks, over a dozen sanctuaries and two closed areas. Most of these areas are open to visitors round the year but are closed briefly during monsoon season.

Details of Main Parks and Sanctuaries are given below:

Behrorgarh Sanctuary

A fairly new sanctuary established in 1983 covering a total area of 229 sq. km. of scrub and dry deciduous forest. Lucky tourists can see here the Leopard, Chinkara, Sloth bear particularly in the month of October to May.

Darrah Sanctuary

This sanctuary was previously known as the hunting ground of the Kota Maharaja. This sanctuary was established in 1955 covering 265 sq. km. to provide protection to rare wild animals like Wolf, Sloth Bear, Chinkara and Leopard.

Desert National Park

This famous national park was established in 1980 having 3,162 sq. km. area. This closed park has shrubs and trees in addition to rolling sand dunes. The famous wildlife wealth comprises of fox, desert cat, hare, spiny-tail uromastix and sandfish. Thousands of sparrows, imperial sand grouse, bustards, falcons and eagles migrate here during the winter.

Jaisamand Sanctuary

Established in 1957, this sanctuary is located beside the man-made lake of the same name. Covering a total area of 160 sq. km. it harbours sloth Bear, Leopard, Chital, Chinkara, wild board and number of birds. Some crocodiles and fish can also be spotted here. Best time to visit is between November and January.

Keoladev Ghana National Park, Bharatpur

Declared as National Park in 1983, this 29 sq. km. park is one of the world's greatest henries. Its shallow, fresh water marsh attracts thousands of migratory birds. Over 10,000 nests of egrets, darters, cormorants, grey herons and storks hatch nearly 20,000 to 30,000 chicks every year. There are an infinite variety of migratory birds. Mammals like the Sambhar, Black Buck, Chital, Nilgai, Fishing Cat, Otter and Mongoose also roam freely here. Best time to visit is August to February.

Kumbhalgarh Sanctuary

The majestic fort of Kumbhalgarh overlooks the 578 sq. km. sanctuary. The Aravali Hills, which remain barren for most of the year, turn green during rains and provide shelter to sloth gear, leopard, flying squirrel. It is also the only sanctuary where the Indian wolf is breeding successfully. Best time to visit is March to May and September to November.

Mount Abu Sanctuary

The highest point of the Aravalis, the Guru Shikar lies in this 289 kms. sanctuary. Established in 1960 this provides shelter to the common Langoor, wild Boar, Sambher and Leopard. The Grey Jungle Fowl can also be spotted here besides a number of lowering trees enhance the beauty of this place. Best time to visit is March to June.

Location of Tourism Industry in Rajasthan

Rajasthan is an open air museum where it has something for every kind of tourist, those looking for active action packed holidays for wildlife lovers and for those who have interest in history, art and culture. These places can be classified broadly in three categories.

Traditional Spots

Those places which were known and frequently visited by all the tourists coming to India. Such places are well-known for their historical, natural, artistic workmanship and cultural importance, which include Forts, Palaces, Temples, Monuments etc. Brief resume of such palaces has been provided tourist circuit-wise in undergoing paragraphs.

Jaipur-Amer Circuit

Kachhawah Rajput Maharaja Sawai Jai Singh founded Jaipur the Pink City in 1727. The city is considered to be a marvel of town planning. Traditional art like jewellery, metal work, enamelling, tie and die, stone carving, blue pottery, miniature paintings were patronised by the rulers and still continue to flourish today. The wide straight roads, streets, lanes and uniform rows of shops on either side of main bazaar arranged in rectangular shape in accordance with the principles of town planning set down in the 'Shilpa Shastra' gives the city a very beautiful look.

City Palace, the royal residence is built in a blend of the Rajasthan and Mughal styles. The projected balconies, arches, slender pillars and marvellous entrances with floral motifs in gold and coloured stones deserve appreciation from every visitor. The palace houses a museum with super collection of Rajasthani Costumes and armoury of Mughals and Rajputs including swords of different shapes and sizes. Some of them inlaid with enamel and embellishing with jewels and encased in magnificent scabbards. There is an art gallery in the palace with an excellent collection of miniature paintings, carpets and rare astronomical work in Arabic, Persian, Latin and Sanskrit.

A stone observatory with its complex instruments, whose settings and shapes are scientifically designed, represents the high-points of medieval Indian astronomy is also situated in the city palace complex. Hawa Mahal, the palace of winds, built in 1799 with the aim of enabling ladies of the royal households to watch the everyday life and royal processions of the city. Ram Niwas Bagh outside the city walls is a green lush garden. The majestic Albert Hall a fine example of Indo-Sardonic style of architecture design is an exquisite collection of sculptures, paintings, decorative wares, with an Egyptian mummy and the celebrate Persian carpets.

Nahargarh or the Tiger Fort provides some stunning views of the city and a royal retreat for the maharanis. Jaigarh, the fort of victory is a rugged fort. The world's largest cannon on wheels lies here. Also of interest is the intricate water supply and storage system which is considered as a marvel of planning. Maharani Ki Chatri and Gaitor are royal funeral grounds. There are some fine cenotaphs with intricately carved marble columns and lattices. Govind Deo Ji Temple, Birla Planetarium, Galta Ji and Dolls Museum are also of great interest.

Amer was the former capital of the Kachhawah rulers of the old state of Dhumdher. The beautiful complex of palaces has some very interesting apartments, the likes of which are not to be found in the country. Jai Mandir, Sheesh Mahal, Sukh Niwas, Ganesh Pole, Shila Devi Temple are some of the prominent places of interest in the fort. Elephant riding here also attracts the visitors. Old township of Amer lies at the foothills of the palace, where Jagat Shiromani Temple, Narsingh Temple, Panna Meena Ki Baori are worth visiting.

Jodhpur-Bikaner-Jaisalmer Circuit

Jodhpur: Rao Jodha founded Jodhpur, the former capital of Marwar State in 1459. Jodhpur is a tourist-trading center of wood, cattle, camels, etc. Maharangarh Fort is a majestic fort and is one of the most impressive and formidable structure. Within the fort are some magnificent palaces with marvellously carved panels, latticed windows and evocative names. Noteworthy of these are, Moti Mahal (Pearl Palace), Phool Mahal (Flower Palace), Sheesh Mahal (Mirror Palace), Sieeh Khana (House of Armoury) and Daulat Khana (Royal Treasury). These palaces house a fabulous collection of trapping of Indian Royalty including a superb collection of palanquins, elephant howdahs, miniature paintings, musical instruments and costumes. Jaswant Thada a cenotaph built in the memory of Maharaja Jaswant Singh. Ummaid Bhawan Palace was built under the famine relief programme to provide employment to famine struck population is a grand impressive building constructed in sandstone. Other important places of interest in the nearby area are Mandore, the ancient capital of Marwar State, the Hall of Heroes has fifteen figures carved out of the rock on the wall, which represents the Hindu deities. Maha Mandir, Kailana Lake and Balsamand Lakes are very attractive.

Bikaner: Bikaner was inhabited by Rathore Prince Bikaji, the eldest son of Rao Jodhaji of Jodhpur in the year 1486. The fortified town encircled by a moat and has some beautiful palaces within. The palaces made of red sandstone and marble, make a picturesque view of the court yards, balconies, kiosks and windows dotted all over the structure. Chand Mahal or the Moon Palace is decorated with marvellous paintings, mirrors and carved marble panels, Phool Mahal or Flower Palace ornate with glass and mirror work are worth-notable. Anup Mahal, Dungar Niwas, Ganga Niwas, Gaj Mandir and Rang Mahal are other spots of interest. Lalgarh Palace has beautiful lattice work and filigree work. Camel Research Farm, Devikund, Gajner Wildlife Sanctuary, Karni Mata Temple, Kolayaji and Kalibanga are nearby excursion spots.

Jaisalmer: Jaisalmer foundation of township was laid by the Bhati Rajput Rawal Jaisal as a new capital in the year 1156, prior to this Lodru was the capital of the Jaisalmer State. The golden hued fort is a sentinel to the bleach desert scape from its 80 meters high perch on the hill, housing the entire township within its rampart Nathmalji Ki Haveli and Patwon Ki Haveli are most decorate and magnificent of all the havelies in Jaisalmer with exquisitely carved pillars, extensive corridors, chambers and splendid miniature paintings. The fort has three Jain temples dedicated to Rishabhdeo, Sambhavnath and Parshavnath and a Library—Gyan Bhandar—with some of the oldest manuscripts of India. Lordruva, a Jain pilgrim spot and old capital town, Wood

Fossil Park at Aakal for 180 million year old fossils, Sam Sand Dunes where the ripples on the wind-caressed dunes that create an enchanting mirage are surely delightful, Amar Sagar, Bara Bagh and Mool Sagar are near by spots, one cannot avoid to see.

Udaipur-Chittorgarh-Mt.Abu Circuit

Udaipur: Udaipur, the beautiful city of lakes was founded by Maharana Udaisingh in the year 1559. Overlooking the Pichhola Lake, the city palace on a hill surrounded by crenulated walls is majestic architectural work. The main entrance is through the triple arched gate, the Tripolia with eight marble porticos, Suraj Gokhade the balcony of sun, is where the Suryavanshi Maharanas of Mewar presented themselves to the people in time of trouble to restore their confidence. The 'Mor Chowk' known to its exquisite peacock mosaic in glass 'Chini Chitrashala' noted for its blue and white ceramics. Jagdish Temple most beautiful temple with its noteworthy sculpted images. Saheliyon Ki Bari (Garden of the maids of Honour) is a small ornamental garden, royal ladies used to come for a stroll. Garden has many fountains and delightful pools. Pratap Memorial on the top of Moti Magari or pearl hills overlooking the Fateh Sagar Lake—in the middle of lake is Nehru Park— a lovely island garden. Jag Mandir and Jag Niwas (Lake Palace) on the Pichhola Lake are of breathtaking magnificence. Sajjan Garh the Monsoon Palace dominating the skyline offers a panoramic view of city and lakes. Ekling ji, a beautiful sculpted temple complex with 108 temples within its high walls. The temples are dedicated to Lord Shiva, the main deity of Mewar rulers. Magela is renowned for Sas Bahu Temples for its architecture and carvings and Jain Temples Adbu ji, Haldi Ghati the battle field of Maharana Pratap and Mughal Emperor Akbar. Nathdwara temple dedicated to Shrinath ji or Lord Krishna and Kankroli Temple of Dwarikadhish are worshipped by the Vallabhacharya sect. Rajsamand and Jaisamand are beautiful lakes. Kumbhalgarh is among the major forts in Rajasthan after Chittorgarh.

Chittorgarh[15]: The pride and glory of Rajasthan, Chittorgarh echoes with tales of romance and valour unique to the Rajput tradition. Chittorgarh Fort is a massive structure with many gateways built by Maurya rulers in 7th century on a 180 metre high hill, it sprawls over 700 metre area. The fort has many magnificent monuments, all fine examples of the Rajput architecture. **Vijay Stambh** (Victory Tower) a 37 metre high structure with nine storeys covered with exquisite sculptures of Hindu deities depicting episodes from Ramayana and Mahabharatha. Maharana Kumbha built it to commemorate his victory over the muslim rulers of Malwa and Gujarat. **Kirti Stambh** (Tower of Fame) 22 metre high tower by a wealthy merchant in 12th century dedicated to first Tirthankar Adinath Ji of Jain sect. **Kumbha Palace** a ruined structure of great historical and architectural work. It is believed that Maharani Padmini and other women committed Jauhar here. Padmini Palace is built beside a pool, the palace is magnificent one, here the Rana Ratan Singh showed a glimpse of Queen Padmini to Alladin Khilji. Rana Kumbha built Kumbh Shyam Temple for Meera Bai, wife of prince Bhojraj, who was an ardent devotee of Lord Krishna. Kalika Mata Temple, dedicated to mother Goddess Kali, the symbol of power and valour, was originally a Sun Temple later in the 14th century it was converted into Kalika Mata Temple. Jaimal Patta Palace ravines witness to the gallantry of these Sisodia Warriors. The magnificent Fateh Prakash Mahal, presently a fine Museum with an exquisite collection of sculpture from temples and buildings in the fort is worth a visit.

Ranakpur: Ranakpur, 90 km. away from Udaipur, is a beautiful sculptured temple lie in a tranquil valley of the Aravalis. The main Chaumukha Temple is dedicated to the Tirthänkar Adinath has 29 halls supported by 144 pillars, all distinctly carved. Neminath Temple, Parshavnath Temple and Sun Temple are also noteworthy.

Mt. Abu: Mt. Abu is a green oasis in the barren desert-scape is situated at the southern tip of Aravali range. The hill retreats its cool climate to its rich flora covering the entire hillside that includes coniferous trees and flowering shrubs. An ideal resort for a reverie at an attitude of 1,220 metres. Following are the major sites to visit on the mount.

A natural spring flowing through a sculpted cow head gives the shrine a name the temple is dedicated to Lord Shiva nearby is a magnificent marble image of Nandi. Nakki Lake is a picturesquely set amid the hill it is believed that it was scooped out by gods with their finger nails 'Nakh' therefore the lake was given this name. Delware Temples, a cluster of Jain temples, built between 11th and 13th century, are sheer elegance in marble, dedicated to Jain Tirthankaras. The Vimal Vasahi Temple is the oldest which dedicated to first Tirthankara. There are also temples dedicated to Rishabhdeo, Neminath and other Tirthankaras. With door easiness, pillars, architras and sculptures on porticos of these temples are fine specimen of craftsmanship. Adhardevi temple is carved out of a huge rock. The temple is dedicated to mother goddess Arbuda Devi. Sun set point is spectacular height of the setting sun when the hills are carved in the golden glow can be viewed from here. Honeymoon point offers an enchanting view of the verdant plains and valleys. Raghunath ji Temple overlooking the Nakki Lake with the beautiful image of Raghunath ji. The famous Hindu preacher Shri Ramanand constructed the temple in 14th century. Museum, Ashok Vatika, Gandhi Park, Municipal Park, Terrace Garden etc. are some of the noteworthy spots to visit.

Ajmer-Pushkar-Circuit

Ajmer: The city of Ajmer was founded by Raja Ajay Pal Chauhan in the 7th century and continued to be a major center of the Chauhan power till 1193 when Prithvi Raj Chauhan was defeated by Mohammed Gauri and captured by him.

Since then Ajmer become home of many dynasties, which came and left, leaving behind indelible marks of their cultures and a blend of Hinduism and Islam. Hindus as well as Muslim pilgrims equally pay tributes at Dargah-Sharif-Tomb of the Sufi Saint Khawaja Moinuddin Chisti. Major places to visit are detailed in the following paragraphs.

The Dargah is a spending tomb of the Sufi Saint Khawaja Moinuddin Chisti, more popularly known as Khawaja Saheb or Khawaja Sharif. The shrine is next only to Mecca or Medinas for the muslims. Buland Darwaja was built by the Nizam of Hyderabad. The two massive Deghs in the courtyard are of particular interest. Adhai Din Ka Jhunpra is a remarkable structure, this is a masterpiece of Indo-Islamic architecture, said to be constructed only in two and a half days. Originally it was a Sanskrit College built within a temple in 1193, Mohammed Gouri converted the building into a mosque by adding a seven arched wall in front of the pillars hall in just two and a half days. Taragarh fort was the city of the military activity during Mughal period, later used as a sanatorium by British. Ana Sager the Museum and Nasia (Digambar Jain Temple) other places worth visiting.

Pushker: The Pushker lake, nestled in the hills, is one of the holiest pilgrim center of Hindus. According to legends, the origin of this lake back to the time when Lord Brahma was on his way in search of a tranquil land to perform 'Yagna'. A lotus fell down from his hands into this valley and lake sprang up on this spot and was dedicated to Lord Brahma. Rangnath Temple, Brahma Temple are other places to visit at Pushker.

Development Spots[1]

Those places, which were later on, developed to attract the tourists. Rajasthan Tourists Development Corporation has provided facilities for the tourists coming to visit Rajasthan.

Alwar: Silisera Lake and Palace is 13 km. away from Alwar is a beautiful lake with a marvellous palace. The palace offers boating and sailing facilities.

Sariska: Sariska is a thick reserve forest in the picturesque valley of Aravalis. It is an excellent tiger sanctuary. Sambher, Cheetal, four horned antelope, wild bore and Nilgai can also be seen. Sariska palace has been converted into a hotel now-a-days.

Barmer: Kiradu (Kirat Koop) had been the capital of Panwars. The ruins of five ancient temples of Lord Vishnu and Lord Shiva are of interest to archaeologists and art lovers. In Jasal Hindu Temple is ornamented with fine sculptures which were brought from Jain Temple of Lord Mahaveer and Jain Temple are worth visiting. Meva Nagar is well-known for its Nakoda Parshavnath Temple of Jain community. The temple of Lord Vishnu is also worth visiting.

Banswara: Mahi Bajaj Sager Dam is built on river Mahi 18 km. away from Banswara. The Dam has a number of islands at intervals. The Mahi Dam and Kagdi Pickup have a picturesque view. Madareshwar a temple of Lord Shiva set amid natural beauty and other temples are praiseworthy. Arthuna, 55 km. away from Banswara, the ruins of cluster of Shaivite and Jain temple of 11th, 12th and 15th centuries are found in this village. The Manduleshwar temple was built in 1080 by Chamunda Raja Parmara chief is noteworthy. Tripura Sundari is an ancient temple of the goddess known as Tartai Mata. The idol of the goddess riding on a tiger is magnificent one in black stone, the temple is one of the Shakti Peeth of Hindus. Mangarh on the Gujarat border is a

Jahianwala Bagh of Bangar. British soldiers opened fire on the followers of Guru Govind a well-known reformer among Adiwasis.

Bharatpur: Jawahar Burj and Fateh Burj. A few of the eight towers erected by the Jat rulers. These two were built by Maharaja Surajmal to commemorate his victories over Mughals and British respectively. Lohgarh Fort was built in the 18th century with its impregnable defences sustained itself even after a number of British attacks. The fort has three palaces within its precincts—Kishori Mahal, Mahal Khas and Khothi Khas are of great interest. Keoladeo National Park is a royal hunting preserve of the princes of Bharatpur, is one of the finest bird sanctuaries in the world incubated with over two species of water birds exotic migratory birds from Afghanistan, Central Asia, Tibet as well as Siberian cranes from the Arctic and China come here in the months of July/August to spend the winter in the warmer climate and they breed till October/November.

Deeg: The summer resort of the rulers of Bharatpur is an interesting town with stunningly beautiful garden and magnificent palaces is worthy of a trip.

Bundi: Bundi is one of the unexplored cities with a rich history. Bundi is surrounded by the Aravali hills on three sides and is circumscribed by a massive wall with four gates. Bundi is very famous for its intricate carvings and murals.

Taragarh: Taragarh is one of the most impressive forts of Rajasthan perched on thickly wooded hill. The palace is a fine example of Rajput architecture. Chitrashala is a fascinating pavilion and gallery of miniature mural emburish the palace. Colourful paintings on the walls depict scenes from the 'Ragamala' and 'Raas Lila' the Radha Krishna Story. Chhatar Mahal, Ratan Daulat, Nawl Sager, Rani Ji Ki Baori, Sukh Mahal and Phool Sagar are other nearby spots to visit.

Dungarpur: Rawal Veer Singh founded Dungarpur in the year 1282, when he took over this part of State from the Bhil chieftain Dungaria. Dungarpur is famous for its unique style of architecture as seen in its palaces and noble residences adorned by jharokhas built in stone. Udai Bilas Palace is a veritable example of the Rajput architecture ornate with intricately sculptured pillars and panels, impressive balconies bracketed windows and marvellous arches. Juna Mahal is a seven storeyed structure—resembling fortress with crenellated walls, turrets, narrow entrance and corridors to slow down the enemy. Frescoes, miniature painting and glass mirror work makes it impressive. Baneshwar at the confluence of the Som and Mahi rivers, Deo Somnath, Galoakot and Poonjpur are other nearby places of great charm.

Rajasthan Tourist Development Corporation has provided financial assistance for tourist development to the entrepreneurs and has developed old palaces and fortress, excursion and resort centers, where the tourist enjoys a royal style of life. These are, Pushker Palace, Pushker (Ajmer), Neemrana Fort Palace, Neemrana (Alwar), Sariska Palace, Sariska (Alwar), Bhanwar Niwas, Lalgarh Palace and Basant Vihar Palaces of Bikaner, Laxmi Vilas Palace of Bharatpur, Castle Bijaipur (Chittorgarh) Bhairawati Palace, Dausa, Raj Palace, Bisau Palace, Rajmahal Palace, Narain Niwas Palace, Samod Haveli and Khasa Khothi, Jaipur, Ramgarh Palace, Jaipur Karni Bhavan and Ajit Bhawani Palace (Jodhpur), Fort Chandava (Jodhpur).

Dunilod (Jhunjhunu), Castle Mandawa (Jhunjhunu), Narayan Niwas Palace Jaisalmer, Khinusar Fort (Khinusar Nagaur), Rohit Fort (Rohit Pali), Sardar Samand Palace (Pali), Narlai Rawala Narlai (Pali), Deogarh Palace (Deogarh, Rajsamand), Sawai Madhopur Lodge, Sawai Madhopur, Kama Rajputana Club Resort, Kanaught House and Palace Hotel Mt. Abu (Sirohi) Fateh Prakash Palace, Shikar Badi, Shiv Nivas Palace and Laxmi Niwas Palace (Udaipur).

Hidden Spots[16]

These are the places, which are well-known among the local people, but the tourists have yet to see. These places include natural, archaeological, religious and cultural sites some of them have been enumerated in the following paragraphs:

Ajmer: Prithvi Raj Memorial Garden and statue of Prithvi Raj is a new excursion spot on way to Taragarh, Baradari on the banks of Anasagar gives a picturesque view of the lake.

Alwar: A picturesque garden Purjan Vihar (Company Garden) laid out by Maharaja Shiv Dan Singh in 1868. The lush surroundings and the cool shades make it idyllic visiting spot during summers. Vijay Mandir Palace built by Maharaja Jai Singh in 1918 is overlooking the lake makes it a fascinating sight Jaisamand Lake provides a splendid view during monsoon, sprawling greenery all-around makes it visual treat.

Banswara: The ruins of cluster of Shaivaits and Jain Temples constructed during 11th, 12th and 15th centuries are of archaeological and historical importance. A beautiful life size statue of Lord Brahma is worthy of a visit at Chhinch.

Bharatpur: The summer resort of the rulers of Bharatpur and second capital of the region Deeg is a fortified stunningly beautiful town with magnificent palaces and gardens. Keoladeo National Park is the another attraction for the wildlife lovers. Over 400 species of water birds come here from Siberia and Central Asia.

Bikaner: The extensive remains of the pre-Harappan and Harappan civilisation found in Kalibanga of Hanumangarh district are of immense interest to archaeology and enthusiasts.

Jaipur: Palace of Samod has been rebuilt and renovated, is a fine example of Rajput Haveli architecture and an ideal spot for outing. Jai Singh Pura Khor and Madhogarh Tunga Forts are praiseworthy.

Jaisalmer: Desert National Park, a peculiar landscape dominated by rolling sand dunes and scrub covered hills. Black Bucks, Chinkara, Desert Fox and the great Indian Bustard are the prominent fauna of the park.

Jhalawar: A picturesque wooden cottage on the banks of the Kishan Sagar Tank known as Rain Basera is an idyllic haunt for the tourists, is 6 km. away from the district headquarters. Dag is renowned for some 12th century temples and Rani Ka Maqbra etc.

Kota: Beautiful rock paintings are found in the hillocks on the bank of river Alniya. Darrah wild life sanctuary 50 km. away from Kota is a thickly wooded mountain range. The wildlife variety includes Panther, Spotted Deer, Tiger, Wild Bear, and Bear.

Rajsamand: Wild Life Sanctuary at Kumbhalgarh spread over an area of 586 sq. km. houses a rich variety of wild life like Sloth Bear, Wild Boar, Four Horned Antelope, Panther and Crocodiles in the lake are attractive.

Sawai Madhopur: An 8th Century Ganesh Temple is of great attraction for the devotees at Ranthambore. An impressive fort was built in 994 on the top of a steep high creek 200 metres above sea level. Ruined pavilions, walls, chattries and splendid monuments are interspersed within the majestic fort Ranthambore National Park spread over 392 sq. km. over undulating terrain of

DIRECTION TO DEVELOP TOURISM

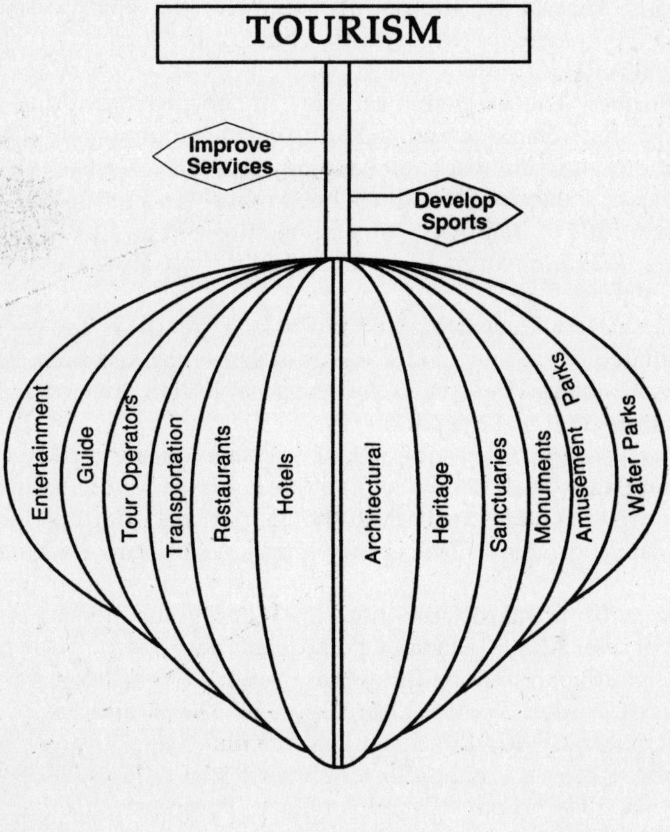

Fig. 2.2

(Designed and Compiled by the Authors)

Aravali and Vindhyan ranges is one of the finest Tiger reserves in the country under the Project Tiger.

The majestic predalors, assured of protection, roam freely during the day time and can be seen at close quarters. The sanctuary has a large number of Sambher, Chital, Leopard, Nilgai, Chinkara, Langur, Wild Bear and Peafowl. There are three lakes—Padam Talab, Rajbagh and Milak Talab along with a number of anicuts in the Padam Talab. Jogi Mahal is an attraction on the banks of Padam Talab.

Udaipur: West Zone Cultural Centre has developed Shilp Gram amidst the Aravali ranges near Fateh Sagar. The atmosphere is a quite rural hut of different states and artisans working there can be seen. Cultural programmes are also held. Water park is another attraction near Goverdhan Vilas for excursion.

Special Facilities[16]

Infrastructure of R.T.D.C. at Tourist Centres in Rajasthan

Table 2.2: Infrastructure Facilities of R.T.D.C.

Sl. No.	*City*	*Name of the Unit*
01.	Jaipur	Palace on Wheels
02.	Jaipur	Beer Wholesale Trade
03.	Jaipur	Gangaur Hotel
04.		Teej Hotel
05.		Swagatam Hotel
06.		Transport Unit
07.		Jheel Ramgarh
08.		Fairs and Festivals
09.	Ajmer	Khadim Hotel
10.		Khidmat Hotel
11.	Alwar	Meenal Hotel
12.	Bikaner	Dholamaru Hotel
13.	Bharatpur	Saras Hotel
14.	Behror	Motel
15.	Barr	Motel
16.	Balotra	Motel
17.	Bundi	Vrandawati Hotel
18.	Barmer	Khartal Hotel
19.	Chittorgarh	Panna Hotel
20.		Padmani Menal

(Contd.)

(Contd.)

Sl. No.	*City*	*Name of the Unit*
21.	Deeg	Motel
22.	Devgarh	Motel
23.	Dholpur	Motel
24.	Dausa	Motel
25.	Deshnok	Karni Yatri Niwas
26.	Devli	Motel
27.	Fatehpur	Havli Hotel
28.	Gogunda	Hotel
29.	Gulabpura	Motel
30.	Haldighati	Rest House
31.	Jodhpur	Ghoomer Hotel
32.	Jaisalmer	Moomal Hotel
33.		Sam Dhani
34.	Jaisamand	Jaisamand Hotel
35.	Jhalawar	Chandravati Hotel
36.	Kota	Chambal Hotel
37.	Mahuwa	Motel
38.	Mount Abu	Shikhar Hotel
39.		Purjan Niwas
40.	Nathdwara	Gokul Hotel
41.		Yatrika Mangla
42.	Nagaur	Kurjan Hotel
43.	Pushkar	Sarovar Hotel
44.		Tourist Village
45.	Pokhran	Godavan Motel
46.	Pali	Panihari Hotel
47.	Ranakpur	Shilpi Hotel
48.	Rishabdeo	Gavri Hotel
49.	Ratanpur	Motel
50.	Ratangarh	Chinkara Motel
51.	Sawai Madhopur	Jhoomer Bavri Hotel
52.		Vinayak Hotel
53.	Siliserh	Lake Palace Hotel
54.	Sariska	Tiger Den
55.	Shahpura	Motel
56.	Udaipur	Kajri Hotel
57.	New Delhi	Package Tour
58.		Central Reservation Office
59.	Mumbai	Tourist Information Bureau
60.	Kolkata	Tourist Information Bureau

Palace on Wheels[16]

Palace on wheels is an enchanting experience run by the R.T.D.C. and the Indian Railway. The Palace on Wheels is a novel thrilling holiday concept of a railway cruise. This fully air-conditioned train is a legend on wheels dazzling in the area of gleaming brass, with ceilings of painted silk and walls adorned with old paintings and all a glow with the warmth of yesteryears. Journey by this train provides travellers wise exotic experience of Pink City Jaipur, Heroic Chittorgarh, Lake City of Udaipur, Desert Citadel of Jaisalmer and Jodhpur, Keoladeo Ghana National Park, Bharatpur and Agra, the fascinating city of Tajmahal.

It is in operation for six month from October to end of March every year. Twin bedded accommodation, with comfortable lower sleeping beds, modern toilets with running hot and cold water and shower facilities, a small lounge and kichtinnette in every saloon two dinning cars offering continental and Indian cuisine, observation car with a bar-cum-library, sound system for announcements and music in every saloon, laundry service at Jaipur, Udaipur, Jodhpur. It is a royal train in its gala and glory.

Rajasthan Tourism Development Corporation and Railway Department is running another train known as Fairy Queen on this line. State Government is also thinking to run orient trains for the tourist purposes.

The analysis of table reveals that Palace on Wheel is emerging as an important source of foreign exchange earning to the State and is gaining popularity among international tourist coming to Rajasthan.

Golden Pass Scheme

R.T.D.C. in collaboration with R.S.R.T.C. has announced various schemes for tourist coming to Rajasthan. Various package tours has been designed to and from the tourist destination suiting the pocket of every tourists and will include accommodation, catering, sight seeing, transportation, guiding and other facilities. The charge will be Rs. 1,000 per person per day.

A pass known as Golden Pass will be issued to the tourist and he or she would be entitled to travel by R.S.R.T.C. deluxe buses and accommodation and catering and other facilities would be provided by R.T.D.C. "Nashta" package scheme would also be adopted to avoid rush at the midways. "Friends of Rajasthan Tourism Project" is also launched.

A special scheme to attract the foreign tourists and NRI's on line of V. USA (visit USA) cards has been announced at package rates inclusive of to and fro travel with accommodation anywhere in Rajasthan (known as Ind. State Gold Pass costing US 160 dollars).

Package Tours

R.T.D.C. is operating a variety of package tours from Delhi to Rajasthan. However, tourist can join in from Jaipur. Different package tours offered by the corporations are:

A. Package Tour from Udaipur

1. Udaipur, Kumbalgarh, Ranakpur, Gogunda, Udaipur
2. Udaipur, Chittorgarh, Udaipur
3. Udaipur, Mt. Abu, Udaipur

B. Package Tour from Jaipur

1. Jaipur, Sariska, Sellisette, Jaipur
2. Jaipur, Sawai Madhopur, Sellisette, Jaipur
3. Jaipur, Ramgarh, Jaipur
4. Rajasthan visit
5. Char Dham
6. Doo Dham

C. Package Tour by R.T.D.C.

Table 2.3 : Package Tour by R.T.D.C.

Sl. No.	*Name of the Tour*	*Days*	*Destination*
1.	Hawa Mahal	3 days	Delhi-Agra-Fatehpur Sikeri-Bharatpur-Deeg-Sariska-Jaipur-Delhi
2.	Desert Triangle	7 days	Delhi-Bikaner-Jaisalmer-Jodhpur-Barmer-Jaipur-Ajmer-Pushkar-Delhi
3.	Mewar Tower	6 days	Delhi-Jaipur-Chittorgarh-Udaipur-Haldighati-Ranakpur-Nathdawara-Ajmer-Pushkar-Delhi

(*Contd.*)

(Contd.)

Sl. No.	*Name of the Tour*	*Days*	*Destination*
4.	Golden Triangle	3 days	Delhi-Sariska-Jaipur-Bharatpur-Deeg-Fatehpur Sikeri-Agra-Delhi
5.	Rajasthan Package	15 days	Delhi-Bikaner-Jaisalmer-Jodhpur-Mt. Abu-Ranakpur-Haldighati-Nathdwara-Udaipur-Chittorgarh-Ajmer-Pushkar-Jaipur-Bharatpur-Sariska-Delhi
6.	Wild Life Package	4 days	Delhi-Sariska-Ranthambore-Bharatpur-Delhi

Source : Annual Reports 2003-04, Department of Tourism, Rajasthan.

Rajasthan Tourism Crowns the following Seven Jewels

1. Bill Clinton, the President of U.S. visited and re-visited Rajasthan.
2. Hotel Raj Mahal at Jaipur bags one of the finest hotel in the world.
3. In 26th January, parade Rajasthan Jhanki "Sonar Killa" won the first prize first ever.
4. Jaipur "The Pink City" is designed as Heritage City of India.
5. The only State, which has trained tourism Tourist Police to grab "Lapka" looter of the tourist.
6. Jaipur airport converted into International Airport.
7. The largest State of India not only in area but also for tourism traffic and centers.

REFERENCES

1. *Welcome to Rajasthan*, A Rajasthan Tourism Publication, Jaipur.
2. *Forts and Palaces of Rajasthan*, A Rajasthan Tourism Publication, Jaipur.
3. *Rajasthan Crafts and Paradise*, A Rajasthan Tourism Publication, Jaipur.
4. *Gems and Jewellery of Rajasthan*, A Rajasthan Tourism Publication, Jaipur.
5. *Discover Rajasthan*, A Rajasthan Tourism Publication, Jaipur.

6. *Folk, Music and Dance of Rajasthan*, A Rajasthan Tourism Publication, Jaipur.
7. *Fairs and Festivals of Rajasthan*, A Rajasthan Tourism Publication, Jaipur.
8. *Dungarpur Banswara*, A Rajasthan Tourism Publication, Jaipur.
9. *Ajmer Rajasthan (Taragarh Fort)*, A Rajasthan Tourism Publication, Jaipur.
10. *Desert Festival Jaisalmer*, A Rajasthan Tourism Publication, Jaipur.
11. *Ganguar Festival*, A Rajasthan Tourism Publication, Jaipur.
12. *Mewar Festival Udaipur*, A Rajasthan Tourism Publication, Jaipur.
13. *Marwar Festival Jodhpur*, A Rajasthan Tourism Publication, Jaipur.
14. *Colourful Rajasthan for all Seasons*, A Rajasthan Tourism Publication, Jaipur.
15. *Chittorgarh*, A Rajasthan Tourism Publication, Jaipur.
16. Annual Report 2002-03, Tourism Department, Rajasthan, Jaipur.
17. New Tourism Policy 2001 of Government of Rajasthan, Jaipur.

Chapter III

ORGANISATIONAL SETUP AND PLANNING PATTERNS IN TOURISM INDUSTRY

Introduction to Tourism Organisation

For any industry to develop an "organisation" is a must as it plays a vital role in planning, development and growth.[1] Organisation is the process of combining the work, which the individuals or group have to perform with the facilities necessary for its execution, that the duties so performed provide the best channels for the efficient and systematic functioning of any particular organisation.[2]

The term organisation also means the structure or form of an enterprise and the arrangement of all parts thereof in a manner suitable for use and services.[3]

Organisation in variously used in management. It is the behavioural science concerned with human relationship, group activity and enhances social structure. "Organisation" compasses all former and informed relationships, inside and outside the enterprise, which are concerned with the behavior of the employees.[4] On the above criteria, which have been put forth by Chris Arguros, the tourism organisation deals with behavioral aspect of the industry, which determines the "enterprise" to accomplish the goal of increasing the tourist arrival, to generate employment, to promote trade and accelerate transport activities and to earn the foreign exchange for the overall development.

"Tourism Organisation" relates to the structure of the Tourism industry, and is concerned with the issues involved in and the approaches to tourism.[5] Robinson emphasizes that the industrial structure of the tourism in the primary stage involves attractions, accessibility and amentias. It is the origination task to achieve this success.[6] Tourism is to be organized as an industry segment and trade association. The industry segment of tourism organisation is Accommodation, Marketing and Transportation. The 'Trade associations' are identified as 'Travel Agency' the Tour Operator or Restaurants Organisations, Entertainment and Recreational Associations, Shops and Publicity Organisations. This is the broad demarcation, as to how the tourism industry can be classified.[7] Tourism organisation can facilitate in reducing the distance, and the managerial ability to sell the commodity, to promote production and sale in the right perspective.[8] Thus accommodation, restaurant services, transportation, travel agencies, handicrafts, shopping establishments, financial institutions can be seen under the preview of the 'Primary Enterprise' while construction industry, plants and equipment, making and advertising come under the Secondary Tourist Enterprises".[9]

Organisational setup in the Department of Tourism Govt. of Rajasthan

The ministry of tourism, art and culture presides over the affairs relating to tourism, art and culture in the state. The promotional aspect[10] is looked after by the Directorate of Tourism and the commercial side falls under the Jurisdiction of Rajasthan Tourism Development Corporation (R.T.D.C.). The ministry is responsible for policy formulation and the Directorate of Rajasthan Tourism Development Corporation has to look after field organisations and implementation of policies and programmes.

The Department and Tourism[11] in its efforts is to promote Tourism promotional activities like the development of tourist sites, bringing out promotional literature, brochures and folders on different tourist destinations, holding of fairs and festivals, bring out films and video tapes on various themes, exploiting the new tourist destinations, encouraging and assisting the private parties to establish new hotels, restaurants and transport units. Presently Tourism Department has sixteen Tourist Information Bureau within the state and six outside the state (New Delhi, Calcutta, Chennai, Mumbai, Ahmedabad and Agra).[12] As an assisting wing of tourism department, the Rajasthan Tourism Development Corporation (RTDC) looks after the commercial side and operates tourist bungalows, midways, cafeterias and provides transport facilities. To make tourism glamorous the RTDC operates luxury train "Palace on Wheels" from October to March every year with the assistance of Indian Railways.

Tourism at the National Level

Modern tourism is a big source of economic development providing employment to million of workers in host countries and foreign exchange earnings for the country. Therefore government is taking interest to play an active role in tourism activities. Tourism has the potential to do damage to the ecosystem cultural pattern of the host communities, if allowed to develop unplanned and unregulated. Ministry of Tourism and Civil Aviation, Government of India can be described as the National Tourist Organisation of the country. The primary task of the department of tourism is to formulate the policies, collect related data, attend to enquiries related to tourism and India as a destination, brand.

Similarly there are a number of tourist offices abroad, which work in liaison with Air India for promoting India as a destination. The India Tourism Development Corporation,[13] (ITDC) a public sector organisation working under the ministry of tourism and civil aviation, was set up in 1966 and entrusted with the management and operation of all government owned hotels, motels and other similar properties. In addition it offers publicity and consultancy services to tourism organisations, operates an India-wide transport network and runs duty-free shops at international airport. ITDC was set up when the private sector was shy of investing in hotels and similar tourism projects. ITDC performed excellently during the early years. However, now the private sector has come of age, and there is a strong demand that the facilities given by ITDC may be best left to the private sector.[14]

Presently ITDC plays a major role in tourism promotion, travel and infrastructure development, within the country. Unlike the department of tourism, ITDC is a commercial profit earning organisation. The corporation[15] has been prime mover in the progress, development and expansion of tourism infrastructure in the country and provides tourism facilities such as accommodation; travel services, surface transport, duty-free shopping, and production consultancy service as well.

ITDC has four regional offices[16] at New Delhi, Mumbai, Chennai, Kolkata. Broadly the main objectives of the corporation are:

A. To construct, market and manage hotels, beach resort, travel lodges, restaurants etc.

B. To provide transport, entertainment, shopping and conventional services.

C. To render consultancy-cum-managerial service in India and abroad.

A significant step was taken by the Government since 1986 by setting up the National Committee on Tourism, which has representatives from both public and private sector.

Tourism at the State Level

Tourism has been put on a concurrent list by the government to be handled both by the union and the state government. The states have realized the importance of tourism and are playing an effective role by investing in tourism projects and activities from their own resources in a big way. States have followed the Central Government's directions while setting up tourism committees. State level tourism is managed between private sector and public sector and has assumed the role of mixed economy. While planning and monitoring are in the hands of Government, real services in this trade lies with private entrepreneurs. In India every state has a separate tourism development cooperation to promote tourist trade in the state. These corporations are working under Ministry of Tourism on the pattern of the India Tourism Development Corporation (ITDC).

Function of State Tourism Development Corporations

STDC's have started commercial activities while the work of publicity and development of new tourist places in the State remains in the hand of state directorate. The main functions State Tourism Development Corporations (S.T.D.C.) are as under.

1. To provide comfortable accommodation facility to tourists both from and within the country at star Hotels, Motels, Tourist Bungalows, Tourist Huts, Holiday Camps Rest Houses, Circuit Houses, Tented accommodations managed by STDC's etc.
2. To provide catering facilities to tourists by way of Hotels Restaurants, Cafeterias, Canteens, Coffee Houses which are managed by STDC's.

3. To provide cheep accommodation to middle class or low-income tourists at various places by way of youth hostels, waiting room facilities at railway stations and airports, camping sites, pavillions and dormitories, etc.
4. To provide better transport facilities to tourists by establishing travel and transport units, within states. STDC's have their own tourist buses, coach's, taxies.
5. To provide entertainment to tourists by organizing fairs and festivals, dances, music, nights clubs, sports, swimming pools (sound and light shows) at various tourist attractions in the states.
6. To provide shopping facilities by establishing and managing shops at various places of tourist attractions to the tourists in the state.[17] On the pattern of central government, the state government and union territories have their own Tourism Development Corporations.

Local Bodies and Tourism

Initially the role of local bodies in tourism development[18] was not accounted for by the planners and developers. The policy formation was done at national or state level and the local bodies were ignored in this regard. The tendency has been to thrust project from above leading to complaints later on that the local body is not cooperative or creates hurdles. Most of the local bodies also are not aware regarding their functions and responsibilities. In this regard, of late they are becoming conscious regarding their role and rights. Their relevance in destination development and sustainability is being recognized at top level also. In fact there is a direct correction between tourism and local bodies. It is acknowledged that tourist resort, motels and other place of historical significance and natural beauty are possibly able to attract large number of tourist if the environment around the site is hygienic, well developed, neat and clean and properly maintained. Local bodies constituted by the Government can play a violent rate in this regard. Following are the areas that have to be managed properly by the local bodies for the tourism development:

- Roads, traffic signs and directions
- Neat, clean and well maintained shopping centres
- Sanitation and toilets

- Local Transportation
- Water Supply
- Security, Law and Order
- Pollution Control
- Health Hazards and Medical Aid

Role of Department of Tourism, Art and Culture, Jaipur

The Department of Tourism is solely responsible[19] for promoting tourism in the state of Rajasthan. It deals with planning and coordination at the state level. It undertakes promotion and publicity work for tourism and is also responsible for regular functioning of various tourist activities. The State Department of Tourism acts as a coordinator and a catalyst for all developmental and promotional activities in the field of tourism, with the objective of putting Rajasthan predominantly on the tourist map of the world, the state Department of Tourism has been active in developing infrastructural facilities within the state. The efforts made in the past Thirty-three years have started paying dividends and the inflow of tourist to the state has seen vertical growth year after year. The functions of the tourism department are both promotional and organisational in its approach.

Objects of the department of tourism, Art and Culture, Jaipur Rajasthan[20]

1. To motivate a greater number of foreign and domestic tourists to visit Rajasthan.
2. To put the state of Rajasthan prominently on the tourist map of the world.
3. To provide infrastructural facilities both for domestic and foreign tourists.
4. To develop and motivate private agencies like travel agencies, hotels, transport units in the state to accelerate the growth potential.
5. To coordinate the functioning of other government departments and private agencies.
6. To conduct surveys and compilation of the art and cultural heritage available in the rural area of Rajasthan.
7. To preserve the culture of Rajasthan for Tourism.

Functions of Department of Tourism, Art and Culture

The Department of Tourism has several functions[21] to perform. The manifold functions fall under the broad heads as are given below:

1. Collection, compilation and dissemination of tourist information in India and abroad and attending to enquiries from international tourists, tour operators and travel industry, such as airlines, steamship companies and hotels.
2. Co-operation with international travel and tourist organisations at government and non-government levels.
3. Development of tourist facilities for national international tourist.
4. Publicity at home and abroad with the object of creating an overall awareness of the importance of tourism.
5. Simplification of frontier formalities in respect of international tourists.
6. Regulation of activities of various segments of the travel trade, such as hotels, youth hostels, travel agencies, wildlife outfitters, guides, tourist car operators and shopkeepers catering to the needs of the tourists.
7. Compilation of statistics and market research on international tourist traffic to India and their utilisation for more effective tourist promotion.

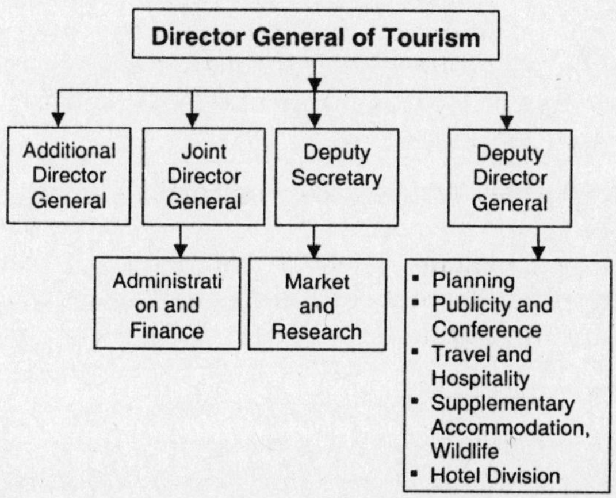

Fig. 3.1 : Organisational Chart of Department of Tourism Art and Culture, Jaipur

Directorate of Tourism

The second agency in the organisational hierarchy is the Directorate of Tourism, which works under the Secretary, Department of Tourism Art and Culture. The functions of directorate are as under:

(*i*) To deal with establishment matters relating to the non-gazetted staff of the department like appointments, transfer, promotions, resignations, leave, special pay and allowances, pension and gratuity cases under Rules 35 to 50 of Rajasthan Service Rules.

(*ii*) Preparation of policies at the initial level for tourism development and publicity.

(*iii*) Preparation of budget for the directorate and various district units, advance loans for purchasing store and articles.

(*iv*) Supervision and control of the directorate including district and other units both, within and outside of the state.

(*v*) Co-ordination of directorate with other Government agencies.

(*vi*) Participation and arrangement of various conferences, committee, exhibitions, fair and festivals.

As for as Department of Tourism, Art and Culture of Rajasthan is concerned the department has started working independently since 1956 at the secretariat level. The department is headed by the Secretary, Tourism and under him Director, Tourism, Tourist officers work for assisting and implementing the policies so formulated by the cabinet or in consultation with or without the central Government. Rajasthan Tourism Department is also having following agencies under him:

1. Rajasthan Tourism Development Corporation Ltd. (RTDC)
2. Rajasthan State Hotels Corporation Ltd. (RSHC)
3. Rajasthan Institute of Tourism and Travel Management (RITTMAN).

The main role of Department of Tourism, Art and Culture is:

1. To promote touristic infrastructure for speedy tourist traffic and full utilisation of tourist resources.
2. To co-operate with private sector for the development of new tourist sites and destinations and to encourage private participation in this regard.

3. To organize and promote folklore, handicrafts fairs and festivals, rural tourism to further boost the tourism activities of the state.
4. To develop international airport at Jaipur and prepare infrastructure for civil aviation at other important tourist destinations.
5. To promote and provide publicity of tourist products at the national and international level.
6. To prepare tourism policies and programmes for speedy and sustainable tourism development.
7. To provide tourist police force for safety and security of tourists.
8. To provide consultancy to private sector.
9. To provide grant for tourism research.
10. To provide tourism and hotel management education through hotel management institutes which are running at Jaipur, Jodhpur, Ajmer and Udaipur.
11. To organize seminars, conferences and exhibitions.
12. To develop regional tourist circuits through Divisional Commissioners.
13. To link tourist offices and destinations through Computers.
14. To develop and take care of existing tourist infrastructure.

Recently the department has widened its role by signing M.O.U. (Memorandum of Understanding) with Archaeological Survey of India to preserve the identity of Jaisalmer fort for four years and released 4.5 crores for expenditure in this regard. Apart from that similar nature M.O.U. was organized with Chirag Deep International Film Co., Gujarat Tourism Development Corporation, I.T.D.C. and many such other programmes of similar nature are under consideration. The department of Tourism has set up as single window agency to process and to expedite all government permission and clearances as the role of facilitator.

Role of Rajasthan Tourism Development Corporation (RTDC)

On the basis of the recommendations of the central survey team and following the pattern of the India Tourism Development Corporation the Government of Rajasthan established "the Rajasthan Tourism Development Corporation" at Jaipur under the provision of Companies Act, 1956 and it started operating properly from April 1, 1979.

The Rajasthan Tourism Development Corporation (RTDC) is a pioneering and popular unit to promote tourism in the state of Rajasthan. Its primary function is to provide infrastructural and service facility such as accommodation, transport, catering etc. Keeping in view the vast increase in tourist traffic the corporation has planned and commissioned new units. The work of expansion in different existing units is also undertaken and it is working effectively and efficiently. The state government realizes that tourism is neither a compact entity nor it is a cognate activity. With this feeling multi-dimensional functions and operation of tourism necessitated a suitable organisational structure, which could handle its promotional as well as commercial aspects effectively.[22]

Function or Role of R.T.D.C.

The main function of the Rajasthan Tourism Development Corporation is to promote tourism in the state of Rajasthan by assisting to Department of Tourism through various types of activities and facilities to tourists. This function, covers all those facilities, which the corporation provides to the tourists in Rajasthan. The functions and the role of RTDC can be summed up as under:

(*a*) Accommodation
(*b*) Transport Facilities
(*c*) Bar Services
(*d*) Package Tours
(*e*) Bar Shop
(*f*) Booting Facilities
(*g*) Catering Services
(*h*) Palace-on-wheels
(*i*) Sight Seeing Facilities

Table 3.1: Package Tour Offered by R.T.D.C.

S.No.	*Name of the Tour*	*Days*	*Destinations*
1.	Hawa Mahal	3 days	Delhi-Agra-Fatehpur Sikeri-Bharatpur-Deeg-Sariska-Jaipur-Delhi.
2.	Desert Triangle	7 days	Delhi-Bikaner-Jaisalmer-Jodhpur-Barmer-Jaipur-Ajmer-Pushkar-Delhi
3.	Mewar Tour	6 days	Delhi-Jaipur-Chittorgarh-Udaipur-Haldighati-Ranakpur-Nathdawara-Ajmer-Pushkar-Delhi
4.	Golden Triangle	3 days	Delhi-Sariska-Jaipur-Bharatpur-Deeg-Fathepur Sikeri-Agra-Delhi
5.	Rajasthan Package	15 days	Delhi-Bikaner-Jaisalmer-Jodhpur-Mt.Abu-Ranakpur-Haldighati-Nathdawara-Udaipur-Chittorgarh-Ajmer-Pushkar-Jaipur-Bharatpur-Sariska-Delhi.
6.	Wild Life Package	4 days	Delhi-Sariska-Ranthambhore-Bharatpur-Delhi.

Source: Department of Tourism, Government of Rajasthan.

Achievements of Rajasthan Tourism Development Corporation

1. Tie up has been made with Gas Authority of India for food and stay.
2. Accommodation and Catering arrangements were made successfully for International Rajasthani Conclave held at Jaipur.
3. Participated in domestic trade conventions in Delhi and "IATO" for the making and promotion of RTDC Network, Camp Tourism and Palace-on-Wheels.
4. Appointment of marketing agents in thirteen main cities of India for hotel reservation in RTDC units.
5. Started reservation in RTDC units by Fax and E-Mail.
6. Introduced credit card facility in major RTDC units.
7. 50 per cent discount offered in some units of RTDC.
8. Opened a joint office of Deptt. of Tourism and R.T.D.C. in Chennai Tourism Complex.
9. Prepared two authorized web sites by RTDC including necessary information for tourists.
10. RTDC introduced this year a package of "palace on wheels" for India tourists @ 70000 per tour.
11. Expansion of Accommodation, Catering and other facilities, renovation and upgradation of Hotel Gangaur, Jaipur, Motel Behror, Tiger Den, Sariska, Hotel Ghooner, Jodhpur, Hotel Shikhar, Mt Abu, Hotel Kajri, Udaipur and Hotel Khadim, Ajmer.

R.T.D.C. has signed M.O.U.'s for Joint Promotion and Marketing of Tourism with Maharashtra, West Bengal, Karnataka, Himachal Pradesh, Orissa, Uttranchal and Pondicherry states to enhance the better perspectives of the domestic tourism. RTDC has also signed an MOU with India Airlines for tourism promotion in Rajasthan. Similar M.O.U. are also proposed with Air India and foreign International Airlines.

The Rajasthan Tourism Development Corporation (RTDC) has been devising tours and Transport packages and will soon be providing reservations through e-mail. It has already introduced a credit card facility at important tourist locations in the state and has opened an additional office in Ahmedabad for bookings.

Future Prospects of RTDC

1. RTDC acts as catalyst for development of the tourism infrastructure in Rajasthan by constituting a forum having services of experts in the field of tourism crafts, interiors, travel environment etc.
2. New tourist train in joint collaboration with Railways on Delhi-Jaipur-Shekhawati-Bikaner-Delhi sector on the lines of "Palace on Wheels" to be introduced soon.
3. The economy version of "Palace on Wheels" with the same itinerary likely to be introduced.
4. RTDC also plans to tie up with petroleum companies for opening their outlets in the free land available at Hotels / Motels on the highways.
5. Development plans are for Shilpgrams at tourist villages of Pushkar and Jheel.
6. Special Manpower and HRD training programme for RTDC employees.

Tourism Planning and Policy

Planning is the backbone of economic development. No economic activity can generate accelerated growth without proper planning both at the micro and macro level. Tourism planning may be defined as the creation and addition to facilities, and services to meet the need of the tourists. Tourism planning is an essential activity for every destination areas, especially in today's fastly changing business environment. Although some destinations have flourished without any conscious planning, many have eventually suffered serious consequences for most carefully considering future events and their impacts. Planning refers to the selection between alternative courses of action. All planning involves an analysis of the future. It also involves setting the basic goals and objectives for the destination area, which is the point, which other supportive actions follow.[23]

Years of experience have shown that tourism development has to be based on a solid policy and careful planning. Planning in tourism provides a bridge between the present situation and the desired future situations. Its Main objective is to maximize the overall economic, social and cultural advantage of tourism.

There are five essential phases in the tourism planning[24] process and these are follows:

1. Background Analysis Phase
2. Detailed Research and Analysis phase
3. Synthesis Phase
4. Goal-Setting, Strategy, selection and objective setting phase
5. Plan development Phase

Need for Tourism Planning and Policy

All Government for the development of touristic infrastructural are giving priority to tourism policy formation and setting of goals. Policy and planning is essential for every enterprise and service in tourism. Hotels, airlines, travel agencies, tour operators, shopping outlets, local bodies etc, all formulate their own policies and plan of actions.[25] The constituents of the Tourism Industry are also varied and there is intense competition among the destinations to attract tourists. Though many countries may be late entrants in the business of tourism, they have the advantage of evaluating and using to their own benefit the experiences of others in this area. In order to speed up the development process there has to be a policy with identified targets and a plans to achieve them. A new tourism policy,[26] which is Government, led private sector driven and community welfare-oriented was announced by the central government in May 2002. The policy gives direction to position India as a Global brand to take advantage of the burgeoning Global travel and trade and the vast untapped potential of India as a destination. It envisages improvement and expansion of product development in:

(*i*) Cultural Tourism
(*ii*) Eco Tourism
(*iii*) Beach and Coastal Tourism
(*iv*) Cuisine Tourism
(*v*) Cruise/River Tourism
(*vi*) MICE Tourism
(*vii*) Rural/Village Tourism
(*viii*) Health Tourism
(*ix*) Adventure Tourism
(*x*) Festival/Shopping Tourism

It also envisages creation and development of integrated tourism circuit based on India's unique civilisation, heritage and culture in partnership with States, private sector and other agencies. The planning for the development of tourism[27] infrastructure involves an objective assessment of the existing demand for various tourism products and their levels of supply. It is also necessary to make realistic look between demand and supply based on past trends and policy guidelines. The demand can be either actual or potential. The demand, which as already fructified into tourist visits, is the actual demand and that which is yet to be fructified is potential demand. Potential demand is usually assessed in terms of travel plans of target population, positive response rates to advertisements, levels of awareness etc. through market surveys at the source market. The most important consideration in the planning of tourism projects in specific locations is the capacity to absorb tourism. It is assessed through various methods like tangible resource limits, tolerance by host population, satisfaction of visitors, excessive rate of growth or change, cost-benefit analysis and systems approach. The application of any of these methods for the measurement of carrying capacity requires massive data on tourist consumption patterns, resource constraints, changes in the behavioural patterns of population, satisfaction levels of visitors etc. Such data's are usually gathered through special surveys of both the host community and the visitors.[28]

Tourism Planning in Rajasthan

Tourism industry in Rajasthan being a vital accelerator of growth in the state economy needed a well-defined planning which was necessitated by visit of Bill Clinton in 2001. Bill Clinton's visit to Rajasthan helped to turn the world's spotlight on this popular destination as the State is already witnessing an increasing tourist traffic ever since. This welcome development has initiated tourism officials at the government level to form and formulate an effective tourism planning and tourism policy of the state, which can further boost tourism flow in the state. Keeping in view Rajasthan Government formulated Tourism Policy–2001 on the following objectives:

Tourism Policy of Rajasthan—2001

The tourism policy represents "an amalgam of the principles upon which a course of action for tourism development is based."[29] Tourism policy is a part of well-defined planning. Successful planning is depending on the clear, strong and diversified tourism policy. As Rajasthan is one of the most popular tourism states of the country and the share of state in the international tourist arrivals to India is about 25 per cent. Government of Rajasthan, which paid, has declared the tourism policy on 24th September 2001 has emphasis on public-private partnership in almost all areas of tourism sector including the conservation of monuments and heritage. It has been envisaged that the growth of tourism sector of Rajasthan would be driven by private sector and Government would act as a catalyst and pragmatic regulator only. Government has offered a package of incentives to facilitate the rapid and balanced growth of tourism industry in Rajasthan. Tourism policy of Rajasthan aims at poverty alleviation, employment generation, development of remote areas, advancement of women, social integration and above all to bring national and international understanding and peace. This policy is focused on overall social and economic development of state by making tourism a truly people's industry in Rajasthan. This policy will definitely develop and accelerate for the rich and varied products of Rajasthan as– handicrafts, gems and jewellery, leather items, marble statues etc. and to preserve varied bio-diversity of the state on the basis of scientific methods and lines.

Objectives of Tourism Policy (2001) of Rajasthan

1. To increase employment opportunities especially in rural areas for unemployed rural youth.
2. Optimum utilisation of rich tourist resources of the state in order to attract maximum number of domestic and international tourists.
3. To facilitate the growth of tourism in the state so that the private sector contributes significantly in the development of tourism in Rajasthan.
4. Preservation of rich, bio-diversity natural, historical architectural and cultural-heritage of Rajasthan with

special emphasis on conservation of historical monuments in Rajasthan.

5. To develop a ready market for the rich and varied handicrafts and cottage industries of Rajasthan so as to ensure welfare of artisans/artistes.
6. To promote inter-cultural understanding through religious/pilgrim tourism and fairs and festivals.
7. To promote socio-economic development of Rajasthan through tourism with special thrust on backward areas.
8. To make tourism a "People's Industry" in the state.
9. To minimize the negative impact of tourism and promote sustainable tourism.
10. To open new dimensions in tourism like Adventure tourism, Eco-tourism, Camel/Horse Safaris, River and Canal Cruise, House boats in Rajasthan, Educational Tourism, Caravan Tourism and Village Tourism.
11. Jawahar Kala Kendra, Jaipur and other cultural institutions are to be associated with tourism development.

Basic Features of Tourism Policy of Rajasthan—2001

To Ensure Safety and Security of Tourists—To achieve this objective Government of Rajasthan has established tourist police at various tourist destinations of Rajasthan for the safety, security and hassle-free stay of tourists. Government in his policy is also keen to formulate code of conduct for tourists, host community, service providers, guides and other agencies that are directly or indirectly related to tourism.

Promotion of Sustainable Tourism—To promote the tourism industry in the state on the lines of sustainable tourism is the prime focus of tourism policy. In this regard promotion of eco-tourism is the central theme of the policy. Recently after hon'ble Supreme Court of India in his landmark decision to make environmental education compulsory in colleges and schools, will further help in protecting the environment by spreading awareness among general masses. Further this policy encourages tourism advisory bodies at district, divisional and state levels.

Tourism Infrastructure—Rajasthan state is the largest in the country and having the greatest potential for tourism development.

Therefore creation of adequate infrastructure like accommodation roads, airport facilities local transportation, communication links, banking facilities and other important amenities are absolutely essential for the speedy development of tourism activities. This tourism policy will play the catalyst role and encourage private sector participation in developing touristic infrastructure. Efforts will be made to induce external assistance, central assistance and State plan resources with private investment to achieve goals. Government will prepare an Area-based Master Plan on the potential of each destination for development of tourism in the state.

Accommodation—This policy encourages more private, investment in the hotel industry and as per the assessment of the state tourism department 20,000 additional rooms are needed by the year 2005. This policy also encourages establishment of heritage hotels in the state to provide regional accommodation for the tourists and also preserve historical heritage from dilapidation. Paying Guest scheme has been vary popular with domestic and international tourists since 1991 and scope of the scheme has been further enlarged in this policy.

Tourism as a Industry—The central focus of this policy is to provide all the facilities and concessions to tourism units, which are available to other industries in the state as per rule in force. Government of Rajasthan has granted status of the industry to tourism sector in the year 1989.

Tourist Reception Centres (TRC's)—This policy ensures modern well-equipped TRC at important entry points and various tourist destinations. New TRC would be started at Mumbai and Banglore and TRC of Delhi, Kolkata and Channai would be further strengthened and linked by computer networks. Joint sector ventures like interstate packages for trade with state and central public sector companies has been specially emphasized in this policy.

Tourist Information and Publicity—The policy strategy in this regard is to make optimum use of the media for promoting Rajasthan as an attraction for tourists. This policy ensures high quality tourist literature, publishing in foreign languages like French, German, Spanish, Japanese, Italian, Arabic and English. Special efforts would be made for overseas publicity of Rajasthan as a tourist destination. Private marketing and publicity linkage would be established with the help of travel agents and tour operators to promote tourism in Rajasthan in the world tourism market.

Enhancing the Tourist Products of Rajasthan—Rajasthan has a rich and varied heritage of handicrafts, handlooms and other products, which are appreciated and purchased by tourists visiting the State. This policy is a keen indicator of promotion of handicrafts, handloom, cottage and other industries. Efforts will be made to set up Shilpgrams at various tourist destinations with the assistance of Development Commissioner (Handicrafts), Rajasthan Small Industries Corporation (RAJSICO) etc. A Handloom Museum will also be set up at Jaipur. RTDC will also develop shopping arcades in their existing properties and provide space for artisans to display and market their products. Heritage tourism, weekend tourism, adventure tourism, wildlife tourism is also included in this tourism policy.

Upgrading Tourist Support System—This policy ensures human resource development and trained personnel for the tourism sector. Government will encourage setting of the Institute of Hotel Management and Food Crafts Institutes in the private sector to meet the increasing demand for trained personnel in various departments of hotels. Promotion of tourism education has given the special status in this policy dealing with the adverse impact of tourism. This policy proposed to assess the carrying capacity of popular tourist places like Mount Abu, Pushkar, Nathdwara, Jaisalmer, Ajmer etc. Efforts would be made to regulate the tourist traffic without any cultural pollution takes place because of unregulated growth tourism industry.

Role of the State Government—The role of state government is described as a catalyst, promoter facilitator and to provide infrastructure. The state government will also play the role of policy maker, planner and controller/Regulator for law and order, tourist police standardisation of tourism services and regulation of tourism trade. This policy also includes framing of comprehensive Tourism Master Plan of state with regional/sub-area and its execution in a time bound manner with external assistance central assistance live central government and private sector investment.

Tourist Transport—Development of Rail, Road and Air transport services of international standard is included in this policy. Efforts will be made to arrange special tourist trains with convenient timings to facilitate Tourist travel by rail. More and more rail lines are to be converted to Broad gauge. Effort would also be made to launch an economy version of luxurious "Palace-on-Wheels" for budget tourists. Air-conditioned tourist coaches, tourist car and specially desired non-air-conditioned sightseeing coaches as recognized and approved by the Department of Tourism would be encouraged. The State will encourage Air Taxi Operators (ATO) within the state so the tourist visiting the state can see as many places as possible within the available time. Private sector investment would be encouraged in setting up International airports in Rajasthan and special charter flights would be encouraged.

Incentives/Concessions Offered by Central and State Government for Hotel Industry in Rajasthan—This policy recommends various incentives and concessions offered by the central and state Government to boost tourism in the state which includes various tax rebates, stamp-duty exemption, subsidy, simplification of land conversion rules, extension of loans, promotion of film shooting, multiplexes and drive-in-cinema theaters and many more.

Other Features of Tourism Policy, 2001—Apart from the above discussed basic features of tourism policy, 2001, following are the other supporting points, which will definitely boost the tourism traffic in the state:

(*a*) To encourage establishment of hire tags hotels in the state.
(*b*) To Introduce new scheme for camp tourism/Eco-friendly Nature Tourism.
(*c*) Development of Nazool properties having heritage value.
(*d*) To ensure availability of suitable land for development of tourism infrastructure.
(*e*) Utilisation of land belonging to Devasthan Department.
(*f*) To improve organisational backup by constitution of different boards and committees.
(*g*) Establishment of joint venture with Private investors.
(*h*) Enhancement of Paying Guest Scheme.
(*i*) Creation of suitable wayside facilities.

Based on these policy guidelines various departments of state government would formulate detailed action plan to implement the decisions and to achieve the objectives of the tourism policy. Those departments which are directly associated with tourism sector would issue office orders in a time bound manner to ensure compliance of the policy guidelines and decisions contained in departmental action plan.

Rajiv Gandhi Tourism Development Mission–2001

Government of Rajasthan made tourism sector as a central focus in their annual plans by focusing tourism as a multi-sectorial industry and generated massive employment opportunities for almost of all sectors of the state economy. In the direction "Rajiv Gandhi Tourism Development Mission Document" was prepared by the Deptt. of Tourism, Art and Culture, Jaipur with twelve other collaborating agencies, which are related to tourism development. The permanent technically sound advisory committees have been constituted under Chairman, Rajiv Gandhi Tourism Development Mission and their meeting have been held, recommendations have been received which are being implemented by Department of Tourism.

Mission Statement

A mission mandated to ensure optimum utilisation of rich tourism resources of the state to generate employment especially in rural areas, to develop a ready market for the rich and varied handicrafts to preserve and scientifically manage rich natural, historical, architectural and cultural heritage of the state and to accelerate contribution of tourism industry in the financial and socio-economic development of the state by making tourism truly a people's industry in Rajasthan.

Rajiv Gandhi Mission on Tourism Development

Nodal Agency

Department of Tourism, Art and Culture

Collaborating Agencies

1. Rajasthan Tourism Development Corporation (RTDC)
2. Department of Urban Development
3. Department of Archaeology and Museum (A and M)
4. Public Work Department (PWD)
5. General Administration and Civil Aviation (GAD) Department

6. Forest and Environment Department
7. Industries Department
8. Transport Department
9. Devasthan Department
10. West Zone Culture Centre, Udaipur (WZCC)
11. Khadi and Village Industry Board, Rajasthan
12. Archaeological Survey of India (ASI)

Mission Objectives

1. To generate employment in rural areas through development of tourism by conserving and nurturing folk arts; handicrafts and architectural heritage in a planned manner;
2. To ensure equal status to private and public sector in Rajasthan to get active support from private sector:
   (*i*) To improve roads, sanitation, noise pollution as well as the supply of water and electricity around existing tourist sites and heritage hotels;
   (*ii*) To create people's consciousness of Heritage Conservation and management;
   (*iii*) Integrated development of tourist sites/places;
   (*iv*) Installation of Rope-ways and other related recreational facilities for tourists;
   (*v*) Establish an Institute for Heritage management
   (*vi*) Ensuring people's participation for heritage protection and conservation.
3. Dovetailing of resources under various development schemes of State Government for developing infrastructure for Tourism Development and ensure optimum utilisation of resources;
4. To ensure use of available civil aviation infrastructure in the state for tourism development and to get Jaipur Airport upgraded as International Airport.
5. To promote, publicize and market tourism products of Rajasthan at national and international level with the support of private sector and ensure public awareness about Rajasthan as a premier Tourist Destination.
6. To redefine the role of state in general Department of Tourism in particular as Catalyst and not as an obstruction for growth of tourism industry, to implement tourism

policy, rationalisation of tax structure and simplification of procedures.

7. To establish tourism as a people's Industry in Rajasthan and to promote sustainable and eco-friendly tourism (Eco-Tourism, UNO has declared year 2002 as international Eco-Tourism Year);
8. To devise systems and procedures so that cultural tourism can be promoted by utilizing Devasthan and other available government properties all over the State and also outside the state at important places;
9. To promote adventure, pilgrim and water-sports based tourism;
10. To protect, conserve and scientifically manage architectural heritage of six big cities viz. Jaipur, Jodhpur, Ajmer, Kota and Bikaner for developing tourism at these places.

Strategy

1. Promote Heritage Protection for tourism development at school level by involving students.
2. Managing natural, historical and cultural resources as productive assets;
3. For visible results focus on sub-mission (s) at district level and mini-mission for specific sites/heritage hotels;
4. Effective control of Lapkas (Touts) and other anti-social elements hostile to tourists;
5. Aggressive publicity in print, electronic and cyber media.
6. Aggressive marketing at domestic and overseas travel marts and organize Rajasthan travel marts;
7. Adoption of monuments by corporate like Taj Mahal adopted by Taj Group of Hotels (TATAS);
8. Ensure growth of air taxi operations in the state by allowing liberal use of airstrips/helipads owned by the state for promoting tourism industry.
9. Involve Panchayati Raj Institutions (PRIs) for developing rural tourism by promoting Rural Haats, Fairs, Festivals and Shilpgrams;
10. Dovetailing of developmental schemes of State/ Government of India for creation and strengthening of tourism infrastructure;

11. Tourism legislation on the lines of states like Himachal Pradesh, Goa, etc.
12. Creation of authentic Data Bank and Commission Market Research for fine-tuning the tourism products.

Mission Targets

Domestic Tourists	:	To achieve Annual rate of growth from the present 7 to 10 percent.
Foreign Tourists	:	To achieve Annual rate of growth forms the present 5 to 15 percent.
New Circuits	:	One new tourist circuit/destination to be aggressively launched every year from 2001
Job Creation	:	Tourism sector to strive to create jobs as follows.
Rural Areas	:	40,000 jobs every year.
Urban Areas	:	10,000 jobs every year.
Tourist Charters	:	To Study demand/supply to promote Tourist Charter Flights to attract high spending tourists to the State.
Air Taxi Operations	:	Small Plane for Air Taxi and Helicopter Taxis to be promoted rigorously.
Synergy	:	Attempting synergy of tourism sector with Arts, Crafts and Heritage of Rajasthan for ensuring mutual advantage and symbiotic relationship.

Milestones of Rajiv Gandhi Tourism Development Mission

Effort to Raise Tourist Arrivals (Target 2005)

Domestic Tourist	–	11.87 Million
International Tourist	–	1.25 Million

Policy Initiatives by Government

(*a*) Domestic tourists policy—Declared on 24.09.2001
(*b*) Plan of action for implementing tourism policy

(*c*) Notifications for implementation of Tourism policy—13 Notifications have been issued.
(*d*) Simplifications of procedures especially for transport and excise sector.

Aggressive Domestic and International Marketing and Publicity

(a) Domestic

(*i*) Organize Rajasthan Travel and Tourism Mart.
(*ii*) Participate in all major Travel Trade Fairs.
(*iii*) Promote Inter-state cultural and pilgrim tourism MoUs with State Tourism Development Corporations and professional Tourism bodies.
(*iv*) Concerted media campaign for print electronic and cyber media.
(*v*) Promote Rural/Farm Tourism.
(*vi*) Promote Sustainable Eco-Tourism.

(b) International

(*i*) Effective participation of major International Tourism marts at Berlin, London, Frankfurt, Geneva Dubai etc.
(*ii*) Exploring new international markets like Australia, Japan, South Africa etc.
(*iii*) Strengthening existing markets like U.K., Western Europe, Americas etc.
(*iv*) Coordination with Government of India Tourism offices (GOITOS) and India Missions abroad.
(*v*) MoUs with Air India, Pacific Asia Travel Association (PATA), Travel Agents Association of India (TAAI) India Airlines WTTC, ITDC, Gujarat Tourism, Pondicherry Tourism have been done.

Organizing International Fairs like Stonemart (2000) at Sitapura (Jaipur) Venue

2004 – Rajasthan Gems, Jewelry and Textile Mart
2005 – Rajasthan Stone Mart

Awareness and Professional Management of Heritage

- Establishing an Institute of Heritage conservation and management at Jaipur.
- Marking Heritage Protection and Development of Tourism part of school curriculum.

Ensuring Hassle-Free and Pleasant Stay of Tourists in Rajasthan

- Tourist police sat Jodhpur, Udaipur, Mt. Abu and Jaisalmer (Budget Allotted).
- Code of conduct to be devised and implemented Voluntarily for tourists and hosts.
- Drive against LAPKAS (touts) and Hostile elements to tourists (Launched at Udaipur).
- Tourist Legislation (Facilitation and Regulation of Travel Trade Act).
- Promoting Sociologically, Culturally and ecologically sustainable tourism practices.

Tourism Promotion through Cyber Highway

- Connecting all tourism information Bureaus (TIBS) Tourist Reception Centres (TRCs) within state and outside through computer Network.
- On line information and bookings for the services of Department of tourism (DTO) and Rajasthan Tourism Development Corporation (RTDC).
- Cyber café's at all TIBs, TRCs and RTDC Hotels.
- Launch of cyber version of Rajasthan Tourism magazine Rajasthan Athithi.
- Interactive CDs and other cyber tools for promoting e-based tourist facilitation.

Public Private Partnership

- Lease out premier heritage properties like Khasa Kothi Anand Bhawan etc. to the internationally acclaimed hotel chains by inviting competitive bids.
- To encourage conversion of lesser-known cultural

properties in far flung areas for spreading the economic benefits of tourism at the grass root level.

- MoUs with International Hotel Chains/Travel Agents for marketing and publicity.
- Float permanent Forum for public-private partnership in the state (Tourism Guild of Rajasthan).
- Encourage hospitality education in private sector for professional human resource in tourism.

Mobilize Resources for Heritage Conservation

- Promote Adopt a monument Scheme for Corporate and institutional donors.
- Launching monuments as center for learning and cultural events.
- Promoting museums as seats of learning and cultural exchange.
- Promote private museums by liberal grants and publicity in departmental literature.

Rural Tourism for Generating Employment in Rural Areas

- Identify 50 rural tourism sites, preferably one in every district.
- Motivate Panchayati Raj Institutions (PRIs) to participate activity in promoting rural tourism.
- Establishing rural Arts, Crafts and cuisine centers (Ship grams).
- Promoting Traditional Rural theatre, Folk Arts and performers.
- Promoting Souvenirs from rural areas for the domestic and international tourists.

REFERENCES

1. Batra G.S. and A.S. Chawla, *Tourism Management—A Global Perspective* (2000), Deep and Deep Publications Pvt. Ltd. New Delhi, page xii.
2. Wiley and Sons, *The Philosophy of Management*, New York, 1980, p. 32.
3. Cornell William B., *Organisation and Management in Industries and Business*, Ronald Press, New York, 1947, p. 36.

4. Argyris Chris, '*Personality and Organisation*', Harper Row, New York 1957, p. 239.
5. Robinson H., "*A Geography of Tourism*", MacDonald and Evans, 1976, p. 81.
6. *Ibid.*, p. 81.
7. Raina A.K., "*Tourism Industry in Kashmir*", 2002, Shipra Publications, Delhi, p. 64.
8. Koontz Harold D. and Cyril J.O. Connell, '*Principles of Management*', McGraw Hill Book Company, New York, Third Edition, p. 208.
9. Mridula, Narayan Datt, *Ecology and Tourism*, Universal Publishers Distributors, 1991, Delhi, p. 104.
10. Department of Tourism, Govt. of Rajasthan, Jaipur.
11. Sharma K.C., *Tourism Policy Planning, Strategy*, Pointer Publishers, SMS Highway, Jaipur, 1996, p. 98.
12. *Ibid.*, p. 98.
13. Seth Pran Nath and Sushma Seth Bhat, *An Introduction to Travel and Tourism*, Sterling Publishers Pvt. Ltd., New Delhi, p. 54.
14. *Ibid.*, p. 54.
15. *Ibid.*, p. 69.
16. Gupta Sunil, S.P. Bansal, '*Tourism Towards 21st Century*', Deep and Deep Publication Pvt. Ltd., New Delhi, 2001, p. 69.
17. *Ibid.*, p. 70.
18. Batra G.S., A.S. Chawla, *Tourism Management, A Global Perspective* (2001), Deep and Deep Publications Pvt. Ltd., New Delhi, p. 186.
19. IGNOU, *Study Material Ts-1 Foundation Course in Tourism*, 'Tourism Planning and Policy', Vol. 8 (April 1995), p. 35.
20. Sharma K.K., *Tourism in India* (Centre State Administration), Classic Publishing House, Jaipur, 1991, p. 59.
21. *Ibid.*, p. 61.
22. Sharma K.C., *Tourism, Policy, Planning, Strategy*, Pointer Publishers, Jaipur, 1996, p. 67.
23. *Ibid.*, p. 99.
24. Mill Robert Christie Al Astair M. Morrison, *The Tourism System, An Introductory Text*, Prentice Hall Inc., Englewood Cliffs, New Jersy, 1985, p. 285.
25. *Ibid.*, p. 293.
26. E. Murphy Peter, "*Tourism a Community Approach*", Mithun, New York, p. 153.
27. *Highlights of Tourism Arrivals in India—2002*, Department of Tourism, Govt. of India, New Delhi, p. 9.
28. IGNOU—*Study Material Ts-1 Foundation Courses in Tourism*, Vol. 2, 'Tourism as an Industry' (July 1994), p. 49.
29. *Ibid.*, p. 49.

Chapter IV

FINANCIAL IMPLICATIONS OF TOURISM

> "The entire Travel and Tourism Industry has been galvanised and the Tourism Environment has been infused with new dynamism, new dedication and new foresight. It is now looking to future with great confidence and sense of mission."
>
> —Jagmohan

Tourism is one of major industries in India. It is one of the fast growing industries with the increase in number of tourists and investment. Many of the industrial houses are investing a huge sum of amount in this industry. Any business house, which takes a decision to invest, calculates the return. Tourism, as we see the history, in past, only a social/cultural obligation, but, in the present times, the entire situation has changed and its future is very bright from investment point of view due to following reasons:

- It is one of the fast growing/expanding industries in the world.
- The barriers of international boundaries are no more, as the world has now become a global village.
- People are more mobile than ever before.
- "Seeing is believing" is believed now.
- Adventuresome/risk-free generation.
- No credit, instant cash turnover.

In tourism the term financial implications in relation to business fall into three broad groupings. One defines the finance function in a tourism business, as simply the task of providing funds needed by the enterprise on terms that are most favourable in light of its objectives. Similar meaning of the word "finance", this approach is concerned almost exclusively with the procurement of funds. It is, of course, widened to cover a discussion of the instruments, institutions and practices through which funds are obtained. It also covers the accounting relationships between an owner and its sources of funds. This approach assumes that the expenditure decisions, giving rise to the demand for investment, are made elsewhere within a business and the owner is left with the task of determining how these funds can be raised.

Although this definition has the merit of highlighting the core of finance function-keeping the business supplied with enough funds to accomplish its objectives—its is generally considered that such a definition is too narrow to be of any use. Finance implications is certainly broader than that of funds procurement of supply.

At the other extreme is another definition which considers that finance is concerned with cash, and that since nearly every business transaction involves cash directly or indirectly, finance is concerned with everything that takes place in the conduct of a tourism business. Obviously, such a definition is too broad to be meaningful.

The third approach—more acceptable for the purpose of our discussion—envisages finance function as procurement of funds and their effective utilisation in business.

Classification and Description of Financial Implication

Financial implication may be classified into two groups: Executive and Incidental. The executive implication is sort termed because it requires administrative skill in planning and execution, and the incidental implication is so-called because, for the most part, it covers routine work, chiefly clerical, that is necessary to carry into effect financial decisions at the executive level. Some of the basic executive finance functions are given as under:

- Establishing asset-management policies.
- Determining the allocation of net profits.
- Estimating and controlling cash flows and requirements.
- Deciding upon needs and sources of new outside financing.

- Carrying on negotiations for new outside financing.
- Checking upon financial performance.

Investment Decisions for Financial Implications

1. Establishing assets management policies
3. Estimating and controlling cash flows and requirements etc.

Financing Decisions

4. Deciding upon needs sources of new outside financing etc.
5. Carrying on negotiations for new outside financing etc.

Profit Decisions

2. Determination of the allocation of net profits.
6. Checking upon financial performance etc.

Cost of Capital

(a) Financial Decisions
(b) Investment Decisions
(c) Dividend Decisions

The under-mentioned table gives estimated investment requirement for infrastructure in Rajasthan on the basis of new tourism policy of State.

Table 4.1: Estimated Investment Demand

(Rs. in crores)

Activity/Years	*2002*	*2002-07*
Hotels	25	100
Restaurants	5	10
Airlines facilities	20	80
Air Taxis/Charters/Helicopter Services	20	40
Taxis/Tourist Coaches	80	140
Wayside facilities	15	50
Monuments conservation	7	10
Sanctuaries	8	20
Amusement/Theme/Water Parks	12	30
Others	10	50
Total	**202**	**530**

Source: Projections by Researchers on the Basis of Demand of Tourist Traffic in Rajasthan.

Infrastructural Investments in Tourism is also Important for

- Employment Generation
- Poverty Alleviation
- Empowerment of Women
- Survival of Rural Artists
- Upliftment of Rural Artisans
- Improvement of Urban and Rural Infrastructure

To meet above estimated investment requirement, resources/ facilities are available in the State as under:

Financial Assistance from State/Central Government

A new method of funding by way of grant-in-aid towards project cost was introduced during 1996-97. As per the scheme, 28 per cent of the project cost is provided by the Central Government and the State Government provides 12 per cent. The balance 60 per cent has to be raised as loan from financial institutions or banks. This method of funding is applicable to bankable projects requiring large investments.

It is expected that the State Governments would be able to mobilise more resources from financial institutions for investment in tourism projects through this method. In the initial years, the State Governments did not show much interest in this method of funding as they were generally interested in availing loan facilities for putting-up development projects. It was therefore, proposed to re-allocate a major part of the funds provided for the scheme to normal funding schemes. The remaining budget was proposed to be used to meet the committed liabilities in respect of already sanctioned projects. However, some of the State Governments became aware of the significance of the scheme and came up with new projects for financial assistance.

The scheme is therefore, being continued along with the normal funding scheme. All bankable projects with substantial financial requirements are funded under this scheme while the developmental projects which are not requiring heavy investments are funded under the normal scheme.

Procedure for Financial Assistance

The State Governments desirous of availing the Central assistance prepare a list of projects proposed to be taken up during a particular year and discuss the same with the Central Ministry of Tourism during the beginning of each financial year. On the basis of these discussions, a number of projects which conform to the norms of approved schemes and useful from the point of view of tourism are short-listed or prioritised.

The State Government/Union Territory Administration are required to submit the project proposals in prescribed 'C' form along with following documents.

- A certificate to the effect that the developed piece of land is readily available and the same is in possession of the State Government (State Tourism Department) and the land/title of the land will be transferred in favour of Government of India free of charge and free of cost. The certificate should also indicate the exact location of land with site measurement, name of the place and district, etc. along with and undertaking in prescribed format from the State Government, as given in 'C' form.
- Blueprints, drawings, details of the proposed facilities to be created with rate per sqm. and estimated cost of each of the facility.
- Estimates, prepared/vetted by the CPWD/State PWD (approved Civil Engineering Wing), as the case may be.
- A map of the proposed project along with tourist map of the State.

Description about the tourist center along with tourist traffic of the last three years, facilities already available, if any, and full justification for creation of the proposed facility.

The projects and proposals received with the above details are scrutinised with reference to the norms of approved schemes, sources. The project satisfying the existing guidelines are then approved for financial assistance.

The actual releases against the sanctioned projects are made in 3 to 4 instalments. The first instalment is normally released as an advance and the subsequent instalments are released on submission of utilisation certificates in respect of the funds already released. The total release made to any State Government in a year thus depends upon the efficiency of that State in executing the projects.

Loan Facilities from Banks/Institutions

Table 4.2: Projected Loan Facilities from Banks/Institutions

(Rs. in crores)

Banks/Institutions	*2002*	*2002-07*
Banks	132	320
Financial Institutions	50	100
Non-Banking Financial Institutions	10	50
State/Central Government through NGOs	10	60
Total	**202**	**530**

Source: Classification on the Basis of the Projections.

These agencies are providing finance/assistance to the tourism industry on the basis of their operational viability and future prospects.

Operational viability does not mean only financial/monetary benefits and return but has to be studied from social cost benefit too, from macro and micro base with short, medium and long term implications, as shown in the following table :

Table 4.3: Calculation of Social Costs and Benefits

	Macro Base	*Micro Base*	*Implications*
Short Term	-1	0	(-) 1 Below/at par
Medium Term	+1	+1	(-) 2 Profitable
Long Term	+2	+1	(+) 3 Highly Profitable
Implications	+2 Profitable	+2 Profitable	

Implications +2 Profitable/+3 Highly Profitable

As per the details above, any proposal/project for short term may not be viable from macro/micro base, but gradually, with the time span in medium and long-term, it jumps from profitable to highly profitable.

Even when BEP is calculated, we have to consider the social cost benefits and ratios for operational viability. In the present study, has taken following formula has been considered for calculations.

Social cost and Benefits ratio ⇨ $\frac{\text{Total benefits at present rate}}{\text{Total cost at present value}}$

Result of above:

>1 = Project/proposal is sound/viable
=1 = Can be considered
<1 = Needs reconsideration

Example

Chokhi Dhani, Jaipur is one of the tourist resorts with five star hotel facilities, lacks transportation. If a tour operator starts providing bus service in the morning hours from Ajmeri Gate to Chokhi Dhani. The impact and implications of BEP has been calculated as ahead:

Table 4.4: Calculation of Cost Benefit of Regular Bus Service from Jaipur to Chokhi Dhani

Year	*Investment + Operation cost = Total cost*			*Monetary return + Social return** = Total return*			*Discount at 10%**	*Present cost*	*Present profit*
1	7	3	10	8	0	8	0.909	9.09	7.27
2	6	4	10	8	2	10	0.826	8.26	8.26
3	5	5	10	8	4	12	0.751	7.51	9.01
4	4	6	10	8	6	14	0.683	6.83	9.56
5	3	7	10	8	8	16	0.621	6.21	9.93
Total								**37.90**	**44.03**

* Future profit has been discounted @ 10 per cent.

** Social return includes—other intangible benefits like employment generation, increase in cultural value, income derivations and others.

Social cost benefits ⇨ $\frac{44.03}{37.90}$ ⇨ 1.16%

It shows that though, at the initial stage, it is below BEP and not profitable, whereas, in long run, taking into consideration other social aspects, it is profitable and viable.

While calculating the expected dividend from any of the projects/proposal, opportunity cost and shadow price has been considered and then, the use of discounting factor, as is shown in the above table.

True benefits of tourism can be appreciated only on a broad basis, which include all the above and should also be taken into consideration of following incentives.

Incentives[1]

Interest Subsidy

Three per cent interest subsidy is available to hotels of one to three star category on loans sanctioned by financial institutions. Five per cent interest subsidy is available on loans if tourism units are constructed in Jaisalmer, Jodhpur, Bikaner and Barmer.

Income Tax Incentives

- Section 80 HHD of the Income Tax Act: This is available to hotels on their foreign exchange earnings. Fifty per cent of profit derived by hotels, travels agents and tour operators in foreign exchange is exempted from income tax. The balance 50 per cent of profits in foreign exchange is also exempted, provided it is reinvested within a period of 5 years in new hotel projects or expansion of existing units. In an amendment of this section in the budget proposals of 1999, the balance amount can also be invested in equity shares of eligible issue of capital. This would be by a public company and the entire proceeds of issue should be utilised for new hotel projects or for facilities for growth of tourism as prescribed by the Central Government.
- Section 80 IB of the Income Tax Act: Section 80 IB of Income Tax Act, 1961 gives income tax exemption not related to foreign exchange earnings. This is because hotels are like an infrastructure facility contribution to the economic development of an area. This section was

earlier known as 80 IA and has been renamed as Section 80 IB in the budget proposals of 1999. All hotels that start operating between 1.4.1997 to 31.3.2001 will be eligible for income tax deductions as under:

- Hotels located in the hilly areas, rural areas, places of pilgrimage or a specified place of tourist importance will be allowed 50 per cent deductions from their profits/gains.
- In respect of hotels located in other places, the deduction allowed is 30 per cent only, except in Metro cities of Kolkata, Chennai, Delhi and Mumbai, where no deduction is allowed.

These benefits are only available to hotels approved by the Ministry of Tourism. The hilly areas, rural areas and places of pilgrimage have been defined as:

Hilly Area: The term "hilly area" means any area located at a height of 1,000 meters or more above sea level.

Place of Pilgrimage: A "place of pilgrimage" means a place where any temple, mosque, gurudwara, church or other place of public worship of renown throughout any state is situated.

Rural Area: It means any area other than:

- An area which is comprised within the jurisdiction of a municipality (whether known as a municipality, municipal corporation, notified area committee, town area committee or by any other name) or a cantonment board and which has a population of not less than ten thousand according to the preceding census of which relevant figures have been published before the first day of the pervious year.
- An area within such distance not being more than fifteen kilometres from the local limits of any municipal or cantonment board referred to in as the Central Government may, having regard to the stage of development of such area including the extent of, and scope for, urbanisation of such area and other relevant consideration specify in this behalf by notification in the Official Gazette.

Incentives by State Government

- *Remission in Stamp Duty*: To the extent of 50 per cent on transfer of deeds relating to land purchased in municipal areas and to the extent of 100 per cent on transfer of deeds relating to land purchased in Panchayat area of such hotels.
- *Remission in Land and Building Tax*: Hundred per cent for hotels for 5 years in municipal area.
- *Remission in Luxury Tax*: Fifty per cent for 5 years in municipal areas and to the extent of 100 per cent for 5 years in panchayat areas.

The above remissions shall be considered only if such new hotels shall invest at least Rs. 1.00 crore during the period between 1.4.2000 to 31.2.2001 and start functioning by 31.12.2001.

On violation of the above conditions the hotel owner shall be liable to pay entire amount of stamp duty, land and building tax, and luxury tax with penal interest of 24 per cent per annum.

Facilities for Land Conversion

- *In Urban Area*: This is being done under Rajasthan Land Revenue (Industrial Area Allotment) Rules, 1959 on 99 years lease.
    - *Competent Authority*: (*i*) Collector in the districts, (*ii*) In Jaipur District, Director of Tourism, Art and Culture, Jaipur.
    - *Development Charges*: (*i*) Rs. 1,500 per acre at Jaipur and Kota within 15 miles radius, (*ii*) Rs. 500 per acre at places having population of 3 lacs and above except Jaipur and Kota, (*iii*) Rs. 300 per acre at places having population of 50,000 and above but below 3 lacs, (*iv*) Rs. 200 per acre at places having population below 10,000 and above but below 50,000, (*v*) Rs. 100 per acre at places having population below 10,000.
    - *Conversion Charges*: (*i*) Rs. 250 per acre for areas having population of 3 lacs and above, (*ii*) Rs. 150 per acre for areas having population of 10,000 and above but below 3 lacs, and (*iii*) Rs. 75 per acre for areas having population of below 10,000.

- In Rural Areas: Conversion of agriculture land for non-agriculture purpose in rural area for construction of tourism units is being done under Rajasthan Land Revenue (Conversion of Agriculture Land for Non-Agriculture Purpose) Rules, 1992. (*a*) Competent Authority Collector in the district and (*b*) Conversion charges Rs. 1.00 per sq. metre.

- For Heritage Hotels
  - *In rural area*: No conversion charges
  - *In urban area*: Conversion charges will be charged on the built-up area and equivalent land as per rates specified under Rajasthan Urban Improvement Trust Rules, 1974.

Tax Exemption to Films

Films are now exempt from entertainment tax to the extent of 50 per cent for a period of one year, as are picturised in the State of Rajasthan, subject to the following conditions viz.

- That the film shall not have anything, which is against communal harmony and national integration.
- That the film shall not have any objectionable scenes in it.
- That the procedure of the film shall be required to submit in advance, copies of shooting schedule to the Director, Art and Culture and the Deputy Secretary, Finance (Tax) Department, Government of Rajasthan.
- That the minimum 50 per cent of the reel length of the film shall be shot in the State of Rajasthan and be verified by a committee comprising the Director, Art and Culture, the Director Public Relations and the Deputy Secretary, Finance (Tax) Department.
- That such exemption would be subject to recommendations of a committee consisting of the State Minister of Tourism, Art and Culture. The Commissioner, Commercial Taxes or his representative, the Special Secretary, Home, the Director, Public Relations and the Deputy Secretary, Finance (Tax) Department.

Establishment of Land Bank[2]

A land bank has been established at the level of tourism department so that land can be made available quickly for tourism units at suitable revenue. Urban and rural land is being identified to be included in this land bank.

Rajasthan Institute of Tourism and Travel Management[3]

Special heritage preservation and restoration bodies on the pattern of ICCROM would be set up in the state very soon. Efforts are also being made by RITTMAN to provide trained staff in the tourism sector in the state.

At the end it can be stated that while analysing the financial implications of tourism, we should not see that tourism as merely a trading activity but also treat it as a phenomenon with a close vision on all types of activities including social, cultural and moral.[4] Therefore, it is significant to note that the benefits of tourism are not to be judged in terms of economic benefits[5] alone. Tourism, as an industry has wider implications encompassing not only economic benefits but also social cultural benefits as well.

REFERENCES

1. Annual Report 2002-03 of Department of Tourism, Government of Rajasthan, Jaipur, pp. 20-22.
2. Annual Report 2002-03 of Department of Tourism, Government of Rajasthan, p. 19.
3. Annual Report 2002-03 of Department of Tourism, Government of Rajasthan, pp. 16-17.
4. Kuchhal, S.C., *Financial Management*, Chaitanya Publishing House, Allahabad.
5. Sinha, V.C. and Pathak, N.P., *Business and Managerial Economics*, Mayur Paper Backs, 1999.

Chapter V

SOCIAL AND ECONOMIC IMPLICATIONS OF TOURISM

"Tourism must no longer remain the flower of the surplus economies."

—P. Defert

The numerous tourist ramifications defies the estimation of its total impact on all sectors of the economy with which it has direct and indirect links. A tourist has been considered both—a friend and a foe in the process of socio-economic transformation depending upon the nature of development reflexes unleashed by his association with the destination area. Very often visitor propels/ dispels the change in the setting of host area through social and economic dimensions of his personality.

Social Impact—Tourism

Tourism enables to have look into the past and learn about different ways of life. Social tourism is a great force in education and enlightening the people. "It is recognised that tourism has considerable social impact and visitor is highly sensitive to local atmosphere".[1] The spread effects of social tourism through the demonstration of a 'lifestyle' of a tourist have visible influenced the social moorings and attitudes of destination population.

Life is meaningful in the social set up. Social impact on life is regarded as the elixir of human existence, as man by nature has shown inclination in tours, visits, movements, etc. The tourism is a social endeavour. Appreciation of social impact of tourism has been to some extent neglected so far, however, Sir George Young logically highlighted the importance of considering social impact of tourism on economic activity almost universally have

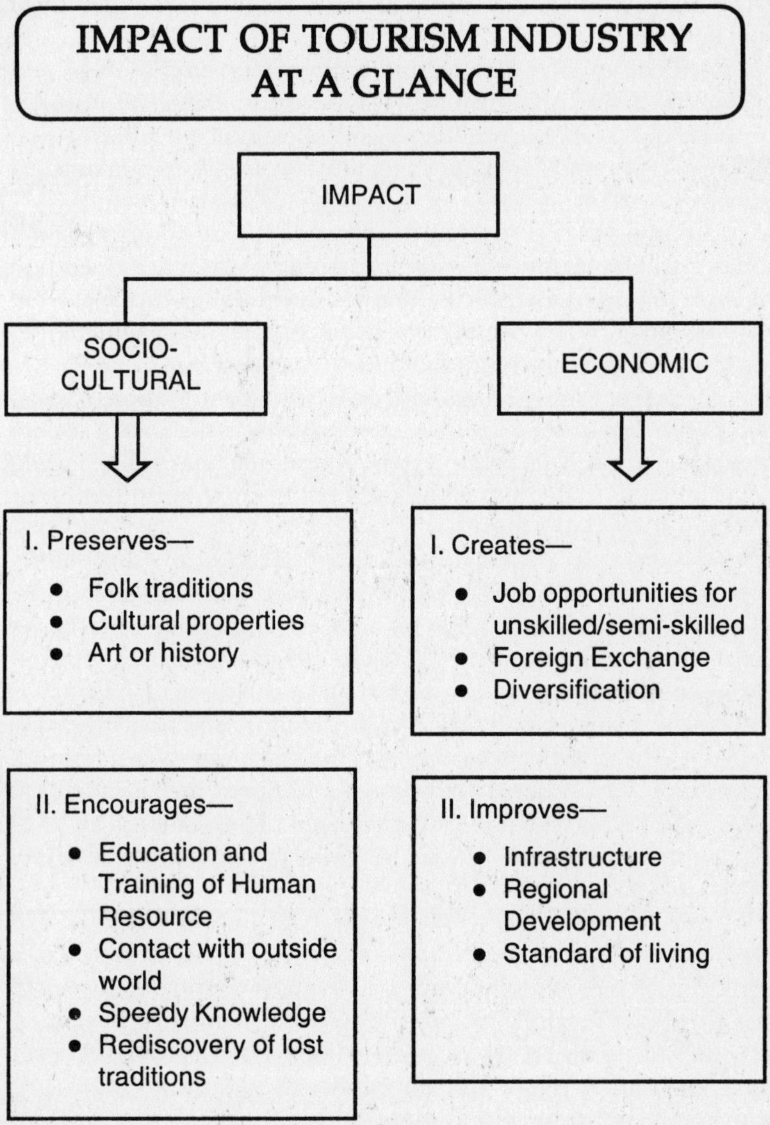

Fig. 5.1

(Designed and Compiled by the Authors)

to be taken into consideration at some stage during growth of that activity.[2]

Tourism impacts directly and indirectly on employment and entrepreneurship opportunities and therefore, affects the attitudes of those dependents on it. Several studies indicate a correlation between economic dependency on tourism and residents support for it.

Liu and Var's study (1986) of resident's attitudes towards tourism in Haveli revealed that respondents strongly agreed that tourism provided many economic and cultural benefits, but were ambivalent about environmental benefits. They were reluctant to attribute social and environmental ethos of tourism.

The present study brings light on tourism contribution to social conditions that many lead to serious problems in the host of society including changes in value system, individual behaviour, family relationship, collective lifestyles, traditional ceremonies or community organisation.

Rajasthan is a historical and archaeological monuments continued to be the biggest draw in attracting international tourists. This fact has been confirmed by a survey undertaken by Pacific Area Travel Association (PATA) in 1994 and also by Tourist Reaction Pattern Survey conducted by Department of Tourism in 1998-99. Rajasthan being rich in history, culture and pilgrim enjoys very wide scope and rich prospects to attract increasing number of tourists, which naturally ensures additional income for local people. With this benefits, the prominence of tourism industry has assumed singular importance—the development of the Rajasthan State.

Tourism indeed is a messenger of different cultures and civilisations and is therefore, a critical actor in presenting a synthesis of socio-cultural values of the host country with that of the originating country. Such a synthetic culture based on appreciation of different cultures and lifestyles in a powerful factor of international peace and development planning would like tourism to embrace whole nation operating as an important unifying force and in broader context finally helps towards creation of single world unit without which human race will not be able to survive very long. Tourism is a vehicle for national and international understanding.

In Rajasthan, tourism is not only an economic activity of huge importance, it is an essential medium of social and cultural development and also of building lasting goodwill and friendship. According to Jawaharlal Nehru "we must welcome these friendly visitors from abroad for economic reasons, for tourism brings foreign exchange but even more so because this leads to greater understanding and mutual appreciation. There is nothing which the world needs today than the mutual understanding."[3] In fact, a tourist with new cultures, new civilisation and new lifestyle triggers off socio-economic transformation of the host country.

Tourism has become an important force for social transformation of the nations. Some of the social implications are being discussed hereunder:

Tourism as Tool for Peace

"The tourist arrives not only with money but with treasures of his civilisation and the history of his country of which he is an ambassador, he is the mirror of the country he belongs as he reflects the social conditions prevailing in their motherland."[4] Tourism draws people and nations closer together, help to dissipate prejudice and corrects misunderstanding, helps in cross fertilisation of international culture which is essential for peace and Rajasthan's effloresce as an open society.

Tourism Promotes Understanding

Face to face meeting of the people erases frontier between the nations and promotes greater understanding and a keen sight into the common problems. It contributes to an open world and free movement of culture and commerce for the benefits of all mankinds. When tourists of different destinations meet it can be the source of new understanding, universal goodwill and replace the present-day tensions, suspicious and mistrust. Tourists bring with them their own ideas, practices and demands; their presence and social background affects the social structure and life of indigenous culture. Tourists are also affected by the experience; they carry back with them habits and new outlook on life.

Tourism has done the Face Lifting of Old Towns

The raw material and finished product of the industry are constituted precisely of the life and the cultural lines of the places concerned. There are many cities and towns in Rajasthan with historical associations, buildings and monuments as resource which cannot be replaced and have retained their best of architecture and other special points of interest for visitors for which tourism has become a new use of old assets. Castles, Forts, Palaces, Havelis, Temples, Museums, Galleries, Monuments as well as streets and squares make up these towns as tourist destinations. New uses of old building in old setting in form of heritage hotels etc. which have outlived their original purpose enables them to be preserved. Thus these towns and village has become an important tourist centre now-a-days. Onsia Mandir and Kiradu Temple are the latest example in the State.

Tourism Rejuvenates the Local Culture

The million of international tourists who are constantly on the move in search of recreation and pleasure support the promotion of such arts and crafts while contributing substantially to the economy of the region. Establishment of heritage hotels is another attempt in Rajasthan to protect our old culture. The concept of heritage hotel came up and number of decaying forts, palaces and castles which were decorated with beautiful frescoes and paintings, furnished with tapestries and furniture were restored back to their original glory which was nearly impossible for the erstwhile rulers and owners to maintain them and continue the rich traditions of the past in the absence of tourist activities. Heritage tourism essentially combines with it the thrill of adventure tourism of which trekking horse and jeep safaris, inhabitants of wildlife, barbecues and flock dances are a pat along with culture tourism which include stays in beautiful Havelies, Palaces, Castles in small towns and villages, participation in local fairs and festivals viewing local handicrafts and experiencing the true favour of India.

Tourism Revives Traditional Arts

The handicrafts and cottage industries of Rajasthan were revived due to the tourism. Marori work of Jaipur the paintings and marble of Kishangarh, woodwork from Shekhawati, figurines from Jodhpur, gems and jewellery of Jaipur, exotic blue pottery, enamelware, brassware, embroided jutis, kota dorea saris, sanganeri printings, tie and dye, odhani, fold paintings, ivory painting phads and pichwair are in great demand among tourists and are the means for crafts and artisans to preserve the art and skill. Number of fairs and festivals are organised now-a-days by the tourism department of Rajasthan so that tourist may have the knowledge of rich culture tradition and customs of the natives.

A New Era for Education

Tourism is an education of other people's habits, society, food, dress, living style without any preceptors professing the desirability of love and goodwill for humanity. A country which succeeds in selling its attractions makes double gain it earns foreign exchange fore what it does not physically exports and it creates a tremendous amount of goodwill in foreign countries which can be measured in terms of money. The tourist will increase their knowledge and learn many new and modern things prevailing elsewhere.

Tourism Provides Spiritual Values

Tourism also provides spiritual values. Tourism can awaken the sense, provide new standards and exposures, art forms and even now belief system. By viewing a range and diversity of societies a wider tolerance for culture of others can be developed, the personal data bank enlarges, level of human experience rises, achievements in many types of learning research and artistic activity is possible.

Tourism Creates a Win-Win Situation

Tourism contributes to the mutual knowledge of man, development of sense of hospitality, reduce distances between the social classes and the human races. It overcomes the isolation of people by encouraging them to vanish in auspicious, prejudices through the encounter of civilisation and culture broading the vision and acceptability for closure ties and mutual understanding a socio-economic cultural integration.

It is a means of social industrialisation. Tourism is a means of social education and social mobilisation in the country itself, as a competing force for fostering better understanding among the nations of the world and for developing close cultural and business relations as a significant factor contributing to world peace.

Economic Impact—Tourism

The contribution of tourism to augmentation of government revenues by way of various taxes is viewed, however, cannot be quantified. Tourism development also contains all the instruments of reducing the regional imbalances. A region may not have the facilities for industrial development but it might be having rich tourism resources in the form of historical monuments, wildlife and other place of tourist interest. An example of miracle performed by tourism development is Jaisalmer in Rajasthan, previously a desert place and now a full-fledged town with every kind of facilities attracting thousands of national and international tourists. Tourism industry thus becomes a nucleus of economic development around which other industries cluster.

The variability factors in tourism have brought about the difference in relative significance in travel trade to different regions of Indian economy. In the State of Rajasthan tourism has acquired a pride of place owing to its significant effect not only to the growth of economy but also on the lifestyle of the people.

Impact of Tourism on Rajasthan Economy

The significance of tourism as a cataclysm of development is well conceived in all types of economies. In the developing states like Rajasthan, tourism has acquired tremendous importance owing to its emergence as an important foreign exchange earner, besides, its numerous direct and indirect social, cultural and economic benefits.

Impact on Industrial Development

Industrialisation has been defined as a process in which changes of a series of strategically process in which changes of a series of strategically production functions are taking place. It involves an

TOURISM IMPACT ON URBAN ECONOMY

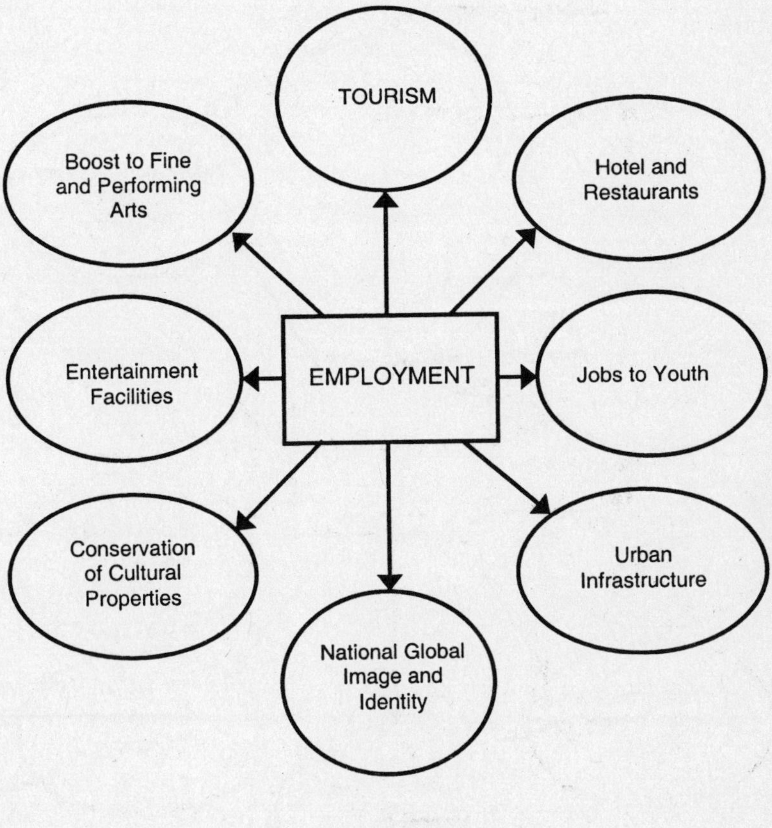

Fig. 5.2

(Designed and Compiled by the Authors)

TOURISM IMPACT ON RURAL ECONOMY

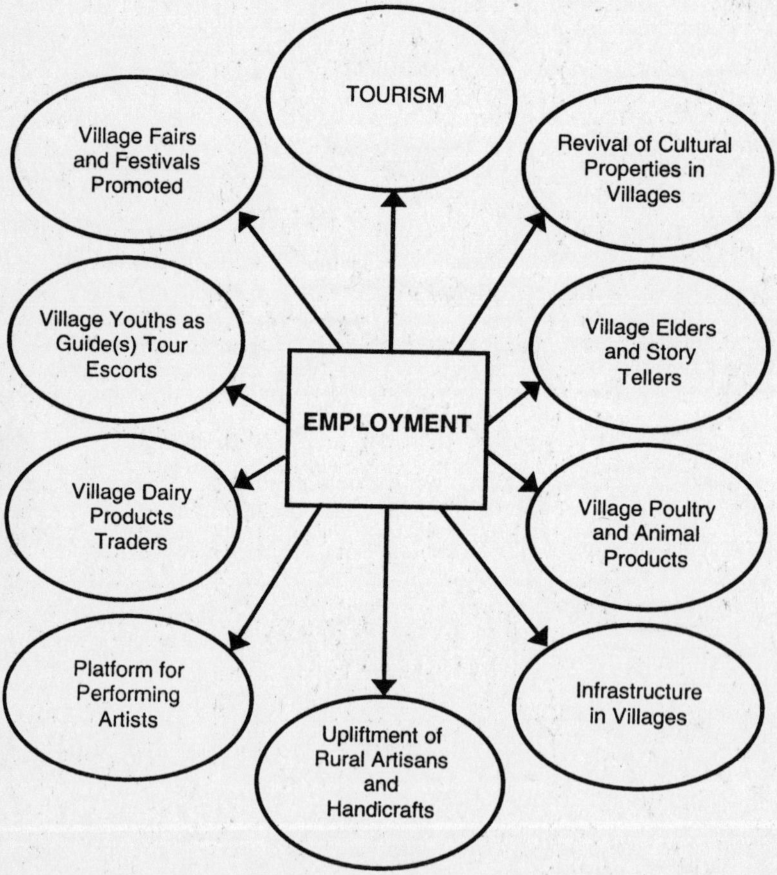

Fig. 5.3

(Designed and Compiled by the Authors)

enterprise, exploitation of a new territory. This is, in a way, a process of "deepening" as well as "widening" of capital.[5] Industrialisation is also understood a process connected with industrial progress, where returns are created, increased and wholly or partially realised. It also lifts the margin of diminishing returns. Increasing returns may be realised because of internal economies, or external economics or both.[6] This is the rationale of industrialisation.

Division of labour leads to discoveries and inventions. The modern organised research suggests and identifies the development through the subdivision of labour[7] and the wise manger attends to the suggestions of the specialised worker. "As a corollary, the store of accumulated knowledge is increased with division of labour."

The industrial development, the primary essential, of which is industrialist, must be aware of the organisational procedures. Organisation spirit is the (*i*) managerial ability, (*ii*) organising ability, (*iii*) administrative or executive ability, (*iv*) special technical knowledge, (*v*) special skill, and (*vi*) physical ability and above all the combination of these qualities. All such qualities when taken into consideration, has drawn a new approach on the "Socio-economic impact of Tourism" in Rajasthan.

Tourism as a Foreign Exchange Earner

The emergence of tourism as an important source of foreign exchange earnings is of crucial importance to State's economy, thereby helping to the national economy. Foreign exchange due from tourism is earned more conveniently than that from manufactured goods. There is no problem of packaging the product and transporting it as the customer brings himself to the point of sale at his own expense, in return takes immediately deliver of the services.

Travel and tourism is one of largest industries in the State of Rajasthan in terms of employment. The study went to say that one out of 25 people is employed in travel and tourism. As a matter of fact, travel and tourism employment investment, output and value added together exceeds those of such major industries as cement, textiles, marble, gems and jewellery etc. Owing to multi-dimensional impact of tourism an accurate estimate of employment generation due to this activity cannot be worked out, however,

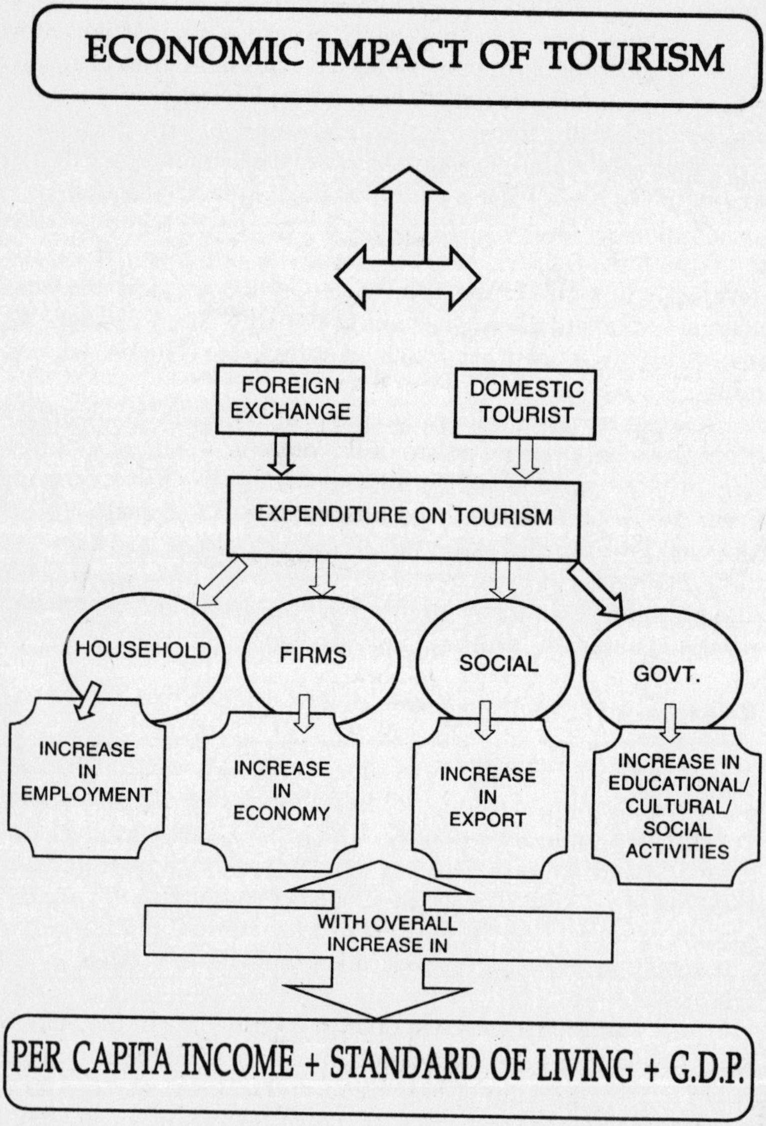

Fig. 5.4

(Designed and Compiled by the Authors)

past study reveals that at least 6 to 7 per cent of workforce is engaged in job connected with or arising from travel and tourism as a matter of fact, tourism is highly labour intensive industry and hence, is a valuable service of employment. It employs a large number of people and provides a wide range of jobs, which extends from unskilled to highly specialised one.

Tourist Expenditure

The structure of tourist expenditure is of crucial economic importance as there is economic mechanism between tourist expenditures and national income, tourist expenditures and employment, tourist expenditures and tax, tourist expenditures and revenue. Expenditures on international tourism were once an unnoticed residual item in a country's balance of payment statistics, now the tourist account balance has become an item of considerable significance, which the Government may seek to manipulate. The tourist expenditure is more pervasive in its economic implications for it acts a stimulant to numerous sections of the economy. The spending behaviour of tourists as per random survey is given below:

Table 5.1 : Pattern of Tourist Expenditure

Sl. No.	*Item of Expenditure*	*% of the Expenditure*
1.	Travelling	20
2.	Boarding	13
3.	Local transportation	7
4.	Entertainment	7
5.	Lodging	24
6.	Shopping	29
	Total	**100**

Source: Field Survey.

Table depicting expenditure pattern of tourists have identified accommodation, food, shopping as the major items of tourist expenditure and accounts for 80 to 82 per cent of tourist spending in the destination area. An identical structure of tourist expenditure is also noticed with respect of India and Rajasthan as is observed from the following table. It is revealed by the analysis of table that expenditure on boarding and lodging, shopping has increased and internal transport has drastically decreased. Table also reveals that home tourist pattern is slightly at variance with that of foreign tourist. All the surveys indicate that foreign tourist expenditure on shopping is higher than home tourists presumably because of their fascination for attractive hand made rare goods.

Table 5.2: Comparative Statement of Expenditure Breakdown in India Under Different Surveys

Item	*1968-69*	*1972-73*	*1976-77*	*1998-99 (Home Tourist)*	*1998-99 (Foreign Tourist)*
Boarding and Lodging	30.23	31.09	33.10	47.60	48.40
Recreation	11.87	13.37	24.40	1.70	3.50
Internal	26.30	25.21	11.24	20.10	13.50
Transport Shopping	28.20	26.00	29.21	30.20	33.30
Miscellaneous	3.40	3.43	2.14	0.40	1.30
Total	**100.00**	**100.00**	**100.00**	**100.00**	**100.00**

Source: Survey Report of Indian Institute of Public Opinion for Department of Tourism, Government of India.

The expenditure incurred by the tourists has their ramification on different sectors of the economy in varying degrees. It also has a wide dispersal effect as against other economic pursuit owing to the complex and multi-faced structure of tourism industry. The tourist expenditure is distributed in the form of salaries and wages to persons employed and as the profit to management engaged in tourists agencies, hotels, cafes, transport companies. Moreover persons engaged in recreation activities, handicrafts also get a due share of tourist expenditure. Apart from these direct beneficiaries tourist expenditure affords an expansion in demand for the products required by tourist servicing sectors. Thus through a backward linkage the suppliers of food, raw material etc. also stand benefited. The consumption expenditure in turn creates further income in the producing sectors, which again is spent on consumption of domestically produced goods and services. As a result of successive chain of income and expenditure, the ultimate increase in income exceeds the initial outlay. The first round of tourist expenditure or the income earned by the tourist serving sectors is thus multiplied through the subsequent rounds of expenditure and thereby raising it to higher level. This growth coefficient of step by step magnification of the impact of tourists expenditure, which gets subsequent multiplied and spread over other sectors is called Tourism Multiplier.

Tourism Multiplier

Tourism multiplier is in fact an attempt to go behind the tourist receipts and find out the expenditure profile of the tourist, nature of his preferences, volume of their transactions, directions in which their spread takes place and the share which goes to various segments of economic activity. The expenditure by the tourist can have beneficial effects on all economic sectors and lead to considerable diversification of industries and other economic activities. Since money circulates through the economy, stimulates it as it changes hand and is spent and re-spent a number of time. Tourism multiplier thus indicates the cumulative force of each currency unit entering the economic.

Besides the direct effects of visitor's expenditure (that is income accruing to factors of production in the tourist sector and in the sectors producing intermediate goods which becomes input of the tourism industry) there are also indirect effects (part of this income is spent on house produced goods and services for personal consumption and this expenditure creates further income which in turn is spent partly on consumption of domestically produced goods. The remainder will be spent on imports and will create further income within the economy or else it will be saved or paid to the Government in form taxes and if Government spends all tax revenue there will be further income generated). In this way ultimate increase in income exceeds the initial increase. This process continues until the additional income generated by new round of spending essentially becomes zero.

The size of multiplier depends on the base and size of the local economy, the need to import goods for consumption by both tourists and local residents, the local residents habits with regard to how much they save rather than spend from any tourist earnings they receive. The intensity which is redistributed to other branches of the economy. The greater the number of hands through which such money passes the greater beneficial effects on the Gross National Product and the National Accounts. The turnover or

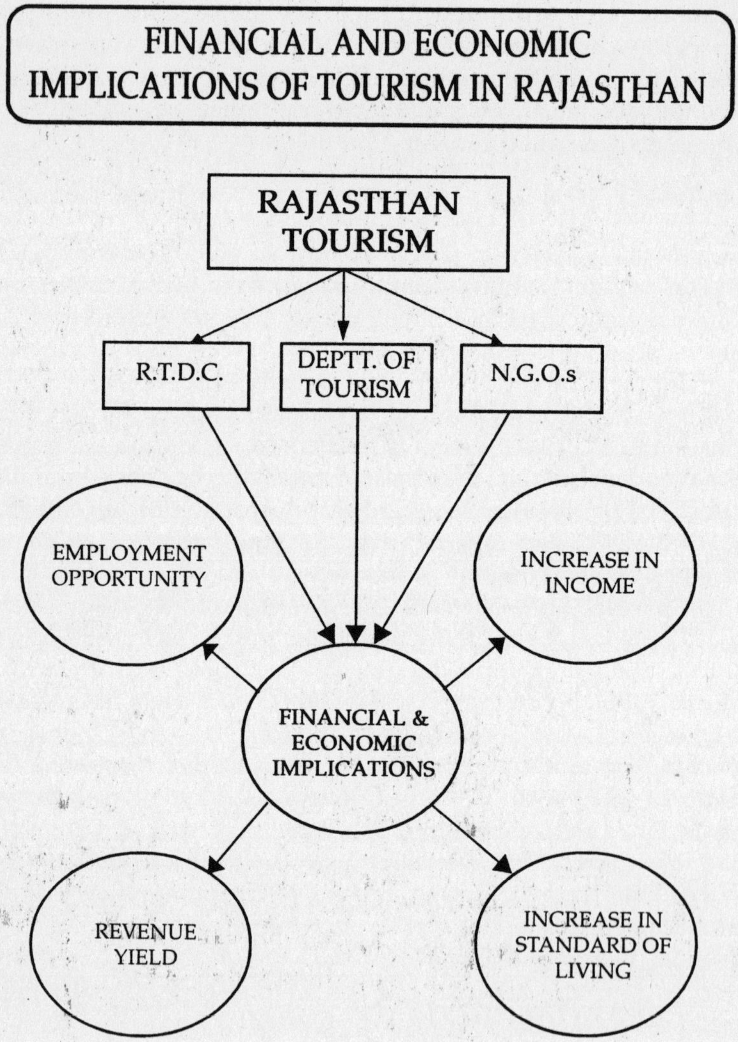

Fig. 5.5

(Designed and Compiled by the Authors)

multiplier effect of the expenditure made by the tourist varies from economy to economy. Each successive round of spending generates less income for the region because of the leakage out of the stream of spending. The leakage are due to...

- The expenditure on import.
- Remittance of profits on foreign capital invested.
- Cost in foreign currency of conducting market activities abroad.
- Savings, travel outside the region, investment abroad and other factors.

The net effect of these leakage is that they generate income and employment in the country in which they are exported therefore the greater the leakage the lower is the value of multiplier and consequently the lower is the benefit to the domestic economy from tourism.

Most developing nations multiplier are lower as compare to developed ones as they are not self-sufficient and depends on imports, similarly at the state or provincial level the multiplier will be lower as compare to the national one as their economics are not broadly based and they have leakage through tax payments to the national government. The Table 5.5 shows the tourism multiplier in various countries.

The table shows that there is a wide fluctuation and variation in the multiplier coefficients of different areas. The difference may be due to:

(*a*) The leakage caused by expenditure on imports for tourist purposes in different, variations in the structure of the economy and structure of consumption etc.

(*b*) The different methods used to calculate these coefficient like.

Paul A. Samuelson, Chairman of the Department of Economics, Institute of Technology Massachusetts, Multiplier[8]

$$K = (1/DC)$$
$$K = 1-(1/DY)$$

K = Multiplier
Y = Change in Income
C = Change in Consumption

MULTIPLIER EFFECT OF TOURISM

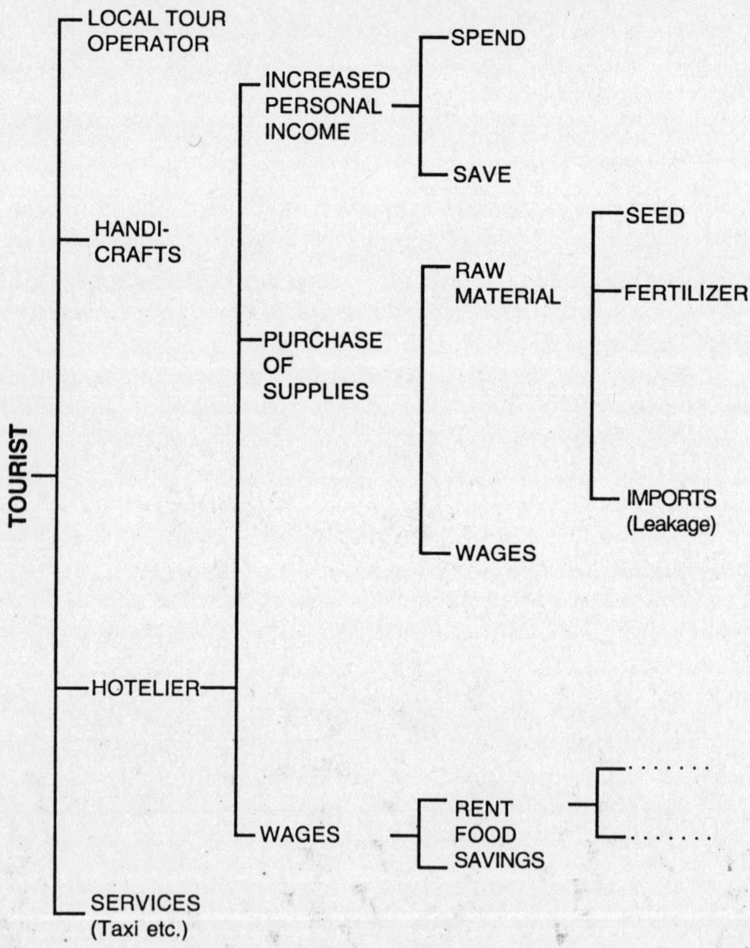

Fig. 5.6

(Designed and Compiled by the Authors)

Peter's Multiplier[9]

$$Kt = [1/(S - ea)]$$

Kt = The Tourist Multiplier
S = The Propensity to Save
ea = The Marginal Propensity to Spend on Tourism abroad by National

Keynesian Expenditure Multiplier

$$K = [1/(S + M)]$$

K = Multiplier
M = Marginal Propensity to Import
S = Marginal Propensity to Save

Table 5.3 : Estimated Tourism Multiplier

Sl. No.	*Country*	*Multiplier*	*Research conducted by*
1.	Greece	1.2-1.4	Daniel B.Suits, An Econometric Model of the Greek Economy 1964, pp. 119-21, Center of Economic Research, Athens.
2.	Ireland	2.7	Study of the Economics of Tourism in Ireland, 1966.
3.	Lebanon	1.2-1.4	Pierre Gorra, Department Nouve le stude, Prospective Sur J' apport, du Tourisme au development Economiquedu Lebanon 1967, Department. Researches et. Documentation, O.N.T. Lebanon.
4.	Pacific and Far East	3.4-4.3	Harry G. Clemen, The Future of Tourism on the Pacific and Far East 1961, Washington D.C.
5.	Brahamas	1.36	Cheechi & Co., Washington D.C.
6.	Pakistan	3.3	Master Plan for Development of Tourism in Pakistan, 1965.
7.	Hawaii	0.9-1.3	Paul G Craig, The future growth of Hawaiian Tourism and Its impact on the State and Neighbour Islands 1963, pp. 105-07, University of Hawaii, ECO Research Center.
8.	New Hampshire	1.6-1.7	Vacation Travel Business in New Hampshire 1962, State of New Hampshire Division of Eco-Development.
9.	India	3.2-3.6	Cost Benefit Study of Tourism.

Source: Tourism and Travel Concepts, J.M.S. Negi.

Tourism multiplier is based upon some unrealistic assumptions like constant ratios of propensity to import and consume taxation to income, factor income share to national income. The chain effects are measured only up to the first or second round of expenditure. While discussing the economic effects of tourism John Bryden[10] says it is upon the multiplier effects that most studies of tourism in the developing countries in the world have concentrated Peter's 1969, Checchi 1961,[11] Zinder Report 1969,[12] Tripartite Survey 1966, Clement 1967,[13] Bryden 1971,[14] Levit Gulati 1970,[15] NCAER 1969,[16] Cost Benefit Study 1975, being the examples. The findings of these reports suggest that countries where there are substantial leakage or slow turnover the money spent by tourist seem to turnover between 3.2 to 3.5 times a year before it disappears. In more highly developed economics there is less leakage and higher limits perhaps 4.3 would probably apply. The multiplier of 3.2 is the lowest that can be produced under any reasonably set of circumstances. When the total estimated expenditure by the tourist is multiplied by 3.2 the result is minimum amount of business generated by tourist expenditure during a period of 12 months.

With reference to Rajasthan due to the limitations of data availability no attempt could be made to estimate relevant multiplier coefficients for the tourist expenditure. For the purpose of estimating the total aggregate state income generated in the economy due to tourism in Rajasthan a marginal propensity to save of 0.12 and marginal propensity to import of 0.16 with multiplier coefficient of 3.2-3.6 can be taken. These coefficients and propensity range are justified considering the developing stage of Rajasthan's economy.

It is now generally accepted that tourism expenditure has a multiplier effect even though there are sharp differences of opinion about the quantum of this effect and how it takes place. There is no doubt that tourism contribution to Rajasthan's economy is far more substantial than it is to the economy of India as a whole in spite of problems of basic data, misplaced aggregation and methodological errors, multiplier effects of tourism expenditure are significant. In the light of these an attempt has been made in the following pages to estimate the income creation, employment generation and revenue yielding effect of tourism activity in the state.

The tourism income and employment multipliers attempt to

measure the total impact of foreign tourist expenditure on the domestic economy. Whenever the multiplier is greater than one, tourist earnings in foreign exchange as a proportion of national income do not fully reflect the benefit of tourism to the economy. The values of multipliers and the value of the benefits to the community in terms of income and employment is reduced to the extent to which there are leakage in the system.

Income Creation Effects

Tourism gives impetus to national income. Tourism constitutes a demand for services and of consumer goods that would otherwise not have been produced. This stimulates the production sectors bringing with it an automatic increase in national consumption, and has a chain reaction effect on the entire national economy. The construction of accommodation, urbanisation for tourist purpose, infrastructure installations, increased tourist transport and equipment etc. are the examples of how tourists transport and equipment encourages investment.

Table 5.4: Sectorwise Contribution in Growth Rate of Rajasthan

Year	*Primary Sector*	*Secondary Sector*	*Tertiary Sector*
1960-61	57.3	17.1	25.6
1970-71	62.0	14.5	23.4
1980-81	52.3	18.0	29.7
1990-91	49.8	17.5	32.7
1995-96	44.7	23.1	32.2
1998-99	43.9	19.5	36.6
1999-2000 (P)	42.7	18.6	38.7

Source: Dr. Jayanti Lal, 'Economy of Rajasthan', p. 272.

Thus, principle of accelerating effect of tourism can be seen in fields like water and electricity supply, sanitation, urbanisation schemes, transportation network, establishment of commercial establishment, increase in production of goods bought by tourists, generation of finance sector, banking insurance and professional services. If we analyse the structure of growth rate in case of Rajasthan, we can find that tertiary sector's contribution is increasing day by day and the reason in the development of service sector facilities like banking, communication, hotels, insurance, road etc. These facilities were developed in the state to cater to the needs of tourist and local of the state. Thus, indirectly the contribution of travel and tourism in state income is boosting gradually.

The national income is matched by total expenditure. The place of tourism in national income can be gauged by ascertaining the contribution of tourist receipts to national income. The multiplier multiplies the estimated total expenditure by tourists in order to get national income created by tourism. This is the minimum amount of business generated by tourist expenditure during one year. The moment the tourists begin to spend there is an addition to national income. The process continues to a lesser degree. Total income from tourism can be estimated by following formulae.....

$$\text{Total Income} : N \times T \times S$$

N = Total no. of tourists per day
T = Average tenure of stay in days per tourist
S = Average spending per tourist per day

Table 5.5: The Average Spending of Tourists Per Head Per Day

Amount	*Average Amount*	*No. of Tourist*	*Total*
< 2,000	1,000	12	12,000
2,000-5,000	3,500	75	26,25,000
5,000-10,000	7,5000	37	2,77,500
>10,000	10,000	51	5,10,000
Total		**175**	**34,24,500**

Source: Random Survey of Tourists by Researcher.

• *Spending Per Family/Group*	*3424500/175*	=	*19568*
• Spending Per Head (Avg. Five Members)	19568/5	=	3913
• Average Spending Per Day (Stay Five Days)	3913/5	=	782

Total income from Tourism in Rajasthan (Year 2000)

No. of Tourists arrival × Per head per day × Average stay

(*Rs. in crores*)

7997491 × 782 × 5 = 3127.02

Tourism contribution to GDP is about 6 per cent. ASSOCHAM forecast that by 2005 foreign exchange earning from tourism will be over 19,000 crore an annual growth of 7.5 per cent is projected. The importance of tourism industry as contributor of economic growth is so widely accepted year after throughout the world that a growing trend of investment contributes to add to its development. It has become a major economic force in the world.

Employment Generation Effects

One of our approaches to the study of tourism is to see the impact on employment. This is very essential problem of the study from the economic point of view. Tourism industry is not based on idealism, it is a dynamic field which covers the involvement of land, labour, capital, organisation including the public finances. Under these heads, the study of tourism is closely knit with the employment generation in the state.

Directly and indirectly, the trading and business communities are integrated with tourism. Tourism has grown to be an activity of international importance. It is a significant industry with the key role of making the tourist spent some of his budget on transport, board, and lodge, sight seeing and making some shopping broadly the functioning of tourism starts with the selection of the distinction and then planning to make the tour a success.

Tourism is a service industry and can be relatively employment intensive for the developing state like ours. The tourism industry not only generates employment once in operation, jobs are also created during the construction of the tourist facilities. When considering individual cases one must not overlook the extent to which tourism can also create secondary employment in other industries. The extent of this employment effect depends on:

- The size and nature of tourist facilities.
- The structural depth of the tourism sector.
- The type of tourism (individual, package, mass, gentle).
- Whether tourism is seasonal or all year round.[17]

The total impact of tourism on employment generation in the economy is related to the income created in the first and subsequent round of spending of tourist rupee on consumer goods industries, the realistic method of apportioning employment by the tourism sector would be on the basis of ratio of aggregate state income to income generated from tourism. Since the total impact of tourism on employment is largely shaped by the income and employment generated at various stages subsequent to the initial spending stage and in various sectors of the economy, *i.e.* agriculture and industry, the apportionment principle based on the overall income employment ratio for the state seems reasonable.

Employment Generation by Tourism in Rajasthan

Tourism is a people's industry one that will create employment for the rural, youth, females, artisans and craftsman. The influx of tourist activity in Rajasthan has resulted in the revival of traditional arts and crafts, carpenters busy with antique looking furniture, the designer's wares, historical weave and pattern in cloth and various other articrafts. State Government has also accorded tourism the status of industry and recognised its importance for poverty alleviation balanced economic development, for increasing the State domestic product and for drought proofing.

The recommendations of the Vyas Committee also focussed on the development of this sector in Rajasthan to curtail unemployment problem. About two lakh peoples are currently directly engaged in the tourism. Many tourism employment generation schemes are in offing like—Paryatan Rozgar Yojana. Some of these opportunities have been mentioned below:

Total income from tourism Rs. 3,127.02 crore as discussed in the income effects.

Table 5.6 : Total Employment Generation (Direct and Indirect)

Sl. No.	*Multiplier Effects*	*Total Income*	*No. of Employment*
1.	1.79	3,127.02	5,59,733
2.	3.20	3,127.02	10,00,646
3.	3.60	3,127.02	11,25,720

Source: Calculated by Applying Income Employment Ratio to the Income Created by Tourism Industry as given in Table.

DEVELOPMENT OF TOURISM AND FINANCIAL AND ECONOMIC IMPLICATIONS

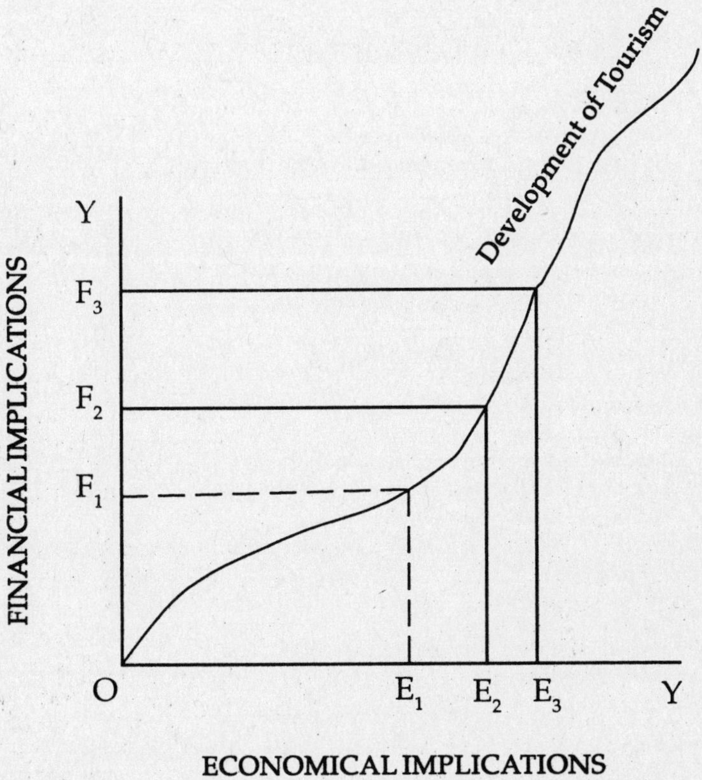

Fig. 5.7

(Designed and Compiled by the Authors)

Employment and Investment Opportunities in the Tourism Industry of Rajasthan:

Sl. No.	*Area*
1.	Adoption of Monuments
2.	Adventure Tourism
3.	Amusement Parks/Water Parks/Theme Parks
4.	Camping Sites of Rajasthan
5.	Elephant Safari
6.	Establishment of Ropeways
7.	Expansion of Accommodation Facilities
8.	Film Industry
9.	Haveli on Wheels
10.	Heritage Liquors—Conservation of
11.	Heritage Properties Available for Private Investment
12.	Horse Safari
13.	Khadi Sector
14.	Land Bank
15.	Museum Development in Rajasthan
16.	Nature Care and Meditation Centres
17.	Air Services
18.	Packaged Food and Culinary Industry
19.	Palace on Waves Industry
20.	Perfumes and Scents of Rajasthan
21.	Polo/Golf Clubs
22.	Promotion of Furniture Industry of the State
23.	Rajasthani Folk Dances and Songs Marketing Through Audio
24.	River Cruise in Chambal River, Kota
25.	Revival of Traditional Transport Modes such as Buggies and Chariots
26.	Rural Tourism
27.	Shekhawati Havelis
28.	Stone Craft Industry
29.	Tax Incentives for Tourism Industry in the State
30.	Tourism Souvenirs Industry

Source: Investment Opportunities in Tourism Sector, Rajasthan, Department of Tourist Art and Culture, Jaipur.

According to the census the maximum number of hotel and restaurant enterprises were in Tamilnadu, followed by Uttar Pradesh, Maharashtra and Kerala; the maximum employment in the hotel and restaurant sector was in the state of Maharashtra followed by Tamilnadu and Andhra Pradesh. The position of Rajasthan State is given in Table 5.7.

Table 5.7: Percentage Share of Rajasthan in Employment in Hotel and Restaurant Sector in India

Region	*No. of OAE*	*No. of Estt.*	*Total No. of OAE and Estt.*	*Employed in OAE*	*Employed in Estt.*	*Total*
India	702178	376128	1078306	1082749	1686576	2769325
Rajasthan	29426	14820	44246	38606	50224	88830
% of State in Total of India	4.19	3.94	4.10	3.57	2.98	3.21

Source: Tourist Statistics, Ministry of Tourism, Government of India, New Delhi.

The above table reveals that hotel and restaurant segment provides the employment opportunity to the teeming millions. In Rajasthan, one person gets a job over eight foreign tourists and one person employed over thirty-two domestic tourists. There are immense opportunities of employment generation through this sector in the state due to its strong tourism base. The following shows the role of tourism in the rural and urban economy of Rajasthan.

- Employment generation.
- Recognition of work.
- Expanse of literacy and education.
- Increase in income.
- Improvement in health and family welfare.
- Eradication of social evils.
- Expanse of cultural values.
- Increase in export/foreign exchange.
- Increase in investment opportunities.

Role of Tourism and Employment Opportunity to the Women

- Employment opportunity to women in manufactured of tourism related goods and services.
- Opportunity for women to interact with tourists as patrons of arts and crafts.
- Inculcate in rural handicrafts and cottage industry.

Revenue Yielding Effect

Besides income creation and employment generation tourism industry is also an important source of state revenue. The revenue yielding effects of tourism inflow has been estimated with the help of following equation.

$$T = Et \times Kt \times P$$

Where

- T Stands for tax revenue
- Et For expenditure by tourists (both domestic and foreign)
- Kt For tourism multiplier
- P For the proportion of state income accruing to the Government through direct and indirect taxes

Or

Total Tax Revenue = Total annual expenditure by tourist × Multiplier × Percentage of taxes with the business generated taxes (airport tax, luxury tax, liquor, tobacco, wine, spirits and Petrol, etc.) from the tourist industry have made it possible for the state to finance major projects like building roads, schools, hospitals and to supply other necessary social services in the state.

It is difficult to estimate the direct contribution of tourism to tax revenue for want of detailed break up of expenditure tax rate, tax revenue etc. for different tourism activities of the state. It has been felt that direct tax constitute only a small fraction of revenue earned by the state hence tax revenue from tourism can be assessed at pro rata basis of total contribution of taxes to the national income. In absence of tourism certainly our government earning will be effected adversely. It was estimated that even 1 per cent rise in our international traffic will bring 3.54 billion US $ to the state. It has been noticed that the developing countries of the world are more or less in doubt in form of aids which cannot be covered by subsidies from abroad. This burden can be reduced by the increase of income by taxation, which come through the promotion of tourism therefore financial contribution of tourism contribution large amount of revenue in the economy of Rajasthan.

According to the Budget estimates[18] for the year 1999-2000, the tax revenue was Rs. 8,712.18 crore and total revenue receipt were calculated at Rs. 12,018.19 crore, constituting 12.18 per cent and 19.57 per cent of the state respectively. The effect of tourism on the tax receipt of the state has been estimated by applying these ratios to the income created by tourism with multiplier coefficient of 1.79, 3.2 and 3.6 as presented in the following Table:

Table 5.8: Revenue Yielding Effect of Tourism

(Rs. in Crores)

Sl. No.	*Multiplier Coefficient*	*Income Effect*	*Tax Revenue Effect*	*Total Revenue Receipts Effect*
1.	1.79	5,597.36	681.75	1,095.40
2.	3.2	10,006.46	1,218.78	1,958.26
3.	3.6	11,257.27	1,371.13	2,203.04

Source: Calculated by Researcher from the Data on Revenue Receipts and Net State Domestic Product.

It thus follows from the analysis of above table that tax revenue from tourist industry was Rs. 681.75 crore, 1,218.78 crore and 1,371.13 crore with multiplier coefficient of 1.79, 3.2 and 3.6 respectively, with the total revenue receipts effect worked out at Rs. 1,095.40 crore, 1,958.26 crore and 2,203.04 crore for the respectively multiplier coefficient.

It has been felt that in spite of all the merits multiplier concept has got certain limitations also like it indicate only some of the gains and losses from tourist income, it does not show the costs (economic, environment and cultural) of receiving that income. It also does not reveal that a high multiplier for one region may seem advantageous to that region but may conflict with the goals of a higher level of development planning.

To overcome all these limitations nowadays Input out Analysis, Cost Benefit Analysis, Structural Analysis Techniques are adopted to study the economic impact of tourism.

The results of the above study suggest that support for the tourism industry in Rajasthan is strong among its residents. Further more, residents not only supported the current magnitude of this industry but also favoured its expansion despite the overall positive feelings towards tourism and the tourism industry.

REFERENCES

1. The then Honourable Chief Minister of Rajasthan, Ashok Gehlot at Inaugural Session of SATTA 2000, Jaipur, 6-8 April, 2000.
2. Young, George, '*Tourism Blessing or Plight*', Hormands Worts, Penguin Books, 1974.
3. Honourable Ananth Kumar, Former Union Minister of Tourism, Inaugural Address at ITTF, New Delhi, 14-27 November, 2000.
4. Paper presented by M.P. Bezbaruah, Secretary, Tourism, Government of India, WTO at Santiago Chile, 1998-99.
5. Pei-Kang, Chang, '*Agriculture and Industrialisation*', p. 69.
6. Kuchhal S.C., '*The Industrial Economy of India*', Chaitanya Publishing House, Allahabad, Chapter 1, p. 1.
7. Kimbal, Dexter S. and Dexter S. Kimbal Junior, '*Principle of Industrial Organisation*', Alight Pacific Pvt. Ltd., Bombay, 1962, p. 86.
8. Sen, Samad A. Paul, "*Interaction between the Acceleration Principles and Multiplier from Review and Economic*", Massachusetts, May 1939.
9. Peters Michael, "*International Tourism*", Hutchinson and Co. Publishers, New York, 1969, p. 235.
10. Bryden John M., "*Tourism and Development—A Case Study of Commonwealth*", Cambridge University, p. 73.
11. Report prepared by Checchi and Company for U.S. Department of Commerce entitled "*The Future of Tourism in the Pacific and Far East*", 1961.
12. Report prepared by Zinder H. and Associates Inc., "*The Future of Tourism in Eastern Caribbean*" for U.S. Agency Commissioned by IBRD, Washington, 1969.
13. Clement H.G., "*The Impact of Tourism Expenditure*", Development Digest, July 1967, p. 71.
14. Bryden and the Mike Faber, "*Multiplying the Tourist Multiplier*", Social and Economic Studies, Vol. 20, No. 1.
15. Karl, Levil and Gulati Iqbal, "*Income Effect of Tourist Spending Mystification Multiplied*", A Critical Comment on Linder Report, Social and Economic Studies, Vol. 19, No. 3, 1970, pp. 326-43.
16. NCAER Techno Economic Survey, New Delhi, 1969, p. 241.
17. Special Article on "*Tourism and Development Countries*" published in Monthly Public Opinion Survey, New Delhi, August, 1997, pp. 7-12.
18. Rajasthan Government papers on Budget estimates 1999-2000.

Chapter VI

INTERNAL AND EXTERNAL FACTORS INVOLVING MANAGERIAL IMPLICATIONS

Just like raw materials get converted into finished products by moving through various machines in a processing system, the different components of tourism supply should be so organised that the expectations of the tourist while planning the trip get converted into full satisfaction and pleasant memories on his/her return. It means there should be perfect coordination and linkages in the availability and performance of all tourism infrastructures.

Tourism management is thus a composite subject and does not necessarily mean the development of only the tourism facilities like hotels, restaurants, recreational activities etc. In fact, creations of tourism infrastructure like roads, water, electricity, sewerage and telecommunication facilities. This aspect was given importance in the Tourism 'Synergy' programme and it was the first attempt in this regard. Subsequently, the State Government was asked to prepare Master Plans for the development of tourism based on the same concept.

A National Strategy for the Development of Tourism was drawn up during 1996 for achieving a greater realisation of the importance of tourism, a consensus on the development needs, positive contribution of all the Infrastructural Departments in a coordinated manner, higher plan allocations and introduction of new schemes for the accelerated development of tourism. The strategy has been endorsed by the Government and a Board of Tourism Industry and Trade has been set up for coordinating the activities of different departments for Tourism Development.

What do we think about tourists?

Tourists

- Are our guest?

- Are our customer?
- Are always cooperative?
- Are well mannered?
- Spend a lot of money in Rajasthan?
- Can be wealthy?
- Are likely to return to Rajasthan in future?
- Are of a high social status?
- Are in Rajasthan only of pleasure?
- Are a valuable part of tourism trade for Rajasthan?

Above informations give, useful information for managerial implications of tourism industry in Rajasthan.

Tourism like other activities furnishes best when it fits into context of managerial policies and programmers designed to lead the optimum growth of tourism industry as a whole. It is an area where opportunity seldom knocks twice, the tourist is often willing to take a chance of a new appealing destinations[1], attracting the tourism, to our country is therefore smallest part of the challenge. Therefore greater stress be paid to develop tourism.

Management is to decide in advance what is to be done when it is be done, by whom it is to be done and how it is to be done.[2] It is an attempt to allocate scare resources between different competitive uses with a view to maximising output, income, employment and to ensure the balanced growth of different sectors. The management programmes, scheduled, procedure and methods for achieving them.

Tourism management may be defined as the creation and addition of facilities, amenities and services to meet the need of the tourists. Management in tourism provides a bridge between the present situation and desired further situation in a destination areas. Its goal is to develop objectives of tourism development and ways to achieve the latter by maximising the overall economic, social and cultural advantage of tourism while respecting the dynamic of balance tourism supply and demand.

Tourism Management

> "Management is, to a large extent, the job of making things happen that would not otherwise happen"
>
> —H. Koontz and C.O'Donnel

The new approach of tourism development must combine planning (the initial goal and development strategy) with management (day to day seasonal operational decisions) because the ability to adjust changing market or seasonal condition is of paramount importance in such a competitive business. Planning must focus on rate of growth of tourism sector, how tourism sector can be fitted for national, regional and local development; role of domestic and foreign capital investment in its development; whether special treatment be accorded to this sector as an industry, whether it should be developed on short term basis. To the extent permitted by the resources of a country efforts should be made for the steady growth in the number of new tourist sites, new tourism dimensions.

W.T.O. has suggested that greater attention should be focussed on three economic criterion in plans which would be used to expand tourism in development nations the gestation period of investment the efficiency of capital investment, capital utilisation and labour intensify investment.

"The methodical progression in planning should be adopted with the short listing of sites which have the potential to be part of circuits, aesthetic beauty, existing infrastructure, environmental sensitive, tourists amenities and no less important connectivity and accessibility. Planning is a tourist product that is economically, socially, environmentally and culturally viable. Tourism projects must be made in a way that maximum use is made of local products and material and encouragement be given to auxiliary tourist facilities like handicrafts and entertainment.

Tourism plans should not be designed only on tangible benefits alone but on the ideals and principles of intangible factor like human welfare, happiness, preservation of natural and cultural resources that attracted the visitors in the first place.

Tourism plans should be flexible so as to adapt to changing conditions and requirements as tourism is an industry that is influenced by subjective consideration like that of economic forces, political and social pressures, psychological attitudes, changes of fashion, etc.

Need of Tourism Management

Management is necessary to coordinate and synchronise the

TRI DIMENSIONAL MANAGERIAL SLOGAN OF TOURISM

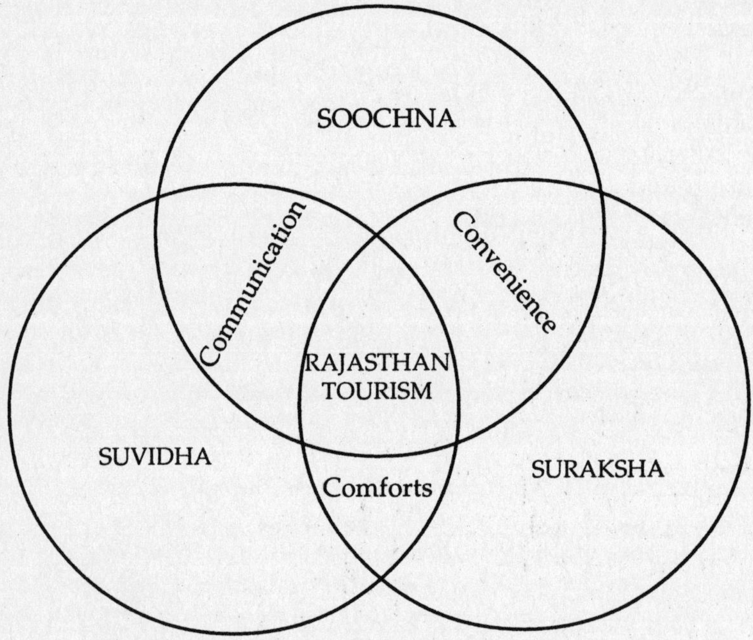

Fig. 6.1

(Designed and Compiled by the Authors)

development of different sectors, to balance competing and sometimes conflicting claims on the same limited resource base, to maximise the positive impacts of tourism development and to minimise its adverse effect. In long run directive measures will usually prove less experienced than corrective ones. It envisages augmented availability and improved organisation of different components of tourism infrastructure to meet the requirement of tourists.

Tourism is a complex and diffused activity. The best solution for any problem is to develop a method or plan to access the present situation, forecast the future situation and select an appropriate course of action to make the most of available opportunities. There are seven basic of stages[3] of internal factors through effective managerial results can be obtained.

Stage 0: Assessment : It helps to discover their present level of ability in and awareness of key competencies by means of self-assessment and self-investigation.

Stage 1: Learning : By reading, discussing information, relevant research, practical guidelines by the story of entire/entrepreneurs about their business and their personal development.

Stage 2: Analysis : This explore appropriate behaviours by examining relevant cases of new business creation and their entrepreneur as role-models.

Stage 3: Practice : This make to apply key competencies to a work-like situation while in experimentation and feedback from peers and coaches.

Stage 4: Application : This give the opportunity to transfer the process to a real life situation with assignments to be made by entrepreneurs from business.

Stage 5: Feedback : After each stage there is a presentation of the results with assignments to be made by entrepreneurs from business.

Stage 6: Evaluation : One have to evaluate their level of improvement on all competence and have to develop new strategies for the next stage of learning.

Stage 7 : Reassessment : To reassess their level of improvement on each competence-level, to redesign their personal development strategy, to repeat from zero.

Each stage creates a new level of competence. The zero stage is the core of self-competence service proper need to start at a level at which they feel comfortable to work developing their present level of competence, each next stage challenging themselves to perform at a higher level. Using the onion as a metaphor for the development of competence.

Principles of Tourism Management

While drawing out the plans of tourism development for the state of Rajasthan following principles must be kept in mind.

Basic Principles

Tourism management must encompass all travel business and pleasure. Planning objectives, process and outcomes very from macro to micro level, integration at all levels must be done, clustering must be adopted and planning must integrate all components of supply side, urban and rural, traffic and pedestrian planning must be integrated.

Environment and Resources

Global environment deterioration demands tourism attention. Sustainable development must be there, resolving of visitor impact management be there, appropriateness and places must be given priority.

Policies and Goals

Tourism planning should not focus on economic development but quality and growth. Efforts must be made to attain greater public private cooperation, regional tourism policies must be designed tourism planning must link government and non-profit organisation.

Processes

In tourism management continuous planning need integration; geography requires destination identification, process technique should be used to identify destination, place making must be there in planning, side scale design must carefully be planned.

Future Challenges

Entrepreneurship, creativity and innovation are essential for future plans. Plans should foster low impact development research and training, proactive environment planning and professional planning.

Factors Involving in Managerial Implications

Without proper management tourism end up becoming part of

construction jungle. Tourism is not always a panacea, over development can generate problems like traffic congestion, inadequate parking, hotel dwarfing, displacement of local community, pollution, etc.

These responsibilities cannot really be blamed on tourism but rather on over commercialisation. It is one of the world's greatest and most significant force the need is to weigh the economic benefit in the light of future degradation human and natural resources. Some of the symptoms of lack of tourism management are:

1. (*a*) *Tangible*: Damage or permanent alteration of physical environment, historical, cultural landmarks and resources; overcrowding and congestion; pollution; traffic problems.
   (*b*) *Intangibles*: Lack of education and training in this field; lack of awareness of the benefits of tourism to the destination area loss of cultural identities, dislike of tourists on part of local residents and less accessibility to services and tourism attractions for local residents resulting in local resentment.
2. (*a*) *External*: Failure to capitalise on new marketing opportunities; erosion of market shares due to the actions of competitive destination area; lack of sufficient awareness in clear markets; cooperative advertising; inadequate capitalisation or packaging opportunities.
   (*b*) *Internal*: Fragment approach of marketing; lack of cooperation among operators; inadequate representation of tourism industry's identity lack of support from local public authorities of common interest to the industry.[4] Centre with Internal and External factors involving management implications.

Inadequate linkage problems; lack of sufficient attractions and events; high seasonality and short length of stay; poor or deteriorating quality of facilities and services; poor or inadequate travel information services.

Advantages of Tourism Management

A well managerial tourism at all levels is essential for achieving successful tourism development and management. Some of the benefits of tourism management are:

A TO Z THEORY OF TOURISM

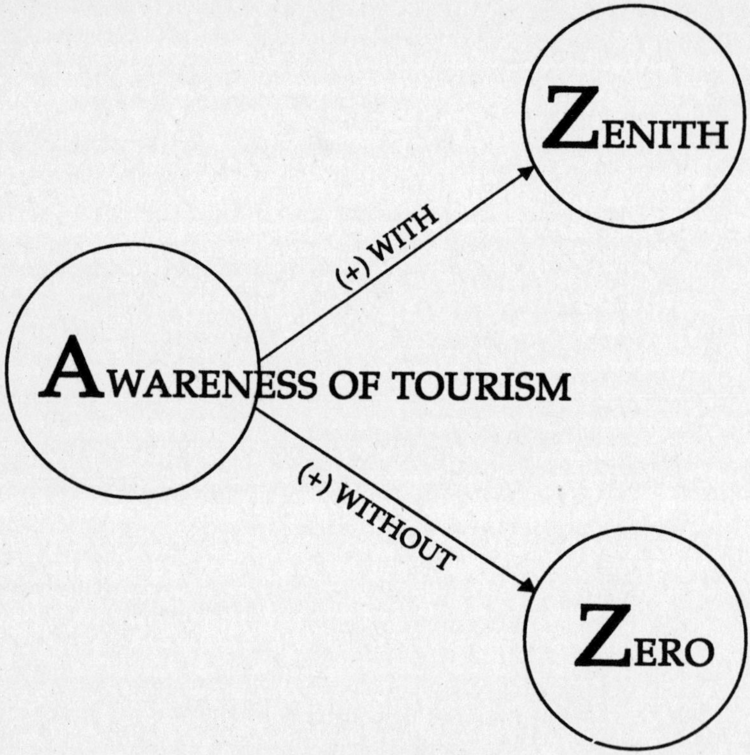

Fig. 6.2

(Designed and Compiled by the Authors)

1. Establishing the overall tourism development objectives and policies.
2. Development tourism in a way that the natural and cultural resources are conserved for future.
3. Integrating tourism with the overall developmental policies and establishing linkages between tourism and other economic sectors.

4. Optimising and balancing the economic, environmental and social benefits of tourism with equitable distribution of these benefits to society, while minimising possible problems of tourism.
5. Providing a physical structure which guides the location types and extent of tourism development of attention, facilities, services and infrastructure.
6. Laying the foundation for effective implementation of the tourism development policy and plan and continuous management of tourism sector by providing the necessary organisational and other institutional framework.
7. Providing the framework for effective coordination of the public and private sector efforts and investment in development tourism.
8. Offering a baseline for the continuous marketing of the progress of tourism development and keeping it on the track.

Thus it can be said that tourism management itself a powerful integrating factor and management skill is need for reasons like:

- To coordinate the role of public and private sector.
- To prevent negative impact of tourism.
- To regulate and legislate matters relating to tourism.
- To improve the quality of services.
- To train human resources in this field.
- To market a destination.
- Demarcate the areas of development and types of tourism to be promoted.[5]

In conclusion it can be said that tourism comprises the activities of persons travelling to and staying in places outside their usual environment for leisure, business and other purposes. These persons invariably seek a pleasant and delectable experience on their trips. The most desirable tourism products should consist of environmental peace, stability, assurance of safety/security, an affable host with requisite services, accessible tourist places with air/internal transport, hotels, restaurants, entertainment/ recreation, shopping/communication facility and basic amenities. There should be a perfect coordination in availability of tourism infrastructure. Therefore, it requires managerial skill to provide all the above mentioned facilities.

REFERENCES

1. Bhatia, A.K., "*International Tourism Fundamentals and Practice*", Sterling Publishing House, New Delhi, 1996, p. 108.
2. Pizam, Abraham, "*The Social Impact of Tourism*", Recreation Research, Vol. No. 2, Publication House, Lucknow, 1986, p. 37.
3. Piffner and Sherwood, "*Administrative Organisation*", Prentice Hall, New Delhi, 1964, p. 89.
4. Mill Robert Christe and Morrison Alastair M., "*The Tourism System—An Introductory Text*", Prentice Hall Inc. Englewood Cliffs, New Jersey, 1985, p. 288.
5. "*Tourism Planning and Policy*", IGNOU, Foundation course in tourism No. V, Aravali Printers Publishers Private Ltd., New Delhi, 1996, p. 56.

Chapter VII

TOURIST PRODUCTS—ITS PROMOTION AND PUBLICITY

Tourism is a multi-dimensional industry with heterogeneous group embracing large variety of trades and industries, which are supplying the tourist needs as their common function. Tourism supply is the combination of natural and man-made attraction, services and goods that are likely to induce people to visit the particular country. Tourism supply is impossible to stock and is to be consumed where it exits, thus, it cannot be separated from time and space. Further owing to variations of weather and other constraints its supply is subjected to pronounced seasonality. The tourism product cannot be transported to other place, it therefore, is to be purchased and consumed at the location. The demand for tourism product originals from outside the area of its location. The increase in demand for tourism product during recent years essentially is attributed to rapid growth of "leisure industries". The growing marginal disutility of work has necessitated combing optimally "work with leisure" and this explains the boom in international tourism. The demand for tourism product is determined by its Quality and level of income of the tourist and can be expressed as:

$$TD = a.\, P_{q.}\, Y_{t.}\, b$$

where, a, b are the scale parameters

With a>0, b>1

P_q = Quality of tourism product;

Y_t = Income levels of the tourists

The above analysis suggest that demand for tourism product is directly related to its quality and income of the tourists because a>0. It also suggests that demand for tourism product is a luxury because co-efficient of co-relation (r) between T D and Y_t is greater than 1. According to Lickorish[1] the income elasticity co-efficient of tourism work out to 1:5. Tourism products[2] are also often located a fair distance from the customers, which requires intermediaries who can influence both the potential tourists and the tourist suppliers. This is the role played by tour wholesalers and travel agencies. Tourism products have to be sold mostly sight unseen by the purchaser. In other words, he or she must spend both time and money before actually using the product or service. Rajasthan is the legendry land of velour and chivalry of beauty and romance, of bustling bazaars and cavalcades of colour. It is the land where the post lingers on and where you are never far from history. Where do you come face to face with the real charm of India, where the people are exuberant and where Hospitality is a way of life. Rajasthan offers diverse tourism products. The tourist, visiting the state, often travels to various places to have a comprehensive experience out of the visit. Following are the main tourism products of Rajasthan state:

Religion

Religion has always played a very important role in the lives of Indian people right from medieval times. Numerous religions practiced by Indians can sometimes be wilder the visitor but a general understanding and tolerance has always existed and accounted for the wonderful cultural unity that has kept the Indian spirit alive what is true for the rest of India is true for Rajasthan as well. Almost all the major religions are represented here. Apart from the Hindus, who from a majority, there are Muslims, Christians, Sikhs and Jains.

Some of the major temples and important religious centers like Pushkar, Nathdwara, Deshnok, Amer exit in the state of Rajasthan. The world's greatest Sufi Shrine–that of Khwaja Moinuddin Chisti— lies in Ajmer. Another pilgrimage center is the Atarki Dargah the tomb of Hamiuddin Nagori at Nagour. Jainism founded by Lord Rishabh and reorganized by Lord Mahaveer (born in 599 B.C.) is one of the oldest living religions of the world. The fundamental principles of Jainism are Ahimsa, Aparigraha, Anekant and the law of Karma. The Jains have built some of the most exquisite temples in Ranakpur, Mount Abu, Shri Mahaveer Ji, Osiam Jaisalmur, Chittorgarm and other parts of Rajasthan. There is also a large majority of Sikhs and Christians who have merged with other communities to give Rajasthan a cosmopolitan flavour. The followers of these religions and the rulers over the period, where instrumental in constructing a number of very important temples, mosques, churches which are built in different parts of the state. Some of the most exquisite carvings on marble stone and wood were created by the believers and exist to this day as a living proof of the creative genius which continues the fascinate by its Sheer brilliance. Other than the structures themselves, the very surroundings of these holy places can give the tourist visitor a sense of peace and calm...[3]

Art and Craft

Rajasthan is among the richest states in the country as far as the field of art and craft is concerned. Rajasthan people over the years have sharpened the creative senses, artistic skills and have created the most opulent and richest of treasures. Stone clay, Leather, Wood, Glass, Brass, Silver, Gold and textiles were given the most brilliant forms to the Rajasthan artists. History of Rajasthan reveals that the kings were patrons of arts and crafts and they encouraged their craftsmen in activities ranging from wood and marble carving to weaving, pottery and painting. For women there is infinite variety–tie and dye fabrics, embroidered garments, enamel Jewellery inlayed with precious and semi-precious stones, leather Joaties. The Rajput rulers encouraged the artisans to set up schools for the propagation of their crafts. Each Rajput principality had its on unique craft and even today, every little town and village has its craftsmen practicing a craft handed down by his ancestors. Some of the popular crafts are Meenakari, Jewellery, Ivory, glass work, sandalwood and wood work, stone work, blue pottery hand block, printing, tie and dye terracotta sculptures painting on camel hide, embroidery, cloth painting, carpets, durries, inlay work on brass and wood to be found all over Rajasthan and the basic attraction for international tourists.[4]

Rajput Painting

Rajasthan's role in the development of Indian art has been very important. The decoration of dwellings and other household objects was but one aspect of the creative genius of the Rajasthan: the world of miniature painting is perhaps the most fascinating and the distinctive styles that have existed here are renowned the world over. From the 16th century onwards there flourished different schools of painting like the Mewar School, the Bundi-Kota, the Jaipur, the Bikaner, the Kishangarh and the Marwar schools representing different styles of paintings.

Each school of painting had its distinctive features of instance, the flowing rivers, dense, forests, lush green fields of Kota-Bundi regions were transferred to the paintings of that region. The Kishangarh school is best known for its Bani Thani painting. A totally different style with highly exaggerated features–long necks, large, almond shaped eyes, long fingers and the use of subdued colours. Jodhpur has a very strong folk tradition and here the figures are mainly robust worriers and dainty women. Painting of the legendary lovers like Dhola-Maru on Camel back, hunting scenes, which included innumerable Horses and Elephants, dominate the painting of the Marwar region. Similarly Bikaner too had strong Mughal influences and developed their own style. In Shekhawati region wall paintings on wall of palaces and the inner chambers of forts, *havelies* are well known all over the world. Artists in Jaipur, Nathdwara and Kishangarh still work on miniatures and some of them produce excellent work. Cloth painting of Rajasthan which include the phads-scroll paintings used by the Bhopas and the pichwais is also very popular tourist product.[5]

Folk Music and Dance

The people of Rajasthan live life to the hilt. After hard work in the harsh desert sun and the rocky terrain whenever they take time off they let themselves go in Gay abandon. There is dancing, Singing, Drama, Devotional Music and Puppet shows and other community festivities which transform the hardworking Rajasthani into a fun-loving and carefree individual. Each region has its own folk, entertainment and the dance styles. Interestingly enough, even the musical instruments are different. Of considerable significance are the devotional songs and the Communities who render these songs. Professional performers like the Bhaats, Dholis, Mirasis, Nats, Bhopas and Bhands are omnipresent across the state. They are patronized by the villagers who participate activity in the shows put up by these traveling entertainers. Some of the better known forms of entertainment are *Ghoomar Dance, Gair Ghoomer, Gair, Ghari Dance, Kachni Ghodi, Fire Dance, Drum Dance, Teerah Taali, Kathputli, Pabuji Ki Pnad, Maand* etc.[6]

Fairs and Festivals

The Rajasthani's love for colour and Joyous[7] celebrations is proved by the elaborate rituals and the gay abandon with which he surrenders himself to the numerous fairs and festivals of the region. In addition to the festival celebrated by the Hindus, Muslims and others, there are also the traditional fairs. There are animal fairs, there are religious fairs and there are fairs to mark the changing season. In fact celebrations occur almost round the year and are a splendid opportunity for the visitor to gain an insight into the life of the Rajasthani. Other than the traditional fairs recently established festivals, which involve Elephants, Camel Race, Dance and Music, are specially organized for the tourists from time to time.

Rajasthani Cuisine

Each region in India has its own traditional dishes and specialties. In the royal kitchens of Rajasthan, as well as most other states, food was very serious business and raised to the level of an art form. Hundreds of cooks worked in the stately palaces and kept their recipes a closely guarded secret. Some recipes were passed on to their sons and the rest were lost forever. It became a matter of great prestige to serve unusual dishes to guests and the royal cooks were encouraged to experiment. Rajasthani's cooking food like dried lentils, beans from indigenous plants like Saugri, Ker etc are liberally used in all over India. Gram flour is a major ingredient here and is used to make some of the delicacies like Khata, Gatta Ki Sabzi, Pakodi, powdered lentils are used for Mangodi, Papad Bajra and corn is used all over the state for preparations of Rabdi, Kheechdi and Roties. Perhaps the best known Rajasthani food in the combination of "Dal Bati and Churma" but for the adventurous traveller, willing to experiment, there is a lot of variety available. Beside spicy flavours, each region is distinguished by its popular sweets—Ladoos from Jodhpur and Jaisalmer, Malpuas from Pushkar, Jalibies from most big cities, Rasgullas from Bikaner, Dil Jani from Udaipur, Mishri Mawa, and Ghivar from Jaipur, Sohan Halwa from Ajmer, Mawas from Alwar and many more.[8]

National Parks and Sanctuaries

Rajasthan is a haven for a wide spectrum of wildlife.[9] The topography of Rajasthan ranges from the barren desert scrub-thorn arid forests, rocks and ravines to wetland and lush, green forests. And each of these areas houses a large variety of animal and bird life, some of them rare while some endangered. Rajasthan is the home of the tigers, black bucks, Chimkara, the rare desert fox, the endangered, caracal, the great Indian bustard, gavial, monitor lizard wild boars, porcupines... migratory birds like the common crane ducks, coots, pelicans and the rare Siberian cranes, imperial sand grouse, falcons, buzzards... flock to this state during the winter months. Rajasthan boasts of two National Parks, over a dozen sanctuaries and two closed Areas. Most of these areas are open to visitors round the year but are closed briefly during the mansoon.

Bhensorod Garh Sanctuary	1983	229 sq. km.
Darrah Sanctuary	1955	266 sq. km.
Desert National Sanctuary	1980	3162 sq. km.
Jaisamand Sanctuary	1957	160 sq. km.
Keoladeo Ghana National Park Bharatpur	1983	29 sq. km.
Kumbhalgarh Sanctuary		578 sq. km.
Mount Abu Sanctuary	1960	289 sq. km.
Ran Thaumbor National Park		392 sq. km.
Sariska Tiger Reserve	1979	

Other Sanctuaries

Sita Mata, Darrah, Chambal, Tal Chapper, Jamna Ram Garh, Kaila Devi, Van Vinar Ramgarh, Shergarh, Todgarh—Rad and Jawahar Sagar.

Adventure Sports and Special Interest Tours

A whole new word of action and adventure has recently been introduced in Rajasthan. The visitors can now gain much more from his holiday in Rajasthan. Fast paced action to a little more staid activity is available all over Rajasthan. The bewitching sights with an equally thrilling sports activity promise an enthralling and unforgettable experience. Ballooning, Camel Safari, Horse Safari, Trekking and Rock Climbing, Hang Gliding, Cycling and Motor Cycling, Fishing, House Boats, Parasailing and Water Skiing are the important adventure sports in Rajasthan for both domestic and foreign tourists.[10]

Palace on Wheels

Travelling on the "Palace on Wheels" is a veritable royal delight ..... An unparalleled experience worldwide made up of vintage salons that once belonged to the erstwhile maharajas, a trip on this train is the closest one can get to princely India. Thus, 7 nights 8 days tour takes the traveller from Delhi to Jaipur, Chittorgarh, Udaipur, Jaisalmer, Jodhpur Bharatpur and Agra back again.[11] Smart uniformed attendants are always on hand to take care of your need and you are treated like a Maharaja throughout your stay on the train. Accommodation available in twin and four bedded cabins with two toilets, hot and cold water and aesthetic furnishing. Indian and continental cuisine is being served to the travellers and to complement the tourist needs, there is a bar and a library to relax in. The "Palace on Wheels" in romantic link with the past and for the tourist there is no better way to feel like royalty for a week.[12]

Heritage Hotels

Rajasthan has been the land[13] of the maharajas and their nobles. The legends that surround these dashing inhabitants have now passed into history—the mythical world of blood and blade, of better won and of their undaunted spirit. But it was not just the battlefield that brought out the best in these brave warriors they gave equal attention to their residence. While the princes built the stately palaces and forts in their state—their nobles were not far behind in building suitably impressive havelies, which were not far behind in building suitably impressive havelies, which were in keeping with their status. All of Rajasthan is dotted with these marvellous monuments, each one an outstanding example of our rich architectural heritage. Most of these palaces here are still being used by the erstwhile royal families; a few have sections converted into museums and hotels thus allowing the tourist a glimpse into the lavish opulence, which was part of the royal life style. With the growing tourism industry and the constant demand for some things different and new for the tourist, the Heritage Hotel concept come on the scene. The department of tourism takes active interest in promoting these heritage hotels.

Table 7.1: Heritage Hotels of Rajasthan

S.No.	District	Classified Heritage Hotels
1.	Ajmer	Pushkar Palace, Pushkar
2.	Alwar	Nimrana Fort Palace, Nimrana
3.		Sariska Palace
4.	Bikaner	Bhawan Niwas
5.		Lalgarh Palace
6.		Basant Vihar Palace
7.	Bharatpur	Laxmi Vilas Palace
8.		Forest Lodge
9.	Chittaur Garh	Castle Bijapur
10.	Dausa	Hotel Bhadarawati Palace
11.	Jaipur	Raj Palace
12.		Bissau Palace
13.		Raj Mahal Palace
14.		Ramgarh Lodge
15.		Narain Niwas Palace
16.		Hotel Khasa Kothi
17.		Samod Havely
18.		Samod Palace
19.	Jodhpur	Karni Bhawan
20.		Fort Chandwa, Lumi
21.		Ajit Bhawan Palace
22.		Bal Samand Palace
23.		Umed Bhawan
24.	Jhunjhunu	Hotel Dundlod Fort
25.		Castel Mandawa, Mandwa
26.		Mukundgarh Fort, Mukundgarh
27.		Rup Niwas Palace
28.		Narain Niwas
29.	Jaisalmer	Narain-Niwas Palace
30.	Nagour	Khivasar Fort, Khivasar
31.	Pali	Rohetgarh
32.		Sardar Samand Place
33.		Rawala Narlai
34.	Rajasamand	Devgarh Mahal
35.	Sawai Madhopur	Sawai Madhopur Lodge
36.	Sirohi	Kama Rajputana Club Resort Mount Abu
37.		Canaut House, Mount Abu
38.		Palace Hotel Mount Abu
39.	Sikar	Golden Castle Resort, Panchar
40.	Udaipur	Fateh Prakash Palace
41.		Sikarbadi
42.		Shiv Niwas Palace
43.		Hotel Laxmi Vilas Palace

Source: Annual reports 2002-03, Deptt. of Tourism, Art and Culture Jaipur.

A Pub-on-Wheel

Trains have always fascinated people all over the world. Rajasthan tourism's luxury train Palace on Wheels is already popular with the travelers. The latest train experience is the Pub-on-Wheels at the Taj Group Rambagh Palace with the colonial steam engine and refurnished carriage, the pub is aptly called "steam". Visitors can be here till after midnight.[13]

Apart from all the tourism products the state has also announced its new millennium tourism products. These include the Chambal river cruise and the Indira Gandhi Canal Cruise, Camel and Horse safaris, Camp tourism, adventure tourism, eco-tourism and rural tourism. In what can be called on innovative, product extension of its Palace-on-Wheels, the state tourism department has now introduce to a Palace of Waves. The Palace-on-Waves scheme will have Shikaras and luxury boats in the Chambal river and the Indira Gandhi Canal. The Palace-on-Wheels already a hit with the international tourist will now have its less-expensive version. Besides there will also be heritage taxis, heritage cars and heritage restaurants in the hotel segment.[14] Plans are also a foot to tap into education tourism where school and colleges vacations can be offered in Rajasthan during the summer season. Rajasthan tourism is already in touch with various schools and colleges in other states and of offering attractive packages to suit the requirements of this niche market. The state is also in the process of working out schemes for the corporate clients where they can be invited in the conservation of monuments.[15]

Tourism Publicity and Promotion

An important component in the promotion mix is the tourism publicity, which plays a crucial role in attracting tourists and promoting tourism. A well-planned publicity programme is found efficacious in the very context. The publicity programme include, regular publicity, stories and photographs to the News Paper, Travel Editor, Contract with Magazine on Stories, ideas and the framing of story outline and picture etc. With the passage of time the tourism publicity has occupied a place of significance. At the initial stage, the information publicity was considered important but of late, the commercial tourist publicity has gained a special significance. This has been due to an increase in the number of tourists and travel frequency. It has necessitated efficient commercial publicity techniques so that a long-term publicity strategy is finalized. The publicity based on motivation force[16] and influencing the imaginative world of the tourists can be referred to as motivation publicity. The holiday maker lives between imagination and reality and the relationship between two influences his judgment on the land visited the most intensive publicity is done for creation, pleasure and cultural travel and the publicity campaign here produce the result on the imagination that the existing need would find the maximum satisfaction in a tourist offer. The publicity may be printed publicity, advertising publicity, project publicity, structure publicity and personal publicity. In the field of tourism, the need for making complete information and facts available to both potential and actual tourists assumes special significance. Tourism promotion is oriented towards creating and maintaining an atmosphere where by traveling public at large is convinced of the advantage of visiting the country or region concerned. International tourism promotion[17] depend heavily on publicity. Media is the most important sources of publicity. The main tools of media publicity are:

- Press releases.
- Informal briefings.
- Presentations.
- Conducted visits.
- Press conferences.
- Sponsored articles.

In the case of a hotel/resort news may relate to the facilities and conventions in the property; events like marriages, seminars, exhibition, inaugurals or sports that may the place in the property and important person who may visit the property. Sponsoring is excellent publicity. A leading hotel group (Taj/ITC/Oberois etc.) might sponsor a cricket match or a TV serial and gain publicity. The another source of publicity[18] is oral publicity. Word of mouth publicity is very effective as for as tourism is concerned. It is said that source of information are credible according to a hierarchy. In descending order of credibility are: according to a hierarchy.

- Intimate family.
- Producer representatives.
- Retailer's representatives.

- Professional colleague.
- Personal friends.

Word of mouth is more effective than advertisements. An endorsement by one who has used the services has more reliability and impact than an advertisement. You ask about the destination from your friend and tell them by one you have experienced. In most cases you search for a person who has experienced the service to seek information like where did you stay? Was the stay comfortable? or how was the bed tea? In the case of tourism, the travel agencies hoteliers, airlines etc. are part of the services and also part of promotion. The personnel in these organization provide service. They also depended upon by the tourists for information and advice. They are a useful 'word of mouth' media.

Following are the basic and main instruments of tourism publicity media:

1. *Printed Publicity*: Composed publicity leaflet, folder, brochure, poster.
2. *Advertising Publicity*: Journals, periodicals daily news papers.
3. *Projected Publicity*: Films, slides.
4. *Structural form of Publicity*: Show cases, window display, participation in fair and exhibition.
5. *Personal Publicity*: Publicity lectures interviews, radiobroadcast, receptions.

The projection and publicity of the tourist attractions[19] of Rajasthan has been one of the most significant tasks of the department of tourism. The department of tourism has adopted the following method for the publicity of tourism in the state:

- Production of promotion tourism literature compressing folder, poster, calendars and brochures.
- Free distribution of publicity literature expect picture postcard, through the directorate and tourist information bureau at 22 centers in and outside the state.
- Sponsored pullouts in travel journals.
- Commissioning travel writer by hosting their visits to Rajasthan.
- Advertisements in travel journals and newspaper.
- Exhibition of Rajasthan tourism attraction and facilities.

- Organizing All-India photographic exhibitions of Rajasthan.

The publicity and promotional wing of the department of tourism, Government of Rajasthan has come up with following features in this direction:

- Advertisements.
- Preparation and distribution of tourist literature.
- International conferences on tourism.
- Preparation of tourist documentaries, Internet, CD, film, photo, etc.
- Seminar and Conferences.
- Exhibition.
- Library on Tourism Literature.
- Welcome and Gift to Tourist as a Guest.

The Government of Rajasthan has published various folders heightening the each tourist event for each tourist destination in the state. The break-up of such folders on fairs and festivals.

- Teej Mela, Jaipur.
- Gangaur Festival, Jaipur.
- Pushkar Mela, Ajmer.
- Kajli Teej, Bundi.
- Desert Festival, Jaisalmer.
- Marwar Festival, Jodhpur.
- Nagour Fair, Nagour.
- Mewar Festival, Udaipur.
- Elephant Festival, Jaipur.
- Camel Festival, Bikaner.

The department of tourism has also published city maps, Indian Airline posters, Rajasthan Tourism Policy, 2001, brochure on cultural heritage of Rajasthan and many more. Most of the tourist literatures, which are being published by the DOT, are provided to the tourists free of cost at all tourist reception centers and tourist offices. In order to heightened the Rajasthan as wonderful tourist destination the government of Rajasthan has selected national and international media for the publicity and promotion purposes. Apart from the publicity in the print media the Government of Rajasthan has also organized various national level conferences, seminars, exhibition, culture programme, annual fairs.

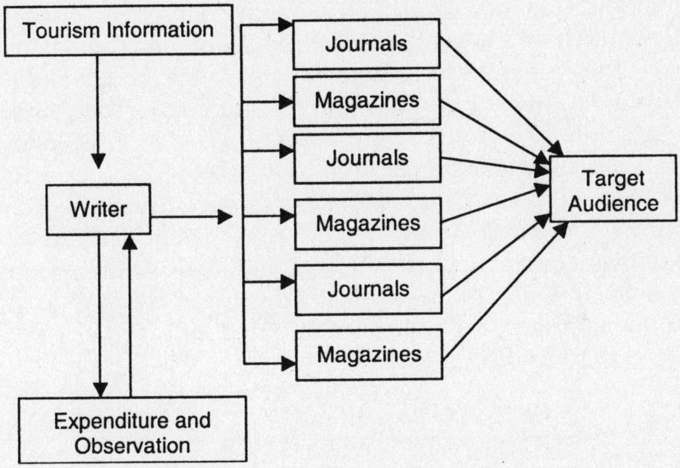

Fig. 7.1

Tourism Information, Experience, Observation and Publicity

Wide publicity is a patent factor in attracting tourist. The Department has its Tourist Reception/Information Centres in 17 districts of the state to provide assistance and authentic information to the tourists. Outside the State, New Delhi has a Tourist Reception Centre while in Mumbai, Chennai and Kolkata have Tourist Information Centre. At these centers, authentic information is provided to the tourists about boarding/lodging facilities and other services available at tourist spots in Rajasthan. Wide publicity is also given through important newspaper, magazines, electronic media etc. about the places of tourist interest/fairs and festivals and other events.[20] Representatives of the Department at National and International exhibitions, seminars, conferences and other appropriate for a make adequate publicity to promote tourism in the state. During (2001-2002) the department represented in the overseas (World Trade Mart, London, Dubai Shopping Festival and I.B.T. Berlin. During (2002-2003) the department representatives participated in the IITM Banglore and Chennai, SATTE (New Delhi) and PATA Festival, New Delhi.[21]

Tourism Promotion

Tourism has assumed an unperfected importance in recent years and therefore efforts have been made at the national and international levels to promote it at a faster rate. More efforts have been planned in the area of publicity and promotion through tourist offices. New schemes have been launched for the promotion of adventure tourism including duty reduction in the import of specialized equipments in new areas of special interest like conversation and incentives are being promoted.[22]

Rajasthan has become one of the major tourism industry with an annual growth of around 11 per cent. This industry helps not only in employment opportunities infrastructure development but also helped India in image-building internationally. Major promotional measures have been adopted and further steps are being taken in this direction.

1. To prepare overall tourist resources in the state.
2. To provide complete safety for tourist.
3. To prepare an integrated mechanism for doing always with the nuisance of touts and beggars.
4. To attend promptly the complaints of the tourist.
5. To gear up infrastructure for development tourism.
6. To give incentives to hotel and other tourism related industry.
7. To develop overseas publicity activities.
8. To promote cultural tourism by arranging holidays and leisure activities like trekking in the Aravalis, camel safari in Thar Desert and many more.

Apart from these mentioned steps some measures should be taken for the domestic tourist as well:

1. Yatrikas, Dharamshalas and Musafirkhanas to be constructed at the religious place.
2. For budget tourist accommodations should very comfortable and as reasonable price.
3. Maximum involvement of private sector by giving a few concession and benefits to them so that to ensure there full cooperation.

It is greatly satisfy that the effort of the Government is putting Rajasthan prominently on the tourist map of the world and gradually it is bearing its fruits. This can be noticed in the development of infrastructure facilities for the tourists both at national and international level. Rajasthan Tourism department should shift from line structure to committee structure by decentralizing the powers and allowing the district head-quarters to formulate the policies for promotional measures in which host communities leaders must be actively involved for overall sustainable development.

Marketing of Tourism Products

The problem of marketing in tourism[23] are somewhat different from the problems of traditional product marketing. The differences are the result of the characteristics of tourism supply and demand. Tourism, first of all, is a service. In manufacturing, goods are produced, stored and sold. The inventory process serves as a way of linking these stages of production and consumption. Tourism supply cannot be stored, airline seats, hotel rooms, or restaurant seats not sold today lose that particular sale forever. A second important factor that makes tourism different from other industries is that it is an amalgam of several products and services. One other factor that makes tourism different from other industries relates to its demand. Tourism demand is highly elastic; seasonal in nature and subject to qualitative factors like taste and fashion as well as objective factors of demand and price. So marketing is a basic problem of tourism industry in India vis-à-vis Rajasthan. Effective marketing is, therefore, a prerequisite for the success of tourism development. There is no other industry, which benefits more from governments marketing efforts than from the tourism industry. It is, therefore, essential that various segment of tourism industry extend their help in marketing.

Profile of Tourist Products

Tourist products profile can be discussed in various forms.[24]

(*i*) Product highly perishable.
(*ii*) Service product.
(*iii*) Users presence essential.
(*iv*) Largely psychological in attraction.
(*v*) Highly risky product.
(*vi*) Demand is unstable.
(*vii*) Supply component rigid.
(*viii*) Product Standard depend on staff.

(*ix*) Not a homogeneous product.
(*x*) Transfer of ownership.
(*xi*) Production and consumption of tourist services are closely related.
(*xii*) A tourist product is assembled by many producers.

Basic components of all tourism products are transport, and accommodation. Although efficient and cheap transport, comfortable accommodation are must yet the attractions and amenities are equally important.

The tourist market may be segmented on the basis of:

- Place or origin of tourism.
- Destinations.
- Purposes of tour-like holiday, pilgrimage, sightseeing shopping etc.
- Economic status and spending tendencies.
- Demographic characteristics-like age, sex, occupation and attitudes.
- Preferences for staying-like camping, luxury hotels caravans etc.
- Preferences of travel-like air, sea road or rail.

Each segment of the market differs in terms of needs and expectations. No organization alone can cater to the needs of the entire segment. Each organization has to decide on the particular segment or segments it would cater to. The segment so identified is called the target segment. The segment identification has to made on the basis of what the organization identifies as its objectives and its capabilities.

Having identified the target market all activities will have to planned and executed keeping this target market in mind. For example, if the hotel is targeting on the domestic tourists in the circuit of religious places, there would be little point in advertising in business magazines or providing foreign cuisine in the restaurant. Simple vegetarian Thali food would perhaps be more satisfying to its patrons.[25] All tourism-marketing objectives as a matter of fact resolve around the market and the following broad lines are therefore typical:

1. Profit maximization in the long-term.
2. Balanced tourist growth and reinforcement of the economic impact of tourism.

3. Security and balance in the social and economic conditions.
4. Maintaining and enhancing the market share in the face of competition in tourism.
5. Enhance the tourist image of the country.[26]

India has a very small share[27] of affluent tourists from the developed nations of the world. Aggressive marketing efforts are required to motivate tourist to India, especially in view of the problems prevailing in some parts of the country. The major role of the overseas offices is to create an awareness of India as an important and attractive tourist destination. Besides the routine functions of answering in queries and providing information, the tourist officer abroad have to maintain liaison with travel trade and by means of advertising and publicity and their visible presence at travel marts and other important travel trade functions. The marketing of tourist's products depends on the development of the destinations. For effective and progressive marketing the worldwide expectation are as under:

1. *Attractions*—natural man-made and cultural or ethnic.
2. *Transport*—easy access particularly to world air routes.
3. *Accommodation*—the commercial sector, the supplementary sector and the informal private sector.
4. *Supportive services*—Shops, banks, medical aid and other resident-oriented products.
5. *Infrastructure*—roads, railways, airports, electricity, sewage disposal and whatever is required to provide support services and facilities.

There are certain factors in tourism, which create a market environment. Favourable examples are easy entry and exit formalities helpful attitude of the Government towards tourism, while unfavourable condition are political unrest, economic instability etc. These factors play a significant role in establishing marketing objectives and goods.[28]

The marketing strategy for any destination or facility has to be formulated on the basis of the extent of seasonality and the capacities available. It would involve special promotions off season prias and development of new products. For example, in case of hill resorts, winter sports can be developed as a special attraction and sold at special off-season prices. The development of new off-season markets to achieve demand substitution by domestic and regional tourists is yet another method of dealing with seasonality in tourism. Thus, a clear understanding of seasonality is a primary requisite in formulating effective tourism marketing strategies.

Constant evaluation is necessary to eliminate ineffective marketing programmers and to strengthen the effective ones. Eventually, the marketing process is completed where it started—with the consumer that is the tourist. It is his satisfaction, which determines the success or failure of tourist marketing campaign. Tourist marketing process cannot be controlled / directed by business enterprises or an organization, howsoever powerful it may be.[29]

Rajasthan has a great tourism potential due to its unique cultural an historical background. The potential has not been fully exploited and whatever any attempt has been made in this direction results have not met expected and desired success. Tourism being unique in its character as tourist belongs from different countries with different socio-economic patterns therefore; their need perceptions are different and vary indifferent degrees. In order to satisfy the tourists psyche the department of Tourism, Art and culture, Government of Rajasthan are branding Rajasthan as one of the unique tourist destinations by marketing aggressively nationally and internationally.

Marketing of tourism needs scientific approach survey-based methodology, futuristic outlook to design, develop and promote tourism in the state of Rajasthan. Identification of market demand pattern is essential in the regard. The Government through its offices can keep track of change in demand patterns and offer a diversified tourism product to suit varying needs of the tourists. As the private sector is guided by the profit motive the state Government will have to engage in market promotion activities to derive full national benefits out of tourism development.[30]

Development of desert destinations, wildlife, sanctuaries, old monuments, forts, revival of art and painting, fair and festivals, folklore are some of the attractions as far as Rajasthan tourism is concerned. These touristic products are unique in its nature and character and can be exploited nationally and internationally to increase the tourist traffic to the state of Rajasthan. All tourist products must have a distinct image. Human resources engaged in the marketing of the tourist products must be harnessed by proper motivation. State of Rajasthan needs well-developed infrastructure, coupled with proper marketing strategy for the promotion of tourism in the state and it will bring the following dividends:

1. Infrastructure development.
2. Regional balance.
3. Revenue yielding effects.
4. Employment opportunities.
5. Promotion of art and culture.
6. Enhancement of fairs and festivals.
7. Encouragement of local artisans.
8. Foreign exchange earnings.
9. National and international image building.
10. Increase in standard of living.

REFERENCES

1. L.J. Lickorish and Rorshaw A.G., *Travel Trade*, Practical Press Ltd. London, 1958, p. 69.
2. Machael M. Coltman, *Introduction to Travel and Tourism an International Approach*, Van Nostrand Rich hold, New York, 1989, p. 299.
3. *Colourful Rajasthan for all Seasons*, D.O.T., Jaipur.
4. *Ibid.*
5. *Ibid.*
6. *Ibid.*
7. *Ibid.*
8. *Ibid.*
9. *Ibid.*
10. *Ibid.*
11. *Ibid.*
12. *Rajasthan Atithi*, March 2003, Vol. 4, p. 19.
13. *Colourful Rajasthan for all Seasons*, D.O.T., Jaipur.
14. *Ibid.*
15. Jha S.M., *'Tourism Marketing'*, Himalayan Publishig House, Bombay, 1995, p. 261.
16. Ibid, p. 263.
17. *"Tourism Marketing and Communications"*, IGNOU Foundation Course in Tourism, Vol. 6, p. 31, Study Material, June 1994.
18. *Ibid.*, p. 34.
19. Sharma, K.K., *Tourism in India—Centre-State Administration*, Classic Publishing House, Jaipur, 1991, p. 54.

20. *Rajasthan Atithi*, September-October, 2000, Issue No. 2, Department of Tourism, Government of Rajasthan, Jaipur, p. 6.
21. *Ibid.*, p. 06.
22. Batra G.S., R.C. Dangwal, *Tourism Promotion and Development, New Advance*, Deep and Deep Publication Pvt. Ltd., 2001, p. 32.
23. Mill Robert Christie, Alastair M. Morrison, *The Tourism System, An Introductory Text*, Prentice-Hall, INE., Englewood Cliff, New Jersey, 1985, p. 357.
24. Jha S.M:, *Service Marketing*, Himalayan Publishing House, Bombay, 1994, p. 18.
25. *Tourism Marketing and Communication*, IGNOU, Foundation Course in Tourism, pp. 31-34, Study Material, June 1994.
26. Batra G.S and R.C. Dangwal, *Tourism Promotion and Development, New Advance*, Deep and Deep Publication Pvt. Ltd., New Delhi, 2001, p. 15.
27. Gupta Sunil, S.P. Bansal, '*Tourism Towards 21st Century*', Deep and Deep Publication Pvt. Ltd., New Delhi, 2001, p. 68.
28. Batra G.S., R.C. Dangwal, *Tourism Promotion and Development—New Advances*, Deep and Deep Publications Pvt. Ltd., 2001, p. 167.
29. *Ibid.*
30. G.S. Batra and R.C. Dangwal, *Tourism Promotion and Development—New Advances*, Deep and Deep Publications Pvt. Ltd., 2001, p. 56.

Chapter VIII

TOURISM AND HOTEL INDUSTRY

Tourism is accelerating growth by employment generation and foreign exchange earning and opening new areas comparing a number of factors. What have always been considered the separate industries, are now integral part of much larger industries of tourism. The most important one is the *Hotel Industry*.[1] In this view it will be noteworthy to consider the report of Lok Sabha Committee (1975-76) that; since the hotels constitute the most important and infect a basic element of tourism infrastructure. The committee feels that the various measures taken and efforts made for tourism promotion will not produce the desired results if the hotel accommodation in the country lags behind.[2] Tourism industry including hotels is a major second largest industry in the world where it has been rightly said—'No Hotels No Tourism' thus hotel industry is essential part of tourism.[3] The expansion of tourism brought inevitable development of the hotel industry. As hotel have significant contribution to make towards tourist trade it is closely linked with tourist industry for it is responsible for 50 per cent foreign exchange earnings. Tourism plays an important role in the development of hotel industry. The guest who comes in the country to know culture and religion they resides in hotels (say five star, Heritage hotels etc.), which do provide the glimpses of our culture. The impact of tourism on hotels is clearly seen by their enormous sophisticated modern techniques. The modern Hotel Industry has become highly sophisticated and equipped with refined and systematized technology.

The tourism industry generates itself sufficient additional resources for inter-linkage inputs and additional economic activity. The hotel industry has inbuilt expansion system, dynamic through its internal cash generation on slow depreciating assets as a result of which could be beneficial without undue diversion resources from other priority areas.[4]

Impact of Tourism on Hotel Industry of Rajasthan

Hotels are the core and essential part of tourism, the largest industry in the world. Rajasthan is a hot tourist destination and with over 1000 hotels and around 50,000-bed capacity, the hotel industry has become the backbone of the state economy. The industry has enough scope to expand further. The hotel industry has been growing its importance from economic and socio-economic point of view. The impact of tourism on hotel industry of Rajasthan focused primarily on economic and socio-cultural aspect. The impact made by tourism therefore depends upon the volume and profile characteristic of the tourists (their length of stay, their preference, purpose of visit travelling styles etc.) together with the characteristic of the Hotel Industry styles (facilities amenities provided, its structure, cuisine etc.) is equally important as it determines the degree of its strength to tourism and tourism development.

1. *Economic Impact*: International tourism is an invisible export that it creates a flow of foreign currency into the hotel industry thereby contributing directly to the economy of the state as well like other export industries. This inflow of revenue creates industry turnover, household income, employment generation and government revenue. The generation process does not stop at this point however. Some portion of the revenue received by the hotel industry, human resource and government creating further rounds of economic activity. Domestic tourism has somewhat similar economic impact upon the host segment. International tourism brings foreign currency into the whole industry, while domestic tourism redistributes domestic currency. Money earned in other segments is spent within the host community so as to create additional resources, job opportunities for semi-skilled and unskilled human resource at tourist destinations. Economic impact of tourism has diversified the economy by creating separate industries—like hotel industry moreover, tourism seems to be more effective than other industries improving infrastructure. Indeed it is in this industry that tourism can make its most significant impact by providing monetary incentive for the continuance of the industry and by creating market for state produce.

2. *Socio-Cultural Impacts*: In addition to the economic impact tourism also imposes socio-cultural impacts on the industry. The culture (the cuisine, the folk, the art, the history) of host communities is often an important factor in attracting tourists to a particular destination. Many tourists are interested in experiencing a culture, which is different from their own[5] indeed the existence of difference between the host culture, and tourist culture is the principle, which stimulates the tourism industry. The culture of the host destination can take many different forms but most examples fall into one of the two categories:
   (*a*) Customs relating to host destination.
   (*b*) Aspects of the everyday life, their history and religion. The first category includes arts and crafts, folk, dance, customs and festivals, colorful ceremonies and carnivals. The second category include not only the local but also the national traditions and customs.

The hotel industry caters to natural, homely environment and warmth. Hotel industry caters to art and history, archaeology, handicraft, literature, music, dance, philosophy of the state. Some of the impacts of tourism on hotel industry are beneficial but some can be considered to be harmful say such effect may be on culture of the host destination known as trivialization.[7]

This terminology can be explained as the degradation and commercialization of the host culture where the economic and socioculture impacts are favourable they can also be explosive. Likewise the impact is seen in the feasts, festivals which tourist are encouraged to attend rather they are being highjacked and encashed by the hotel industry. With good planning however, tourism can provide an impetus for the preservation of ancient cultures, but too often the local way of life degenerates into a commercially organized effigy of its former self. The traditional dances and the skilled crafts give way to cheap imitations to satisfy the needs of the visitors and to obtain money with least possible effort.[8]

Another impact on moral standards of the host population creates deprivation and frustration when they cannot achieve the higher level as foreign tourist. In extreme cases crime, prostitution, gambling and drug traffic are being catered by hotel industry. As Human Resource plays a vital role in the hospitality industry education and training of the resource is must. So it encourages education and training of Human Resource as the industry have to cater to the best products of tourism industry to the tourist. For this the hotel industry has certain duties and responsibilities for resource of the industry.[9]

Tourism and Hotel Industry

Ellsworth M. Statler—The Henry ford of the modern hotels says, "The guest is always right."[10] Some might contradict this but this statement reflects the ultimate challenges being faced by hotel professionals to provide services that meet ever changing need and demands of the guests. The hotel industry is a part of larger

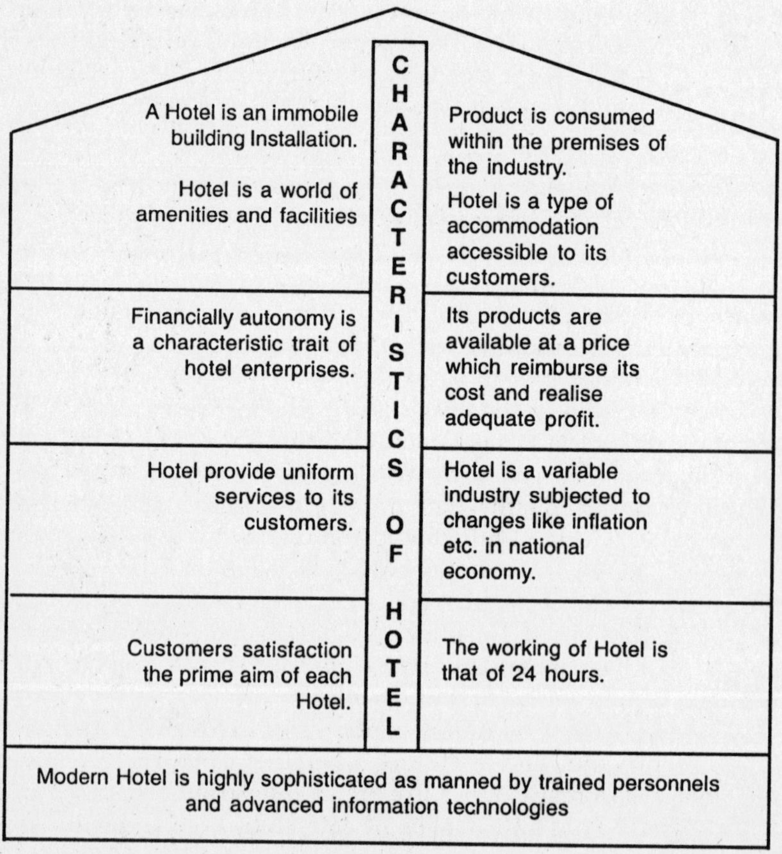

Fig. 8.1

enterprises known as the travel and tourism industry. The travel and tourism industry is a vast group of business with one goal in common: providing necessary or desired products and services to travellers.[11]

Many hotel properties provide food and beverage service, recreational service and more such facilities. As per international standards there are, as estimated 10 million guest rooms available to tourists around the world.[12] According to World Tourism Organisation (W.T.O.) Madrid, Tourism has now become the world's largest industry, ahead of automobiles and petroleum products.[13] Further, with regards to employment, as per the world tourism and travel council report, travel and tourism industry is the largest civilian industry in the world employing one out of every ten person worldwide.[14] As per the WTO report 1,593 million tourist arrivals were recorded all over the world during 2003, registering a 4.6 per cent increase over 2000. International receipts rose to 2,423 billion, registering a 7.6 per cent growth. India, however, commanded just 0.39 per cent of the global tourist arrivals and just about 0.51 per cent of the total receipts.[15]

But it is also notable that this substantial contribution of 0.39 per cent to Indian economy was equivalent to foreign exchange worth Rs. 13,000 crore.[16] Beside, the tourism sector provides direct employment to 80 lakh people and indirect employment to 2 crores people.[17]

The Indian Tourism Industry has been defined to include the following segment.[18]

1. Hotels restaurants resorts and other tourist complexes providing accommodation, food and catering services to tourists.
2. Travel agencies and tour operators.
3. Units providing facilities to tourist on culture adventure, wildlife experiences.
4. Surface water and air transport facilities to the tourists.
5. Leisure, entertainment, amusement sports and health units of tourists.
6. Convention and Seminar Units.

The Ninth Five Year Plan accorded industrialization to tourism. Dr. Negi writes "of the many and diverse components of the tourist industry, hotels constitute the most important segment. Hotels are the vital and essential parts of tourism industry. Without an adequate development of hotel resources all the national scenery, all the climate virtues and all sporting and recreational facilities will not suffice to sustain a good volume of tourists trade".[19]

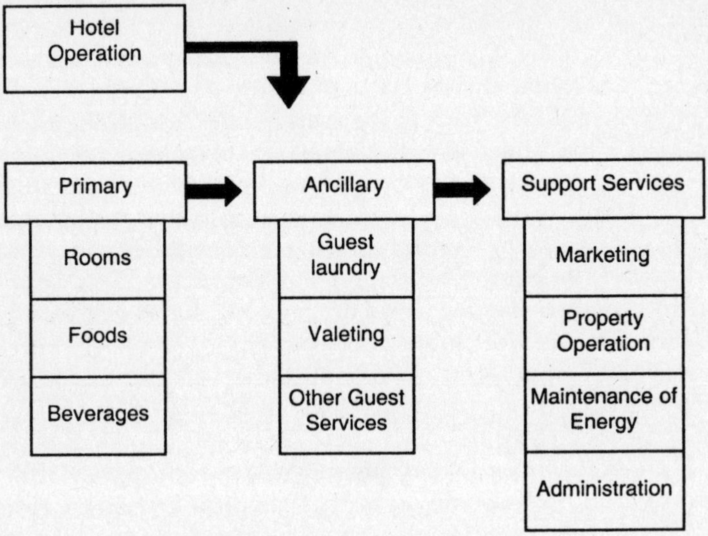

Fig. 8.2: How Hotel Operate ?

Further, Dr. Negi writes, "It has been rightly said, 'No Hotels, No Tourism'. The expansion of tourism will inevitably bring about the development of the Hotel Industry. Hotel Industry is so closely linked with the tourism industry that it is responsible for about 50 per cent of the foreign exchange earnings from tourism".[20]

The employment avenues in the services-oriented hotel industry are quite large. As regards the direct employment it is estimated that the room to staff ratio for a hotel varies between 1:1.5 to 1:3, whereas the committee on unemployment 1993 estimated that on an average one hotel room should expect to provide employment for 2.5 persons.[21] On an average the visit of each foreign tourist provides employment to 1 person, and 6.5 domestic tourist generate 1 job.[22] Further, with regards to indirect employment there are a number of other employment avenues connected to the hotel industry viz supply of food items, various machinery items, from kitchen to air conditioning, laundry equipments computers, furniture, fixtures, cutlery crockery etc. The Bhagwati Committee said it would (indirect) offer nine times employment to the number of persons directly employed in hotels.[23] Moreover, hotel industry seems more effective than other industries in generating employment. The Hotel Industry has direct impact on regional and rural development. The industry has encouraged cottage industries in many ways-handlooms for furnishings, carpets, handicraft etc. "In keeping with the philosophy of self-reliance through indigenous source, the hotel industry has relied predominantly on getting the supplied and equipments fabricated in the country.[24] The hotel industry also provides an opportunity to the guests to know the regional or a country's way of life and culture. In overall terms it has multiple economic benefits, which is an urgent requirement for a developing country like India.

Origin of Hotels—A Brief History

Hotel Industry in India

India, the ancient land of civilization, culture, dance, drama, music, and hospitality has been visited through the centuries by the travellers from many countries. For facilitating the travel, the Kings and Rulers built the Dharamshalas, constructed road, planted trees, dug wells and tanks. With the advent of Muslim rulers, Srai's were introduced. In the reign of Sher Shah Suri and then Mughals it reached a level of perfection. Improvements in the means of transport and communication resulted in the establishment of inns and taverns.

Later with the advent of British the Sarais took the form of western style hotels.[25] It seems that with regard to modern Hotels, it were the British who introduced hotels in India mainly for their own use or for foreign visitors. Dr. Negi writes that the credit for opening the first western style hotel under the name of British hotel in Bombay in 1840, goes to Pallangee Pestongee. He is called the pioneer of the western style hotels in India.[26] The twentieth century was a turning point in the history of hotel industry in India. In this century there was a real growth and development of the hotel industry.

Growth and Development of Hotel Industry

The history of development of hotel industry in India dates back when the necessity and urge to travel either on foot or by horse led to the setting up of places where accommodation and food can be obtained. There are many, historical evidences about the existence of the Dharmshalas and Sarais (Inns). Some of the Sarais were built during the Tughlak dynasties. Sher Shah Suri and Mughals reached to the perfection. Akbar, Jahangir and Shahjahan were great philanthropists, the Sarais built by them were unique. They afforded the best possible facilities to the travellers. Jahanara Begum built the most beautiful Sarai. The Sarai was situated in the garden of Sahibabad or Begumabad in Delhi. Although the sarai is no more, the garden is still there and is known as Queen's Park or Azad Park Jahanara Begum Sarai was a magnificent building.[27] In later eighteenth and early nineteenth century due to the development in the means of transportation and communication inns and taverns[28] were established in the principal cities of the country. The Sarais took the form of western style hotels in some cities during this period. David prince, who visited India in this eighteenth century stayed in one of such Sarais.[29]

The progress made by these hotels in India cannot be underestimated. In spite of the higher initial investment, costlier operating technique and comparatively lower profit margins and a number of other factors, these hotels have a continuous and steady progress. These hotels were first started about 135 years ago mainly for dignitaries and princes. Several hotels came into existence in Kolkata, Chennai, Bangalore, Mysore, Hyderabad, Visakhapatnam etc. The twentieth century was a turning point in the history of the hotel industry in India especially the year 1903 is remembered as a landmark. It is in this century we find the real growth and development of the accommodation industry.[30]

The independently owned hotel were of traditional pattern and the typical first in the industry, but the growth and development of hotel industry has been increasingly associated with hotel groups. Hotels in different locations when placed under central management within a restricted geographical area are said to be grouped hotels. Leased hotels as agents, franchise hotels are being operated by the hotel groups. The hotel groups normally operate hotels owned by them or leased by them from their owners to whom they pay rental. Sometimes they manage hotels as agents for the owners under management contracts, which provide for the payment of expenses/management fees and/or the sharing of profits. The groups may also operate under franchise agreements, which allow one party (the franchisee) to sell a product designed, supplied and controlled by the other party (the franchiser), in return for a fee or a share of profits, in this arrangement a hotel group may be in the role of a franchiser or in the role of a multiple franchises.[31]

The hotel groups are advantageous from various point of view say financial, marketing, managerial, technical etc. groups extend the size resulting into various economies say financial, marketing, buying, managerial, technical economies. The financial economy is the ability of the group to have internal and external capital resources. Because of good security provided by the hotel group to its lenders, lending institutions provide a good finance. The fluctuations in working capital, revenue, and expenditure are being balanced by these financial resources, which can only be obtained by such groups. The size of the group is such that an image is created in the market, which enables the group to obtain, the marketing economies say common name, facilities and standards, public relations, advertising and sales promotion. A hotel groups can achieve economies of buying as goods cost keep pace with the increase in the volume and services are bought in bulk at negotiable price and range. A group can attain the availability of training schemes and benefit from interchange of staff between the hotels in a group. The advantages of group operation such as finance, personnel, purchasing and marketing can be obtained by employing specialists in the group. In a hotel group's managerial economies can be enjoyed as management cost keep, pace with the increase in the volume of business of business. Due to the size of the group various technical economies can easily be achieved which otherwise would not have been possible. As for the Indian Hotel industry is concerned, there are basically six groups or chains of hotels namely.

1. The Ashok Group Corporation	• Indian Tourism Development
2. The Welcome Group	• Indian Tobacco Company
3. Taj Groups of Hotels	• The Indian Hotel Co. Ltd.
4. Oberoi Group of Hotels	• The East India Co. Ltd.
5. Centaur Group	• Hotel Corporation of India[32]
6. Clark Group	

ITDC—Ashok Group

In accordance with the recommendations of Jha Committee (1963), the Government of India set up three separate corporations in 1965 namely. Hotel Corporation of India Ltd. (HCL), India Tourism Corporation and Indian Tourism Transport Undertaking Ltd. After more than a year of their working the three corporations were amalgamate into one composite corporation—India Tourism Development Corporation. This new Corporation (ITDC) commanded functioning with effect from October 1, 1966 with an authorized capital of Rs. 5 crore. Realising the importance of tourism in the country the Government of India created a separate ministry of Tourism and Civil Aviation on 13 March, 1967 under the charge of a Cabinet Minister.[33] Today ITDC provides an incentive to travel and tourism backed by 35 hotels segmented into three different categories—Ashok Elite Hotels, Ashok Classic Hotels and Ashok Comfort Hotels and also Forest Lodges, Travellers Lodges and Beach Resorts.[34] The six 'Elite' hotels of Ashok groups five star deluxe properties that cater 'to up market clientele. The classic' group comprises sixteen units that meet the expectation of the business traveller and mid market guests. The comfort category provides home comfort at eleven locations across the country.[35]

ITC Hotels—Welcome Group

The Indian Tobacco Company (Ltd.) entered the hotel industry in 1957 with the opening of Chola in Chennai. It has been inspired in every case by the Indian historical tradition. The philosophy of ITC is—"We enjoy people with a symbol ITC Welcome Hotels and the emblem of two folded hands in Namaskar done in flowers to be changed everyday at the entrance of every ITC hotel, is the Indian way of welcoming the guests.[36] The Mughal in Agra (1976) is inspired by the red sand stone design of Fatehpur Sikri; the Maurya in Delhi (1977) is inspired by the most famous of the Maurya Emperor Ashoka. Each of the hotel is designed to have an individual character of its own, totally Indian in concept and yet ultra modern in terms of amenities and comfort. Welcome group does not appear willing to build a chain of mass produced hotels.[37] Welcome groups is now rapidly being recognized as the most versatile and quality service hotel. Recently the president Mr. Bill Clinton of USA visited India and stayed at 'Maurya' in Delhi. The company, ITC Hotels presently operates eleven hotels under the Welcome Group banner apart from two other hotels it owns and in all has 17 hotels in its fold.[38] The Welcome Group and Travel Corporation of India Hotels and Resorts (Private) Ltd. signed an agreement to argument the welcome groups chain by working as partners to accelerate the rate of growth of foreign tourist traffic coming to India.[39]

The Taj Groups of Hotels

Shri Jamsetjee Tata who established Taj Mahal Hotel in Mumbai in 1904 incorporated the Indian Hotel Company, Mumbai on April 1st 1902 with an authorised capital of 30 lakh owned. Today Taj Group has 49 properties in 33 destinations with more than 6000 rooms in India. It is India's largest hotel chain offering Luxury hotels, Business Hotels, Leisure Hotels, which comprise Palaces, Resorts, Garden Retreats, and Cultural center hotels. To further consolidate its position in the industry it has won international acclaim for its quality hotels and its excellence in business facilities, service cuisine and interiors. Today, there are many hotels in the chain including Taj Mahal, Inter Continental, President Hotel, the Fort Augada Beach Resort, the Lake Palace (Udaipur), the Rambagh Palace (Jaipur), the Taj Coromandel, the Fisherman's Cove, the Pandyan Hotel, the Taj Mahal (Delhi) and the Taj Palace (New Delhi) in all the Taj Group has total of 55 Properties in India and abroad.[40]

Oberoi Groups of Hotels

Mr. Oberoi the propounded of Oberoi group of hotels was a clerk in Cecil Hotel, Shimla who soon became a partner in the Clerk Hotel Shimla. He took over Grand Hotel, Calcutta in 1933. The Oberoi Hotels Pvt. Ltd. was established with a capital of Rs. 5 Lakh in 1946.[41] since then several hotels were built and added to his chain of hotels like Mount Everest (Darjeeling), Mount View (Chandigarh). Maharaja Hari Singh's Palace in Srinagar etc. Oberois further extended their activities internationally since 1964. They have been successfully going on with numerous ventures abroad. Kathmandu (Nepal), Singapore, Sudan, Figi, Egypt, Indonesia Mauritius and acquired Menna House in Cairo Oberoi Aswan at Elephantine Island in the middle of Nile, Hotel Ya Bhawani at Zanzibar Hotel Dammam in Saudi Arabia. In 1973 Oberoi Sheraton was opened in Bombay. The Oberoi group has its own school of Hotel Management in Delhi, recognized by the International Hotel Association, Paris.

It has an exchange programme with Lycee Technique Hoteller in France.[43]

The BHEL is also moving into hotels in collaboration with Oberois and heading to established hotels at Chennai, Coimbatore, Bangalore, Pune and other commercial cities of India.[44] Oberoi has played a place setting role in developing the hotel industry since 1947. They acquired international name with elegance, personalized service and luxurious living. Mr. Oberoi, the winner of the 'Agastya' Award for promotion of tourism in India the 'Victory Pillar' for promotion of hotel and catering industry, may justifiably be called the founder, promoter and builder of hotel industry on this sub-continent.[45]

Air India—Hotel Corporation of India

The airlines generate a substantial quantum of traffic, which feeds the hotels with business and tourist travellers. The air-passengers natural choice is certain to be influenced by the carrier reputation and associated facilities offered by it. Therefore, Air India considered it proper to enter into and give a new direction, to the Indian Hotel Industry.[46] Air India in July 1971, set up a wholly owned subsidiary called Hotel Corporation of India (HCI) with a capital of US$ 6.5 million. Its flight kitchen is famous for the craft of crockery. The Baby of the chain HCI Group opened centaur hotel at Santa Cruz (presently Shivajee) Airport Mumbai and hotel Centaur at Delhi's Indira Gandhi International Airport. In addition, there are two beach resort operating in collaboration with the TCI. The Centaur Beach Resort at Port Blair, Andaman and Centaur Beach Resort at Bangaram.[47]

Clarks Groups

Clarks Hotel, Varanasi, was established in the eighties of the nineteenth century. In 1948 the present owner, the U.P. Hotels and Restaurant Ltd, acquired it. Within 13 years of its establishment it made a tremendous progress by establishing four luxurious hotels at Jaipur, Calcutta, Khajuraho and Kathmandu. There are plans for opening three more luxury hotels at Delhi, Patna and at a few Buddhist places.[48] Among the other Hotels the prominent ones are Holiday Inn, Bombay having its franchise from Holiday Inns, Inc.

USA. The New Delhi Hilton is an enterprises of Bharat Hotel Ltd., New Delhi. Asian Hotel Ltd. and Meridian Delhi own Hotel Leela Venture at Bombay and Goa, and Hyatt Regency Delhi, a part of Air France Hotels is there. The quality Inn and Days Inn are also expanding their business in India.[49]

Categorisation of Hotels in India

Categorisation separates accommodation into different classes. Categorising a hotel into a particular group is not easy, because of its diversity. Many hotels do not fit into any single and well-defined category. Government of India, Department of tourism, is doing the widely accepted categorization. The hotel is classified into different star categories, ranging from 1 star to 5 star deluxe. Recently a new category, Heritage hotel has also been added to it. The present system of classification is based on facilities available in the concerned hotels. The Department of Tourism had constituted a committee, Hotel and Restaurant Approval and Classification Committee (HRACC), which inspects the Hotel (the applicant hotel) to assess its suitability, or otherwise for awarding the star category it has applied for. There are five such Committees—the Central Committees and four Regional Committees. The classification or reclassification of 4 star, 5 Star and 5 Star Deluxe hotels is handled by the Central Committees. The classification and reclassification of 1,2,3 star and the regional committees do heritage hotel and approval of restaurants.[50] Further, there are many hotels, which do not apply for classification providing more or less the same facilities what these classified hotels provide. These types of hotels can be named as 'unclassified' hotels. Another category can be alternative lodging properties. It includes Rest Houses, Guest Houses, Tourist Bungalows, and Camping sites, Dharamshalas etc. We are not lagging behind in tourism receipts but we have also not been able to create proper hotel accommodations for the guests. At present we are having only 64,000 rooms.[51] All over India whereas Las Vegas (USA) alone has more than 100,000 hotel rooms.[52] Bangkok, the capital of Thailand provides more hotel rooms than our entire country.[53]

Hotel Industry in Rajasthan

Rajasthan, is favourite destination for all kinds of tourists. Its Forts,

Palaces, Temples, Wildlife, Lakes, Aravalis and Thar, Colourful Fair and Festivals have been inviting tourists to visit Rajasthan. But it seems this 'hot' destination has started loosing its glory. The share of state in tourist arrivals in India has come down to 25 per cent from 33 per cent in recent years.[54]

As the data reveals the most commonly used source of recruitment for hotels in Rajasthan is direct application system. All the Human Resource heads are using the direct application source for recruiting their employees irrespective of group star category. 76.92 per cent have agreed to use friends and relatives working in the hotels as their recruitment source and 38.46 per cent of them have used the advertisement techniques. It is notable that the recruitment sources through 'advertisements' and the lower category hotels are using 're-employment' more. The Five Star category hotels.

Table 8.1: Sources of Recruitment Practice in Hotels in Rajasthan (Response from Human Resource Heads)

S. No.	*Sources of Recruitment*	*Total Respondents (13)*	*No. of Users*	*Respondents*
1.	Direct applicants	13	13	100.00
2.	Friends and Relatives working in hotels	"	10	76.92
3.	Advertisement in daily newspaper	"	5	38.46
4.	Re-employment	"	6	46.15
5.	Campus interviews at FCI or IHM	"	7	53.84
6.	Labour union	"	4	30.76
7.	Employment Exchange	"	Nil	

Source: Field Survey.

As regards re-employment, the 1,2,3, star and unapproved hotels are ahead in this under re-employment head 50 per cent are those employees who left the hotel on their own an roughly 25 per cent are those who were thrown out for disciplinary actions like absenteeism and similar ones. And according to a rough estimate 25 per cent are those who were ousted owing to theft or other illegal activities. But the notable things are that none of the five star deluxe hotels have agreed to reemploy those employees once who have been ousted by them.

Then the smaller category hotels like 1,2,3 Star and unapproved have not shown any belief in unions or union as a source of employment. But 30.76 per cent hotels are using labour unions as a source of recruitment. With regard to campus interviews only 5, star deluxe and 5 star and lastly 4 star and heritage hotels have cast their vote in its favour, while the lower category hotels had either not been up to the mark or say that they cannot afford it. Then the employees were asked regarding the means of their recruitment. The answers were as under:

Table 8.2: Sources of Recruitment in Hotel Industry in Rajasthan (Responses from Employees)

S.No.	*Sources of Recruitment*	*Respondents*	*%*
1.	Direct applicants	124	29.52
2.	Friends and Relatives working in hotels	67	15.95
3.	Advertisement	49	11.66
4.	Re-employment	34	8.09
5.	Campus interviews	102	24.28
6.	Labour union	33	7.85
7.	Employment Exchange	Nil	–
8.	Internal sources	11	2.61

Source: Field Survey.

The data reveal that the direct application system with 29.52 per cent is a bigger source for recruiting employees in the hotels. The campus interviews with 24.28 per cent are also a popular source of recruitment. The notable things are that advertisement is not taken as a popular source of recruitment in hotels. It helps only 8.09 per cent to get recruitment in hotels. It may be because nowadays the human resource department has started 'Application Banks.'

A person interested in job, can send application whenever he feels. The concerned human resource department keeps the application, and when the requirement for a candidate comes from a certain department all the applications of that particular area are scrutinized and interview calls are sent accordingly. There is no need for advertisement. Besides the campus interview has also affected the advertisement. A few trends, which have emerged through the data, is, that direct applications, campus interviews, friends and relatives and lastly trade union are the primary source of requirement in five star deluxe, four star and heritage hotels.

But as per the collected information, the senior employees who joined before 1991 have gone in for direct applications, trade union and friends and relatives, whereas the employees who have joined during the last five years have marked campus interviews, direct application. It shows that today the trade union and friends and relatives have lost their importance as a source of recruitment in hotels. Among the 1,2,3 and unapproved category hotels the respondents have marked direct application, friends and relatives, reemployment and advertisement as primary sources of recruitment. These hotels do not like the trade union and no employee from these hotel has marked trade union as a source of recruitment. The overall trend shows that today education and personality are playing an important role in recruitment. The practice of internal recruitment is less prevalent in hotel industry. Only 2.61 per cent employees have shown their source of recruitment as internal recruitment. This practice is more prevalent in 3,2,1 and unapproved category of hotels where the employer wants to pay as less as possible. If a person who is working in restaurant and speaks well and if there is a vacancy at the front office, the owner will bring him in the front office, and will raise his salary by hundred or two hundred rupees per month. If a new recruitment had been done, definitely the employer would have been requited to pay higher salary.

Selection in selection, the management compares the qualification of the application with the requirement of job and eliminates all those who were earlier tempted by the same to apply. To assist in selection there are a variety of tools available to the personnel manager including letters of applications, application forms, interviews, and psychological tests. The tools try to assess a long list of items including punctuality, honesty, integrity, ability etc. When the human resource head were asked as to what steps they undertake in selecting employees for their hotels? The answer were as under:

Table 8.3: Selection Tools Practice in Hotels in Rajasthan (Response by Human Resource Head)

S.No.	*Step*	*Respondents (13)*	*Percentage*
1.	Application Forms	7	53.80
2.	Interview	12	92.30
3.	Psychological tests	Nil	–
4.	Reference check	13	100.00
5.	Medical Examination	6	46.15
6.	Plain Application	6	46.15

Source: Field Survey.

As per the Manager's response more or less all the hotels have interview and plain application (letter) tools though a few owners said that, if the applicant was known or had some kind of recommendation from their family or friends, they would keep him directly. But this is applicable in only 1,2 and 3 starts hotels. The five stars, and five star deluxe and heritage hotels go in for real interview to gather as much information as possible. Some of them have an interview plan also.

The Five Star deluxe, five star and 4 star also follow the step of blank application forms and mostly these are the hotels that ask the applicant to go for physical or medical examination. These hotels have their own contracted doctor and clinics. The 2 and 1 star hotels normally ask for a plain application in which the address of the applicant, his references and the place where he has worked previously are important. The reference part is normally highly used by all in a hotel industry and all the respondents have replied 'yes' to using reference check as a step in selection. No respondent has marked 'yes' to psychological test. The Psychological tests are not at all used in selection of employees in hotels. Further the employees were asked if they knew what tools were used during their selection in the hotel?

Table 8.4: Selection Tools Practice in Hotels in Rajasthan (Response from the Employees)

S.No.	*Selection Steps*	*Respondents*	*Percentage*
1.	Did you fill blank application form	247	58.80
2.	Did you face an interview	386	91.90
3.	Did you appear in any kind of psychological test	Nil	–
4.	Do you know if your references was checked	Yes-180	42.85
5.	Did you go through medical examination	193	45.95
6.	Did you write application on a plain paper.	194	46.19

Source: Field Survey.

The data reveal that 91.90 per cent respondents have gone through the interview process. This indicates that this practice is prevailing more or less in all the hotels for selection of candidates. 58.80 per cent candidates have filled in blank applications provided by the hotels. Here it shows that these employees were from 5 star deluxe, five star, 4 star and heritage hotels. All the respondents said 'no' to any type of psychological test. It is clear that in Rajasthan, while selecting people for hotels there is no system of finding out the working attitude of the employees.

With regard to reference check, 43.33 per cent employees were aware that the reference they wrote in their application was cross-checked but 56.66 employees were not aware that their reference were cross checked. But the notable thing is that there was a 98.8 per cent reference check. More or less all the employers checked the whereabouts of the employees. Yes, reference check in hotels is an important step in selection. It takes little time when the reference is in the same city. Normally it is checked on the telephone, but it takes long to find out if the reference is outside the city. The five star deluxe hotels use their own sources and there are cases when employees were sent back after joining the service.

Then 45.95 per cent went through the medical examination. The employees of 4 star deluxe, 4 star and heritage hotels were also sent for the medical examination. These hotels are having their own contracted private clinics, and the employee is required to go there only. They do not believe in general hospital. The hotels 1,2,3 unapproved category are less interested in the fitness of employees. None of them was sent for medical examination by the hotel. The 46.19 per cent applicants, all from 1,2,3 and unapproved star category, were asked to write an application on plain paper mentioning home address, reference, experiences clearly.

Training and Development

Normally there are three main components that an individual required to perform his job effectively. They are knowledge, skills and attitudes. Effective training can develop each of them. Each component, however, needs different training approach. Knowledge, for example, can be imparted by talks, lectures and films, but these techniques would prove futile in imparting the second component, 'skill'. In this case the practice is necessary. The third component, i.e. a man's set of attitudes, is the most difficult to change, even going through sound training. The human resource heads were asked if they provided any kind of training to their employees? If yes, why? If No, why? The answers were as under:

Table 8.5: Type of Training Provided in Hotels in Rajasthan

S. No.	*Training*	*Respondents (420)*	
		Yes	*No*
1.	Vestibule Training	Nil	Nil
2.	On the Job Training	(129) 30.7%	69.3%
3.	Off the Job Training	(97) 23.3%	76.7%

Source: Field Survey.

The data reveal that no hotel in Rajasthan provides vestibule type of training. It is a type of practice of providing skills, training to the individual after they are hired but before they are assigned to specific jobs. Then 30.7 per cent hotels provide on-the-job or apprenticeship programmes, in which an employee learns with those who are already skilled in their jobs. In this category mostly five star deluxe and government-owned hotels are there. 69.2 per cent hotels do not provide-on-the-job training to their employees. Further, the human resource heads were asked the reason for providing on-the-job training. The answers were as under:

1. Relatively low cost of Training.
2. It is easier to teach supervisors (cum trainers) responsible for providing on the job training to their subordinates.
3. The supervisors and fellow workers provide much of the training. Therefore, it is sure that training relates directly to the work situation.

With regard to off-the job training 23.0 per cent hotels said 'yes' and 76.7 per cent hotels said 'no' among the sample units of Rajasthan. While 'Yes' to off-the-job training programmes (the 23.0%) were asked about the methods used for the training, the answers were as under: 15.38 per cent human resource heads said lecture, talks, film-charts, visual aids, programmed texts and discussions were used. The users of these methods were 5 star deluxe hotels. 7.6 per cent human resource heads said lecture, discussion and programmed texts were used for imparting training to their employees. These were Heritage and four-star hotels.

Later, a question was asked from those employees who had attended any of the two training programmes as to what development could they see from the training programmes? The answers were as under:

The data reveal the 53.09 per cent employees said that they are feeling an increase in their efficiency, and 57.52 per cent said their work knowledge has increased. Now they are able to perform well; earlier their lack of proper knowledge was forcing them to rely on others and was causing delay in services.

Table 8.6: Developments in the Employees after Training Programmes in Hotels in Rajasthan

S.No.	*Developments*	*Respondents (226)*	%
1.	Increase in efficiency	120	53.09
2.	Increase in work knowledge	130	57.52
3.	Development in personality	90	39.82
4.	Increase quality of work	25	11.06
5.	Boost in morale	25	11.06

Source: Field Survey.

39.82 per cent employees said after attending personality development programme they have tried to adopt a few methods used in their training programmes and feel also good about them.

Only a few employees, 11.06 per cent said that because of the above training programmes they do not feel any boost in their morale. 11.06 per cent said, since their work knowledge and efficiency has increased they feel an increase in quality of work they perform daily. But all the above employees also complained that immediately after the training programe they felt a big increase but gradually they started loosing it. In nutshell people felt developments after each training programme, through it did not have tasting impacts.

Performance Appraisal

An appraisal system attempts to ensure some continuity of purpose by checking the validity of individual goals in terms of organizational goals. An appraisal system can promote telephones etc. are there 38.4 per cent sample units consisting of the Taj Group hotels, HRH Group and ITDC are providing more or less the above benefits. Though none of the hotels from the sample units provides 100 per cent benefits. The notable information is that the above benefits are more or less for the higher cadre employees. Then 46.1 per cent hotel are providing staff cafeteria, free laundry for uniforms. And in 15.38 per cent hotels, the situation is worse. There are no free meals on duty, no free uniform and also no free laundry for uniform. In this category mostly unproved category hotels are there.

Protection and Representation

The broad process of protection and representation can be divided into three processes—accommodation process, the collective barraging process, which is mostly found in unionized organizations, and health and safety management process.

The accommodation process refers to the extent to which the management listens or accommodates the needs, the want and complaints (or grievances) of their employer. The human resource heads were asked about the system they are using to manage accommodation process and, the answers were as follows:

Table 8.7: Accommodation Process Practice in Hotels in Rajasthan (Response by Human Resource Hotel)

S.No.	*Systems*	*Users (%)*
1.	Questionnaire	0
2.	Suggestion boxes	15.38
3.	Open Door policy	92.3
4.	Collective bargaining procedure	38.4

Source: Field Survey.

The data reveal that 92.3 per cent hotels in Rajasthan use informal procedure, *i.e.* open door policy to handle employees' grievances. It gives employees access to their supervisors so that the problem can be brought into the open and resolved in a mutually satisfying way. If such discussions do not resolve the issue, employees in some hotels are allowed to take the problem to the higher management. 15.38 per cent hotels especially the group hotels, also use the suggestion box system in which an employee writes his grievances and it reaches the human resource department and sometime to the head of the unit.

Further, 38.4 per cent hotel use collective bargaining process to solve the employee's complaints and grievances. It refers to those events that establish a formal agreement between workers and management, regarding matters as wages and employee benefits, hours, working conditions and grievance procedures. The above 38.4 per cent hotels have use at least 'once' the grievance-arbitration procedure to solve the employee grievances or complaints.

When employees were asked about accommodation process if they have ever used to solve their complaints, grievances or needs, the answers were as under:

Table 8.8: Accommodation Process Practice in Hotels in Rajasthan (Response from Employees)

Systems	*Respondents (%)*
Questionnaires	Nil
Suggestion Box	13.80
Open door policy	9.52
Collective bargaining	16.66

Source: Field Survey.

The data reveal that 9.52 per cent employees have used open door policy to solve their grievances or complaints have ever gone to higher authorities, if they were not satisfied with their supervisor. But the important thing which has come out is that on nearly half the occasions they were sent back to settle the matter with their immediate boss or supervisor and sometimes they had to face repercussions also; the immediate supervisor was unhappy for a long time. With regard to using suggestion boxes, 13.80 per cent employees used this system at least once. But according to some employees this system was prevalent for a short span of time and, that later this practice was closed.

With regards to collective bargaining process, 16.66 per cent employees have used it through their union. In other words, the union has taken up their matter to the management. As per the employees they have also gone through the process of Grievance-Arbitration procedure through 9-10 years before. This is notable that in hotel industry in Rajasthan, especially in 3,2,1 and in unapproved category of hotels, the employees unions have not been allowed to take birth. The employee unions are there in experience in five star Deluxe, Four Star, ITDC hotels.

The health and safety management process attempts to protect the hotel employees from the physical dangers in the workplace. While asking about the systems used in the sample units in health and safety management the answers were as under:

Table 8.9: Health and Safety Practices in Hotels in Rajasthan

Systems	*Respondents (%)*
Meetings with employees	46.1
Availability of first aid stations	13.80
Safety training	30.7
Protective equipment's	61.5
Stress management programs	23.0

Source: Field Survey.

The above data reveal that 46 per cent hotels are meeting the employees for health and safety management system in hotels. 61.5 per cent hotels are using and keeping first aid boxes at various places. Most of the hotels including Five Star Deluxe, ITDC, HRH Group keep their first aid boxes at reception, kitchen and Housekeeping. It has also been found that 3 and 2 star hotels keep them at the reception only. 30.7 per cent hotels have said that they go for safety training programmes using fire fighting drills, posters and sometime inviting guest speakers. These organizations provide safety training to supervisors, employees and also to the managers.

Further, 61.5 per cent hotels said that they use protective equipments. Some of the most frequently used safety devices in hotels are safety boots, gloves, protective clothing etc. Devices used to make the job environment safe are fire-detectors, shower facilities and markings showing exists 23.0 per cent hotels use stress management programmes also showing their concern about stress and how to manage it; these have recently become major issues in safety and health. In this group mostly Taj Group managed hotels, HRH Group hotels are there, using stress management programmes for their employees.

Classification of Hotels

The department of tourism classification functioning hotels under the star system into five categories from 1-star to 5-star. For this purpose a permanent committee the Hotel and Restaurant Approval and Classification Committee has been set up which inspects the applicant hotels to assess their suitability of otherwise for award of the Star category applied for. Based on the recommendation of the HRACC deserving hotels are awarded the appropriate star category and are placed on the approved list of the Department.

Classification of Hotels in Rajasthan

Placing a hotel into a particular group is not easy. Therefore many types of classification are in existence. Here it needs to be noted that the previous researchers had taken into account only those hotels, which exist in directories, especially in Hotel and Restaurant Guide, India, edited and published by the Federation of Hotel and Restaurant Association of India, New Delhi.

For the purpose of the proper analysis of the subject a new hotel classification has been introduced with regard to Hotel Industry in Rajasthan. This classification will cover every hotel unit. It is as under:

1. The classified hotels:
   (*i*) The chain hotels
   (*ii*) Independent hotels
   (*iii*) The government owned hotels
   (*iv*) The Heritage hotels
2. The unclassified hotels:
   (*i*) Registered hotels
   (*ii*) Unregistered hotels
   (*iii*) Alternative lodging properties

The Classified Hotels in Rajasthan

In this category we can keep those hotels, which are classified and approved by the Hotel and Restaurant Approval and Classification Committee, Department of Tourism, Government of India.

The Chain Hotels

In this category the famous hotel chain of India the Taj Group (IHC) operating the famous Lake Palace Hotel, Udaipur (84 rooms), The Rambagh Palace, Jaipur (110 rooms), The Jai Mahal Palace, Hotel, Jaipur (102 rooms), Narain Niwas Palace Hotel, Jaipur (28 rooms) and Ramgarh Lodge, Ramgarh, Jaipur (11 rooms) exist.

Oberoi group (EIH) is comparatively operating less hotels in Rajasthan. At present Rajvilas Palace, Jaipur (120 rooms), The Trident, Jaipur (140 rooms) and The Trident, Udaipur (140 rooms) are in operation.

Heritage Resort Hotel Group (NRH) Udaipur is owned by the royal family of Udaipur. This grouping is owning and operating 10-12 hotels in Rajasthan. The HRH groups in its brochure writes to join them in their Abode of Kings to enjoy the luxury of converted Palaces, Forts and residences of Kings. In Udaipur Shiv Niwas Palace Hotel (33 rooms) Feteh Prakash Hotel (16 rooms), Shikarbadi hotel (25 rooms) are in operation. The famous Lake Palace Hotel (Managed by Taj Groups) is also owned by the NRH Group. Among others Welcome Group (Rajputana Sheraton, 220 rooms) Jaipur, Clarks Group (Clarks Amer, 202 rooms) Jaipur Indo Continental Hotel (Mansingh Hotel with 100 rooms) Jaipur, are in operation.

The Government Owned Hotels

In Rajasthan, the Government owned hotel can be divided into (A) Hotels owned by Central Government. In this category the hotels run by Indian Tourism Development Corporation can be taken such as Laxmi Vilas Palace Hotel (55 rooms) in Udaipur and Jaipur Ashok (97 rooms) in Jaipur.

Hotels Owned by the State Government

In this category there are two types of hotels. First, Hotels run by Rajasthan state Hotel Corporation Ltd., Jaipur. They are Hotel Anand Bhawan (25 rooms) at Udaipur and Hotel Khasa Kothi (36 rooms) at Jaipur. Second the hotels under Rajasthan Tourism Development Corporation (RTDC) set up in 1972. This corporation is running 46 properties including hotels, motels and restaurants in Rajasthan. Kajri (31 rooms) in Udaipur and in Jaipur, Gangaur (62 rooms), Swagatam (34 rooms) and Teej (52 rooms) are included in this category.

Independent Hotels

In this category we can keep those hotels, which are not linked with any hotels chain or are not covered under heritage of government owned hotels but are classified and approved by Department of Tourism, Government of India, New Delhi. They are Rajdarshan Hotel, 3 star with 50 rooms, Hotel Hilltop, 3 star with 60 rooms, Lake Pichola hotel, 3 star with 25 rooms, Chandralok hotel, 2 star with 14 rooms, Lakend hotel, 2 star with 85 rooms, Heritage Resort Hotel, 3 star with 26 rooms. In Jaipur, Kanchandeep hotel, 3 star with 60 rooms, LMB hotel, 3 star with 33 rooms, Hotel Maharani Palace, 3 star with 60 rooms, Hotel Aditya, 2 star with 24 rooms, Hotel Broadway, 2 star with 22 rooms and Hotel Arya Niwas, 1 star with 50 rooms.

Heritage Hotels

Out of the 28 classified heritage hotels in the country, 23 are in Rajasthan. In 1991 Government of India, Department of Tourism declared a new category of hotels—Heritage hotels. Accordingly all the properties more than 50 years old would be included in this category. In Jaipur, Bissau palace with 36 rooms Narain Niwas Palace with 31 rooms, Rajmahal Palace with 11 rooms, Samod Palace (Samod, District Jaipur) with 40 rooms and Ramgarh lodge with 11 rooms find their place in this category. In Udaipur Shivniwas Palace with 33 rooms. Fateh Prakash Palace with 09 rooms and Laxmi Vilas Palace with 55 rooms are registered in this category.

Unclassified Hotels

In this category the hotels can be divided into two parts. One, those hotels that are registered with the Local Hotel Association e.g. Udaipur Hotel Association and Jaipur Hotel Association. Among these hotels a few are the member of (or registered with) FHRAI (Federation of Hotel and Restaurant Association of India) but are not approved and classified by the HRACC (Hotel and Restaurant Approval and Classification Committee). Some hotels are registered under Shop and Commercial Establishment Act, 1958, they are providing services to the Indian and foreign nationals. Vishnupriya Quality Inn with 50 rooms and Parasmahal hotel with 60 rooms are the best illustrations of such category.

Departmentalization in Hotels

Departmentalization represents the pattern of grouping activities. Similar activities intimately related with a distinct function are grouped together to form departments. Departments however differ with respect to the basic pattern used to group activities and there is no single best way of departmentalizing that is applicable to all organizations or to all situations. The aim is to take advantage of division of labour and specialization up to a certain limit. In all categories of hotels, the base for the departmentalization is to function properly. Each major function of a hotel is grouped into a department. Sometimes, the star rating and of ownership also affect the formal existence of a department into a hotel. As per the functions performed in the hotels the following departments generally exist in more or less all types of hotels:

1. Front office department.
2. Food and beverage department.
3. Housekeeping department.
4. Accountants and audit department.
5. Purchase and store department.
6. Maintenance and engineering department.
7. Personnel/Human Resource department.
8. Security department.

Front Office, popularly known as reception is the most visible department in the hotel. It is the focal point of all activities. The front office is responsible for the sale of rooms, which is more than 50 per cent of the total revenue of the hotel. Again, on the basis of the 'function' the front office can be divided into the following sub-departments:

Reservation: It is called the 'key' of the front office department, where the demands of room-reservation are received and processed. A five star deluxe and five star hotels may or may not have a reservation manager but all have reservation assistants.

Registration: It is the focal point of the front office department where the guests are received, registered and assigned keys of rooms. Most governments and states insist on registration, by the guest himself. This is a rule to protect both the hotels and the guests. It is a source of information about the foreigners in the country and also a data source for the hotels. It is done mostly by registration cards. The basic information provided in the registration card includes name of the guest, address, nationality, purpose of visit, duration of stay in the country, passport details, his place of coming and his next place of visit etc.

Information: The main function of this department is to provide information about the hotel, city, the surroundings, transportation etc. and events that are of interest to the guests. The information department also handles the mail of the guests and receive message for the guest.

Cash: The cashier maintains the guests' account, monitors the credit limit, produces guests account statement and is responsible for the proper settlement of the bills. He maintains the accounts for foreign exchange and does other miscellaneous jobs related to the cash.

Night Auditor: A night Auditor, audits all the revenue transactions and reconciles the revenue statements of the revenue generating outlets. They also prepare the various report of the hotel business. Most of the hotels keep the Night auditor, which is an employee of the accounts department. To many hotels the night auditors is a part of the front office. The Night auditor performs more or less the following functions:

- Verifying posted entries to guest and non-guest account.
- Balance all front office accounts.
- Resolving room status discrepancies.
- Monitoring guest credit limits.
- Producing operational and managerial reports.

The Night Auditor Works generally in the night shift, from 11 PM to 7 AM balancing and compiling the transactions of the previous day. Each front office decides, the time when it should be considered the end of its accounting day. An end of the day it is simply an arbitrary stopping point for the business day.

Chart 1: Organizational Chart of Front Office Department in Five star Deluxe Hotel

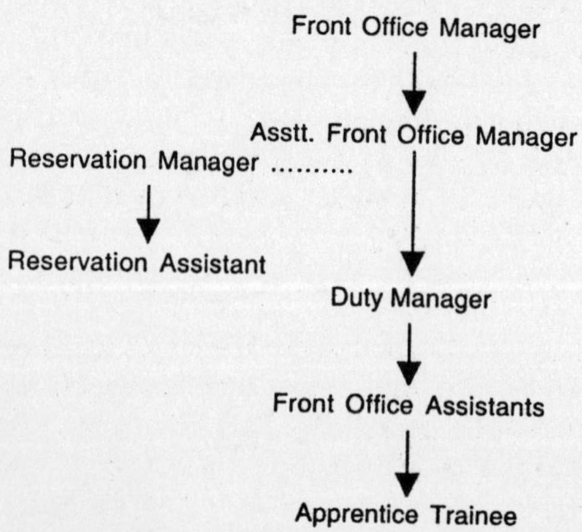

Chart 2: Organisation Chart of Front Office Department in 1, 2, 3 Star and Unapproved Category of Hotel

Front Office Supervisor

↓

Front Office Assistants

↓

Trainees

Food and Beverage Department

The hotel food and beverage department is another important section of the hotel and is considered second to the front office in terms of generating room revenue. Broadly food and beverage department can be divided into two sections—food production and food and beverage service. Food production center basically the 'kitchen' is the place where the craftsmen and artist work to prepare the delicious combination of food. Normally the kitchen are divided into the following sections.

(*a*) Continental section is responsible for the preparation of soups, roast dishes of meat, poultry, grilled dishes of meat, chicken fish and deep-frying of items.

(*b*) Bakery section is responsible for hot and cold sweets including pastries, cookies, cakes, breakfast items like bread rolls, muffin, banana multi bread, plain bread etc.

(*c*) Indian section is responsible for a variety of Indian dishes–rice pulao, biryani, vegetables, egg, fish, and mutton, chicken and tandoor items.

(*d*) Pantry section is the part of main kitchen where all variety of salads (Veg. and Non-veg.) are prepared, this section also supplies tea, coffee, fresh juice, soft drinks, mineral water etc.

(*e*) Butchery section is situated a little away from the main cooking area. In this section the meat items are trimmed up to the first stage, *i.e.* the removal of excess fat, skins and other non-edible parts from the meat items. The organization of the kitchen found in hotels is as follows:

Chart 3: The Organisation of the Kitchen Found in Hotels

Chef de Cuisine

↓

Soups chef

↓

Chef de partied

↓

I commas

↓

II commas

↓

III commas

Food and beverage service section can be traditionally divided in Restaurant, Bar and Room Service.

The restaurant basically provides table and chair for people to sit and eat food prepared by and attached kitchen. These sitting places are equipped with crockery, cutlery and linen.

There are different types of restaurants—coffee shop continental, specialty restaurant, Grillroom, Dinning room, Snack bar, Discotheque etc. The organization of the food and beverage service department, found in hotels is as follows:

Chart 4: The Organisation of the Food and Beverage Service Department

Restaurant Manager

↓

Head Waiter/Captain

↓

Waiter/Steward

↓

Asstt. Waiter/Asstt. Steward

↓

Bus Boy

Room service involves the food and beverage service to the guest rooms. Today room service has become the hallmark of good hotel and most of the hotels try to provide 24 hours room service. The peak period of room service is the morning hours when the "resident guest" orders bed tea and then breakfast in their rooms. The guests call the room service through internal telephones and place their order. The organizational structure of the room service is as follows:

Chart 5: The Organisational Structure of the Room Service

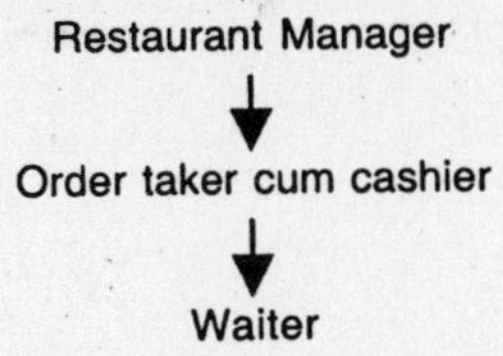

Bar is the place where guest order directly to bar man or other service personal. Food and beverage manager heads the food and beverage department. The organizational chart of a five star deluxe hotel including the heritage is as follows:

Chart 6: F & B organization chart for Five Star Deluxe, Five Star and Heritage Hotels

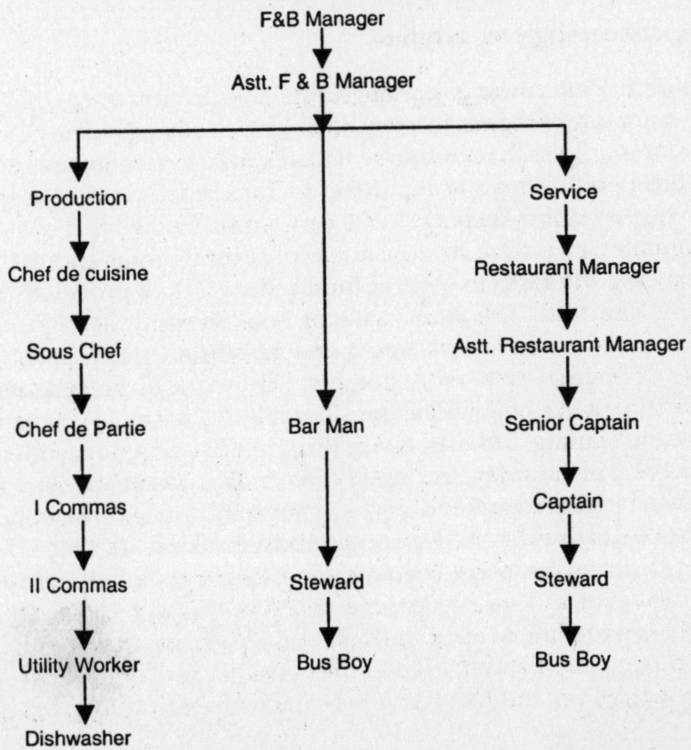

Chart 7: F & B Organisation Chart for 1, 2, 3 Star and Unapproved Category of Hotel

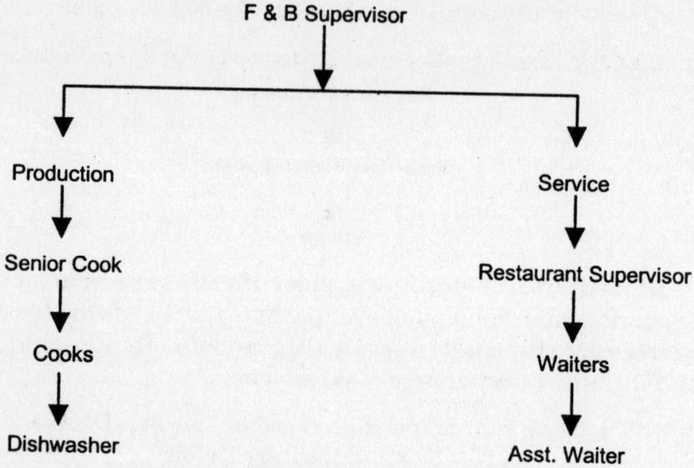

Housekeeping Department

It is perhaps the most important supportive department to the front office for sale of rooms. In a few hotels, especially when the number of rooms are less than hundred, it has been seen that housekeeping is considered a separate department. Conceptually task of keeping of a house (Housekeeping) looks very simple but when it comes to maintaining a palace or large house of several rooms and that too balancing the taste to several hundred guests, it proves to be a Herculean task. The main tasks of housekeeping is to provide cleanliness, aesthetic upkeeping and maintenance that match the taste of several type of customers. The work of housekeeping department in a hotel varies considerable according to star rating. Besides cleaning and decorating the housekeeping department is involved in laundry to the staff uniform, guest dresses and those related to rooms and restaurant linen. Among other things it also takes case of lost and found procedures, floral art, first aid etc. The Head of the housekeeping department is called executive housekeeper in five star deluxe and five star hotels. The other assistants are line keeper, uniform supervisor, room boy etc. The organizational hierarchy found the housekeeping departments of five star deluxe and five star hotel sample units is as follows:

Chart 8: Organisation Chart of Housekeeping Department in 5 Star Deluxe and 5 Star Category of Hotels

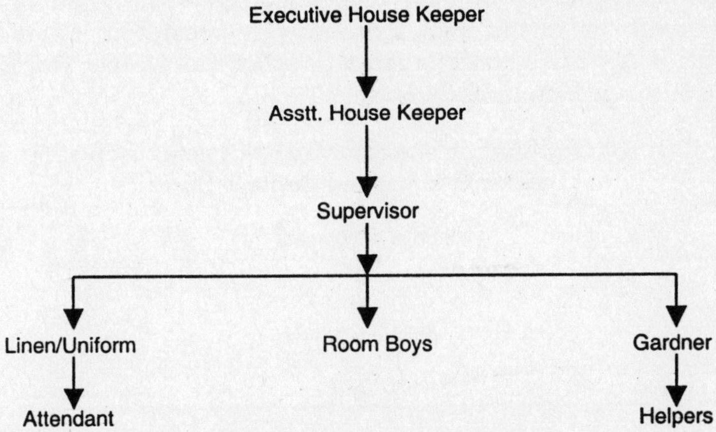

Chart 9: Organisation Chart of House-Keeping Department 1, 2, 3 star and unapproved category of Hotels

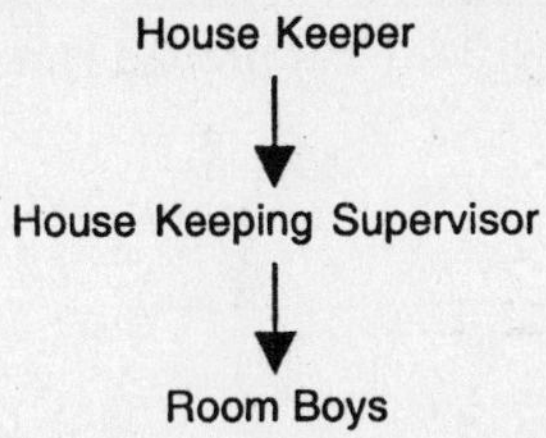

Accounts and Audit Department

The accounts department in a hotel is of vital importance owing to the special character of the business. The accounting department is concerned with the guest bills, payment of wages to the hotel employees, ledgering bills rendered for the hotel purchases and maintaining account books, recording all incomes and expenditure. At the end of the year the accounts department prepares the Balance Sheet and also measures the performance of the hotel business within the year. The accounts department also prepares different statistical reports, which are helpful for purpose of comparison of sale of room's sale of food and beverage outlets and income and expenditure statements. The head of this department is generally called as Chief Accountant or Chief Accounts Officer. Sometimes the Chief Accountants has to act as a dual responsibility; one he has to obey and report to the general manager and secondary he has to listen to the owner or the vice-president, Finance. Organisation of Accounts Department in Five Star Deluxe, Five Star and Heritage Hotel is as follows:

Chart 10: Organisation of Accounts Departments in Five Star Deluxe, Five Star and Heritage Hotel

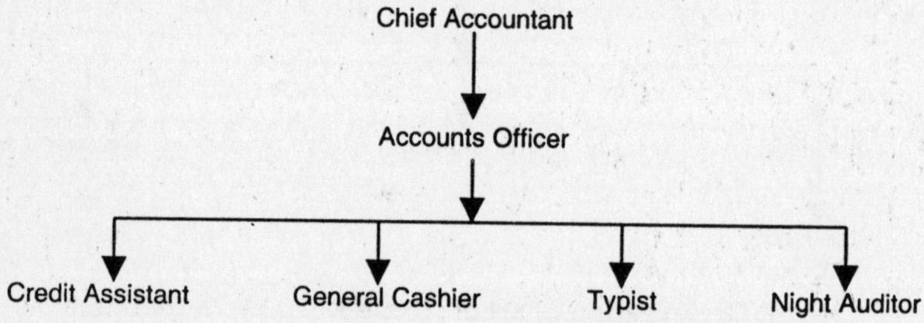

Chart 11: Organisation of Accounts Department in 1, 2, 3 & Unapproved Hotels

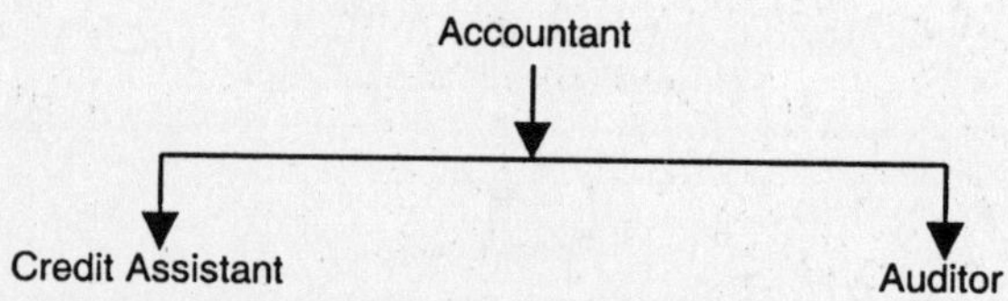

Engineering and Maintenance Department

The engineering and maintenance department in the hotel plays an important role in satisfying the guests demand. A proper service from the maintenance department play a significant effect on the guest motivational patterns and helps to call the guests back. There is a long list of the services provided by the Engineering and Maintenance Department Structural Maintenance. Heating and cooling, ventilation, air-conditioning system, refrigeration, electrical system, television and channel music, telephone and other communication system, water supply including hot water, plumbing, sewage system, swimming pool clearing, maintenance and cleaning of equipment's used by the hotel, maintenance of the furniture and such many other services are looked after by this department. The maintenance department is also responsible for establishment of fire protection procedures within the hotels.

Chart 12: Organisation Chart of the Engineering Department in 5 Star Deluxe, 5 Star Hotels and Heritage Hotels

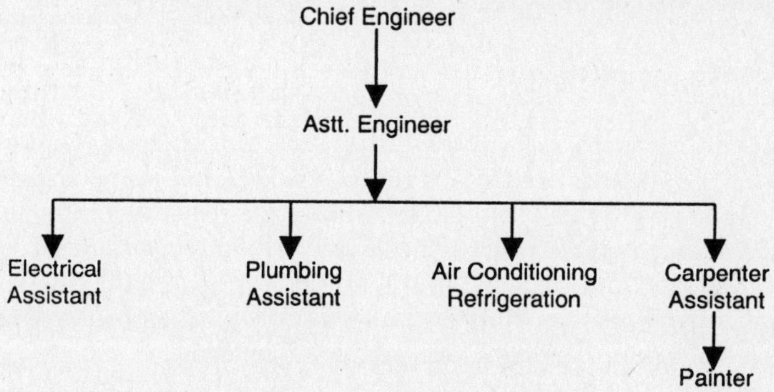

Chart 13: Organisation Chart of the Engineering Department in 1,2,3 and unapproved Hotels

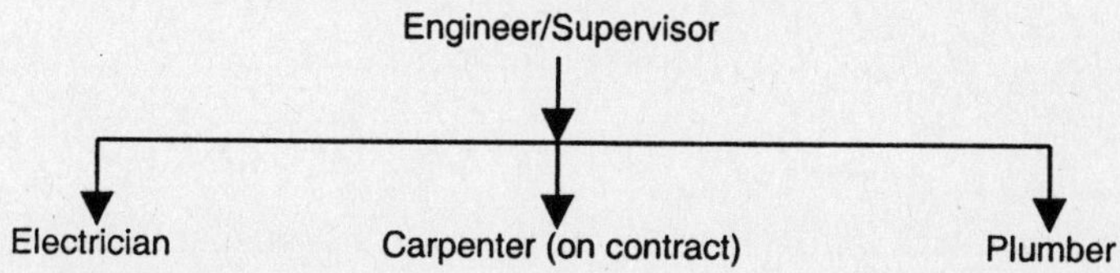

Human Resource Department

The general-purpose department is to acquire, develop and maintain a competent work force, which can accomplish the goal and objectives of the organization what maximum efficiency and minimum expenditure. The human resource department is an integral and important part of the hotel industry but it seems that it has not acquired its due importance. The Management and the employees of a hotel, both are in need of the particular specialized department of recruitment, selection, salary administration, discipline, grievance procedures, staff induction promotion, transfer, training and development, exit facilities, locker facilities identity cards etc. In many one, two and three star hotel there is no such departments in existence. The work of the human resources department is distributed among various persons. For example, the recruitment is performed by the owner and the manager himself. Attendance is done by some other senior person, salary is disbursed by accounts department, provident fund and ESI are looked after by a part time professionals. Thus the hotel associations and other related government officials must look in this direction.

Security Department

The hotel industry is so diverse that it is impossible to set national security standards or to totally rely on the national security system. Therefore to provide a safe and secure environment to protect guest's employees there is a great need for privately owned security arrangement and system. Now a days it is being felt that there is a dual or triple responsibility on the security department as the guests have started looking for safe places/destinations.

REFERENCES

1. Negi J., *Hotels for Tourism Development*, Metropolitan Book Pvt. Ltd., New Delhi, 1984, p. 8.
2. *Ibid.*, p. 4.
3. *Ibid.*, p. 8.
4. *Ibid.*, p. 14.
5. Virender Kaul, *Tourism and the Economy*, Har Anand Publications, New Delhi, 1994, p. 95.
6. *Rajasthan Patrika*, 15 January 2001, p. 14.
7. Virender Kaul, *Tourism and the Economy*, Har Anand Publications, 1994, p. 96.
8. Mohammed Zulfikar, *Introduction to Tourism and Hotel Industry with Special Focus on Font Office Management*, Vikas Publishing House Pvt. Ltd., 1998, p. 60.
9. Written Document of Taj Group of hotels.
10. Floyd Miller, *Statler America's Extraordinary Hotelman*, Statler Foundation, New York, 1968, p. 36.
11. Kasavana, M.L., Brooks, R.M., *Front Office Procedures*, 4th edn., Educational Institute of AHMA, Michigan, 1996, p. 3.
12. Joseph D. Fridgen, *Dimensions of Tourism*, Educational Institute of AHMA, Michigan, 1996, p. 193.

13. *Indian Management, A Blueprint*, Welcoming More Tourists, May 1997, p. 54.
14. *Travel and Tourism: The World's Largest Industry*, World Travel & Tourism Council Report, 1992.
15. *Indian Management, A Blueprint*, Welcoming More Tourists, May 1997, p. 54.
16. *Yojna*, Paryatan Vikas Ke Avsar, Aug, 1998, pp. 52-53.
17. *Yojna*, Paryatan Vikas Ki Sambhavana, June, 1998, pp. 2-3.
18. *Indian Management, A Blueprint*, Welcoming More Tourists, May 1997, p. 55.
19. Negi, J.M.S., *Hotels for Tourism Development*, Metropolitan Book Co. New Delhi, 1997, p. 17.
20. *Ibid.*, p. 3.
21. *Ibid.*, p. 8.
22. *Indian Management, A Blueprint*, Welcoming more Tourists, May 1997 p. 58.
23. Report of the Bhagwati Committee on Unemployment, 1973.
24. Negi, J.M.S., *Hotels for Tourism Development*, Metropolitan Book Co. New Delhi, 1997, p. 9.
25. *Ibid.*
26. *Ibid.*
27. Negi, J.M.S., *Hotels for Tourism Development*, Metropolitan Book Pvt. Ltd., New Delhi, 1984, p. 18.
28. *Ibid.*, p. 19.
29. *Ibid.*
30. *Ibid.*, p. 21.
31. Zulfikar Mohammed, *Introduction to Tourism and Hotel Industry with Special Focus on Front Office Management*, Vikas Publishing House Pvt. Ltd., 1998, p. 77.
32. *Ibid.*, p. 87.
33. Sharma K.K., *Tourism in India* (Centre-State Administration), Classic Publishing House, Jaipur, 1991, p. 141.
34. *Hotels & Restaurants Guide India* '98-Advertisement.
35. Kamra K.K., Mill R.C., Kaushil. *S, Hospitality Operations and Management*, Wheeler Publishing, New Delhi, Allahabad, 2000, p. 27.
36. *Ibid.*, p. 25.
37. Negi, J.M.S., *Hotels for Tourism Development*, Metropolitan Books Co., New Delhi, 1997, pp. 79-92.
38. Kamra K.K., Mill R.C., Kaushil S., *Hospitality Operations and Management*, Wheeler Publishing, New Delhi, Allahabad, 2000, p. 25.

39. Negi, J.M.S., *Hotels for Tourism Development*, Metropolitan Books Co., New Delhi, 1997, pp. 79-92.
40. Kamra K.K., Mill R.C., Kaushil S., *Hospitality Operations and Management*, Wheeler Publishing, New Delhi, Allahabad, 2000, p. 23.
41. *Ibid.*
42. *Ibid.*
43. Negi, J.M.S., *Hotels for Tourism Development*, Metropolitan Books Co., New Delhi, 1997, p. 79-92.
44. *Ibid.*
45. Kamra K.K., Mill R.C., Kaushil S., *Hospitality Operations and Management*, Wheeler Publishing, New Delhi, Allahabad, 2000, p. 23.
46. *Ibid.*, p. 27.
47. Negi, J.M.S., *Hotels for Tourism Development*, Metropolitan Books Co., New Delhi, 1997, pp. 86-99.
48. *Ibid.*
49. *Ibid.*
50. *Hotel & Food Service Review*, Hotel Classification, August 1997, p. 25.
51. *Yojna*, Paryatan Vikas Ke Avsar, August 1998, p. 54.
52. Kasavana M.L., Brooks R.M., *Front Office Procedures*, 4th edn., Educational Institute of AHMA, Michigan, 1996.
53. *Ibid.*
54. Sharma Bimla, "*Foreign Tourists Arrivals Falling*", Times of India, July 2nd, 1997.

Chapter IX

SURVEY AND OBSERVATIONS

The present survey was undertaken with the objective of assessing the financial and economic implications of tourism on the State's economy. In this study an attempt has been made to analyse the need, facilities and problems associated with the tourism benefits. Also an attempt has been made to review the same at various levels—local, regional, national and international. The study endeavours to cover the benefits viz.

- Increase in standard of living.
- Employment opportunity.
- National and international recognition.
- Expanse of literacy and education.
- Increase in income.
- Improvement in health and family welfare.
- Eradication of social evils.
- Advantage of cross culture change.
- Increase in export/foreign exchange.
- Increase in investment opportunity.

The Empirical Study

The research design was formulated keeping in mind the various essentials and requirements of subject of research. Accordingly, questionnaire was prepared and planned in such a way that, as far as possible, all and up-to-date information about the subject could be collected. Therefore, all the sources of information viz., Foreign Tourists, Domestic Tourists, Officers working in various Tour and Trade agencies, hoteliers, businessmen, University teachers and the students, were personally tapped and contacted and an exclusive emphasis was made on gathering first-hand assessment of the situation. In addition to the information collected through the questionnaire, personal interviews were also conducted which enabled me a lot in obtaining substantial conclusions pertaining to this research work. 400 tourists were randomly chosen as respondents. All relevant information was gathered which could be helpful in this work like—travel plan preference, budget, choice for facilities, season, source of spending, spending classification, experience, opinion and recommendations to others, type of service period, number of employees, ownership, investment, income financial support, competition marketing, future plan, tourism awareness, past experience of visit, future plan, centres for selection of state/ spots, tenure, best item, and best age group, Government policy, tourism policy, responsibility, accountability, role of regulating agencies etc.

Initially, the questionnaire was used to conduct a pilot study, later on further informations and questions were matched and revised as per the needs of the situation. All the questions were thus framed in such a way that information, sought could be cross-checked. The questionnaire was internally devisable, but overtly looked one.

The statistical data, so collected, through the questionnaires were analysed in computer through fox pro package. The tables were prepared on the basis of responses received from Tourist's, Service providers, Public and Regulating agencies. These tables were then analysed, at the stage of analysis and interpretation and the chances of imprint and bias are possible, an effort has been made to adhere to objectivity. The questions have been analysed on the socio-psycho and financial economic background to reveal about the implication of tourism in Rajasthan.

Observations of the Study Through Random Survey

Respondents—Tourists

From Table 9.1, it can be seen that tourists prefer to travel in special groups or with the family (43 per cent and 37 per cent respectively), besides 11 per cent alone and 9 per cent with tourist groups.

CLASSIFICATION OF RESPONDENTS OF RANDOM SURVEY

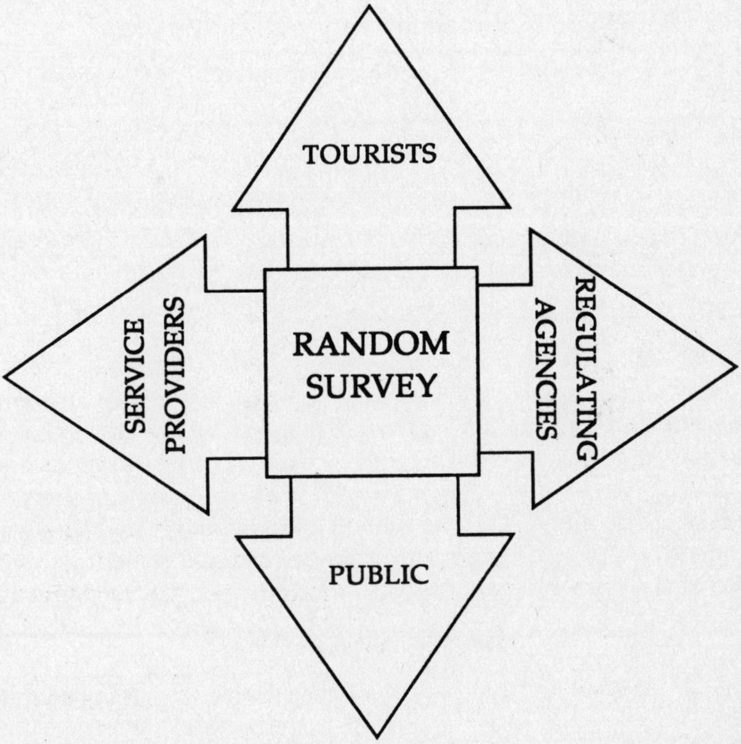

Fig. 9.1

(Designed and Compiled by the Authors)

Table 9.1 : Travelling Style

Sl. No.	Composition	No. of Respondents	% of Response
1.	Alone	19	11
2.	Special group	75	43
3.	Family	65	37
4.	Tourist group	16	9
	Total	**175**	**100**

Source: Field Survey.

Table 9.2: Sources Influencing to Visit Rajasthan

Sl. No.	Advised	No. of Respondents	% of Response
1.	Friends	88	50
2.	Relatives	32	18
3.	Tourist offices	12	7
4.	Travel agent	19	11
5.	Books and Magazine	14	8
6.	Newspaper	10	6
	Total	**175**	**100**

Source: Field Survey.

Rajasthan being a famous tourists spot, major tourists were recommended to visit this place by their friends or relatives (50 per cent and 18 per cent respectively). There is very less percentage of motivation by travel agents, books, magazines, newspapers or tourist offices (only 7 to 11 per cent). It gives message that Rajasthan tourism is not getting proper coverage through media or travel agents. It is high time to consider this aspect and boost up publicity.

Table 9.3: Purpose of Visit

Sl. No.	Reasons for Visit	No. of Respondents	% of Response
1.	Pleasure	75	43
2.	Pilgrimage	42	24
3.	Business/Official	16	9
4.	Academic	14	8
5.	Any other	28	16
	Total	**175**	**100**

Source: Field Survey.

From the above table, it is seen that tourists' majority seeks pleasure (43 per cent) while travelling Rajasthan, besides pilgrimage (24 per cent). To enhance tourist's visits, more infrastructural facilities need to be thrown to pleasure seeking tourists.

Table 9.4: Tenure of Stay

Sl. No.	*Tenure*	*No. of Respondents*	*% of Response*
1.	Very short period < 5 days	89	51
2.	Short period 5-10	28	16
3.	Moderate period 10-15	45	26
4.	Longer period > 15 days	13	7
	Total	**175**	**100**

Source: Field Survey.

It is inferred from the above table that tourists visit Rajasthan only for very short period (51 per cent) against the long stay of only 8 per cent. This suggests that we are lacking somewhere, as tourists prefer only short stay in the State. Tourism is a multi-faceted activity, where all-round development for providing comfort to incoming tourists is involved, unless provided, the staying percentage shall remain very short always.

Table 9.5: Travelling Preference

Sl. No.	*Preference*	*No. of Respondents*	*% of Response*
1.	Museums, Architecture and Monuments	42	24
2.	Customs, Festival and Folklore	38	22
3.	Seeing and meeting people	7	4
4.	Night life	10	5
5.	Country side, relaxing, camping	12	7
6.	Pageantry, photography scenery	28	16
7.	Shopping	19	11
8.	Food and Beverages	19	11
	Total	**175**	**100**

Source: Field Survey.

The table figures out that tourist's major interest lies in museums, architecture, monuments (24 per cent), customs, festivals, folklore (22 per cent), photographic sessions (16 per cent). To upgrade tourism visits, upkeep of museums, architectural monuments like forts etc. besides comfortable facilities is the need of the hour. This aspect should be concentrated upon.

Table 9.6: Choice for Mode of Transport

Sl. No.	*Mode*	*No. of Respondents*	*% of Response*
1.	Air	27	15
2.	Train	57	33
3.	Bus	63	36
4.	Taxi	28	16
	Total	**175**	**100**

Source : Field Survey.

The table reveals that tourists prefer to visit Rajasthan through Trains (33 per cent) and Buses (36 per cent), besides Taxis (16 per cent) and Air (8 per cent). To attract more and more tourists, maintenance of roads and provision of luxury buses and cheap transportation is needed.

Table 9.7: Choice Preference for Lodging

Sl. No.	*Lodging*	*No. of Respondents*	*% of Response*
1.	Stay with friends/relatives	33	19
2.	Choultary	19	11
3.	Guest house	22	12
4.	Paying guest	19	11
5.	Moderate hotel	72	41
6.	Luxury hotel	10	6
	Total	**175**	**100**

Source : Field Survey.

The table reveals that tourists prefer moderate hotels (41 per cent) to stay and stay with friends/relatives (19 per cent), besides guests' houses or as a paying guest, choultary (11 to 12 per cent) only. Here, the role of hotel industry plays major part.

Table 9.8: Opinion About Travel Facilities in Rajasthan

Sl. No.	*Travel Facility*	*No. of Respondents*	*% of Response*
1.	Excellent	19	11
2.	Very good	68	39
3.	Good	78	45
4.	Very poor	10	5
	Total	**175**	**100**

Source: Field Survey.

The ranking given by tourists with regard to travel facilities available in Rajasthan is only Good (45 per cent) and Very Good (39 per cent) with 11 per cent Excellent only. This indicates that facilities are not up to the mark of satisfaction or excellence to the tourists.

Table 9.9: Amount Spent During Tourist Trip to Rajasthan (in group/family)

Sl. No.	*Name of the Benefit*	*No. of Respondents*	*% of Response*
1.	< 2,000	12	7
2.	2,000 to 5,000	75	43
3.	5,000 to 10,000	37	21
4.	> 10000	51	29
	Total	**175**	**100**

Source: Field Survey.

The table shows that tourists visit Rajasthan with varied budget from 5,000 to more than 20,000 (21 to 43 per cent).

Table 9.10: Opinion About the Quality of Food and Beverages in Rajasthan

Sl. No.	*Boarding Facility*	*No. of Respondents*	*% of Response*
1.	Excellent	42	24
2.	Good	108	62
3.	Satisfactory	19	11
4.	Unsatisfactory	6	3
	Total	**175**	**100**

Source: Field Survey.

The quality of food and beverages is rated Good (62 per cent) and Excellent (24 per cent).

Table 9.11: Opinion About Facilities Provided by R.T.D.C.

A. Package Tours

Sl. No.	*Package Tour*	*No. of Respondents*	*% of Response*
1.	Excellent	49	28
2.	Satisfactory	89	51
3.	Satisfactory	28	16
4.	Unsatisfactory	9	5
	Total	**175**	**100**

Source: Field Survey.

The tourists have rated facilities provided under Package Tours as Good (51 per cent) and Excellent (28 per cent). The Corporation should provide this facility in terms of tourism-orientation and not in terms of income-orientation.

B. Midway Facility

Sl. No.	*Midway Facility*	*No. of Respondents*	*% of Response*
1	Excellent	9	5
2.	Good	70	40
3.	Satisfactory	65	37
4.	Unsatisfactory	31	18
	Total	**175**	**100**

Source: Field Survey.

So is the midway facility found rating as Good (40 per cent) and Satisfactory (37 per cent). This area also needs to be given consideration in terms of tourism-oriented facility.

Table 9.12: Opinion About Behaviour of Tourists' Personnel

Sl. No.	*Behaviour*	*No. of Respondents*	*% of Response*
1.	Encouraging	42	24
2.	Informative	42	24
3.	Supportive	42	24
4.	Discouraging	16	9
5.	Cooperative	33	19
	Total	**175**	**100**

Source: Field Survey.

The table gives a satisfactory note that personnel engaged for tourists are encouraging, informing, supporting and cooperative (19 to 24 per cent).

Table 9.13: Opinion About Services of Tourist Guides

Sl. No.	*Service of Tourist Guide*	*No. of Respondents*	*% of Response*
1.	Appreciable	79	45
2.	Satisfactory	65	37
3.	Average	17	10
4.	Unsatisfactory	14	8
	Total	**175**	**100**

Source: Field Survey.

The tourists visiting Rajasthan have found the services of Tourists Guides as appreciative (45 per cent) and satisfactory (37 per cent), besides, lesser problem on others like language front etc.

Table 9.14: Opinion About People of Rajasthan

Sl. No.	*People*	*No. of Respondents*	*% of Response*
1.	Very helpful	23	13
2.	Conservative	28	16
3.	Charming and colourful	31	19
4.	Hospitable and honest	42	24
5.	Language problem	23	12
6.	Indifferent and business minded	28	16
	Total	**175**	**100**

Source: Field Survey.

The people of Rajasthan are known for its hospitality and so are marks received from tourists as 24 per cent.

Table 9.15: Best Season to Travel Rajasthan

Sl. No.	*Name of the Benefit*	*No. of Respondents*	*% of Response*
1.	May-June	28	16
2.	July-August	14	8
3.	Sept.-Oct.	32	18
4.	Nov.-Dec.	52	30
5.	Jan.-Feb.	49	28
	Total	**175**	**100**

Source: Field Survey.

The best season of visit to Rajasthan is considered by tourists from November to February (30 and 28 per cent respectively), besides May to June (18 per cent) and September to October (18 per cent).

Table 9.16: Classification of Spending by the Tourists

Sl. No.	*Spending*	*No. of Respondents*	*% of Response*
1.	Travelling	35	20
2.	Boarding	22	13
3.	Local transportation	12	7
4.	Entertainment	12	7
5.	Lodging	42	24
6.	Shopping	52	29
	Total	**175**	**100**

Source: Field Survey.

The table reveals that tourists visit Rajasthan to buy traditional items and therefore, they spend their funds much on shopping (29 per cent), besides travelling, boarding and lodging and entertainment. This suggests that industry should think in terms of providing more and more entertainment, through different and novel means to attract tourists.

Table 9.17: Purchasing Preference

Sl. No.	*Purchasing*	*No. of Respondents*	*% of Response*
1.	Traditional items	56	32
2.	Leather goods	14	8
3.	Gems and jewellery	40	23
4.	Wooden articles	19	11
5.	Marble stone goods	19	11
6.	Sweets and namkins	27	15
	Total	**175**	**100**

Source: Field Survey.

The table reveals that mostly tourists like to purchase traditional textile fabrics (32 per cent) and gems and jewellery (23 per cent).

Table 9.18: Opinion About Visit to Rajasthan

Sl. No.	*Feeling*	*No. of Respondents*	*% of Response*
1.	Exhilarating	46	26
2.	Enjoyable	65	37
3.	Satisfactory	44	25
4.	Unsatisfactory	15	9
5.	Disappointing	5	3
	Total	**175**	**100**

Source: Field Survey.

The tourists have rated their stay in Rajasthan as enjoyable (37 per cent), exhilarating (27 per cent) and satisfactory (25 per cent).

Table 9.19: Recommendation to Others to Visit Rajasthan

Sl. No.	*Recommendation*	*No. of Respondents*	*% of Response*
1.	Yes	168	96
2.	No	7	4
	Total	**175**	**100**

Source: Field Survey.

The table reveals the liking of tourists to visit Rajasthan, as 96 per cent of them would recommend their friends and relatives to travel Rajasthan. This shows how popular Rajasthan is amongst tourists.

Table 9.20: Ranking of Financial and Economic Implication Factors

Sl. No.	*Factors*	*No. of Respondents*	*% of Response*
1.	Increase in standard of living	19	11
2.	Employment generation	35	20
3.	National/International recognition	15	9
4.	Expanse of literacy and education	19	11
5.	Increase in income	30	17
6.	Improvement in health and family welfare	14	8
7.	Eradication of social evils	9	5
8.	Advantages of cross cultural change	5	3
9.	Increase in Export/Foreign Exchange	19	11
10.	Increase in investment opportunities	9	5
	Total	**175**	**100**

Source: Field Survey.

The above table and the collection of the opinion from tourists reveals that tourism industry is a gold-mine in the economy of Rajasthan as it generates employment (20 per cent), increases income (17 per cent), increases living standard, expands literacy and education, increases export/foreign exchange (all 11 per cent).

Respondents—Service Providers

Table 9.21: Engaged in Tourist Activity

Sl. No.	*Engaged*	*No. of Respondents*	*% of Response*
1.	Exclusively	12	48
2.	Partially	8	32
3.	Occasionally	3	12
4.	Rarely	2	8
	Total	**25**	**100**

Source: Field Survey.

The table shows that 48 per cent of service providers are exclusively engaged in tourist activity and 32 per cent are partially engaged.

Table 9.22: No. of Employees Employed

Sl. No.	*No. of Employees*	*No. of Respondents*	*% of Response*
1.	<5	7	28
2.	5-10	8	32
3.	10-20	8	32
4.	>20	2	8
	Total	**25**	**100**

Source: Field Survey.

The table reveals that 32 per cent each employ 5 to 20 persons in the occupation 28 per cent less than five and 8 per cent more than 20 persons. This shows how employment-generating tourism is.

Table 9.23: Investment in Business

Sl. No.	*Investments*	*No. of Respondents*	*% of Response*
1.	0.50	7	29
2.	0.50 - 5.00	9	35
3.	5.00 - 10.00	6	24
4.	10.00	3	12
	Total	**25**	**100**

Source: Field Survey.

35 per cent service providers have made investment of Rs. 0.50 to 5.00 lakh in their system, 24 per cent have invested Rs. 5.00 to 10.00 lakh and 12 per cent have invested more than Rs. 10.00 lakh.

Table 9.24: Trend of the Business

Sl. No.	*Growth*	*No. of Respondents*	*% of Response*
1.	Growing	9	36
2.	Maintained	6	24
3.	Volatile	6	24
4.	Decreasing	4	16
	Total	**25**	**100**

Source: Field Survey.

The service providers (24 per cent each) opine that income growth of their agency is constant and flexible. However 36 per cent opine that their income growth has increased.

Table 9.25: Opinion About the Best Season to Visit Rajasthan

Sl. No.	*Seasons*	*No. of Respondents*	*% of Response*
1.	Jan. to March	6	24
2.	April to June	6	24
3.	July to September	3	12
4.	Oct. to Dec.	10	40
	Total	**25**	**100**

Source: Field Survey.

The table reveals the best season for tourism as per service providers is from Oct. to Dec. (40 per cent).

Table 9.26: Future Plan of the Business

Sl. No.	*Plan*	*No. of Respondents*	*% of Response*
1.	Expansion	12	48
2.	Change of activity	4	16
3.	Merger with other	6	24
4.	Close down	3	12
	Total	**25**	**100**

Source: Field Survey.

Forty-eight per cent of service providers are interested to expand their business and 24 per cent are interested to merge their business with other activity.

Table 9.27: Opinion About Fairs and Festivals to be Organised

Sl. No.	*Location*	*No. of Respondents*	*% of Response*
1.	New Delhi	3	12
2.	State Capital	8	32
3.	International Capital	4	16
4.	Tourist Spots	10	40
	Total	**25**	**100**

Source: Field Survey.

Forty per cent service providers opined that to promote tourism, fairs and festivals should organised at tourist spots only.

Table 9.28: Rating of Government Help

Sl. No.	*Government helps*	*No. of Respondents*	*% of Response*
1.	Supportive	6	24
2.	Promotive	8	32
3.	Regulative	7	28
4.	Non-supporting	4	16
	Total	**25**	**100**

Source: Field Survey.

Thirty-two per cent service providers recommends role of the State Government as promotive only.

Table 9.29: Opinion About Services After Liberalisation

Sl. No.	*Name of the benefit*	*No. of Respondents*	*% of Response*
1.	Improvement	12	52
2.	No change	4	16
3.	Change as per demand	8	32
	Total	25	100

Source: Field Survey.

Fifty-two per cent service providers said that their services have improved because of competition in the market.

Table 9.30: Ranking of Financial and Economic Implication Factors

Sl. No.	*Factors*	*No. of Respondents*	*% of Response*
1.	Increase in standard of living	2	8
2.	Employment generation	5	20
3.	National/International recognition	2	8
4.	Expanse of literacy and education	1	4
5.	Increase in income	6	24
6.	Improvement in health and family welfare	1	4
7.	Eradication of social evils	1	4
8.	Advantages of cross cultural change	2	8
9.	Increase in Export/Foreign Exchange	3	12
10.	Increase in investment opportunities	2	8
	Total	**25**	**100**

Source: Field Survey.

The above table and the collection of the opinion from service providers reveals that tourism industry is a gold-mine in the economy of Rajasthan as it increases the income (24 per cent) besides, increase in standard of living, employment generation (20 per cent) and expanse of literacy and education, increase in investment opportunities, cross cultural change (8 per cent each).

Respondents—Public

Table 9.31: Awareness About Tourist Spots in Rajasthan

Sl. No.	*Awareness*	*No. of Respondents*	*% of Response*
1.	Yes	161	92
2.	No	14	8
	Total	**175**	**100**

Source: Random Survey.

The table shows that 92 per cent of people from public know tourist spots of Rajasthan/India. This shows how popular tourism is among people, as all of them know the places of interest.

Table 9.32: Experience of Earlier Visit of Tourist Spots in Rajasthan

Sl. No.	*Visit*	*No. of Respondents*	*% of Response*
1.	Yes	75	43
2.	No	100	57
	Total	**175**	**100**

Source: Random Survey.

This table unlike above, gives an ironical statement that 57 per cent of people have still not found the opportunity to visit tourist spots whereas they have full knowledge of tourist spots.

Table 9.33: Future Plan to Visit Tourist Spots in Rajasthan

Sl. No.	*Future visit*	*No. of Respondents*	*% of Response*
1.	Within 3 month	14	8
2.	Within 6 month	28	16
3.	Within 12 month	42	24
4.	After 12 month	91	52
	Total	**175**	**100**

Source: Random Survey.

The table reveals that most of 52 per cent of people plan their visits after 12 month, 24 per cent within 12 months and 16 per cent in 6 months.

Table 9.34: Priority in Visit of Tourist States

Sl. No.	*State*	*No. of Respondents*	*% of Response*
1.	J & K	7	4
2.	M.P.	19	11
3.	Rajasthan	50	29
4.	Tamil Nadu	19	11
5.	West Bengal	22	12
6.	Other specify	58	33
	Total	**175**	**100**

Source: Random Survey.

The above table conveys that 29 per cent of people out of 75 are interested to visit Rajasthan and M.P., Tamilnadu and West Bengal have equal but lower investment to visit (11 per cent to 12 per cent).

Table 9.35: Arrangement for Source of Spending

Sl. No.	*Source*	*No. of Respondents*	*% of Response*
1.	Domestic savings	98	56
2.	Facility from employers	42	24
3.	Incentives from others	28	16
4.	Borrowing	7	4
	Total	**175**	**100**

Source: Random Survey.

Table 9.35 reveals that almost 56 per cent people prefer travelling out of their domestic savings, 24 per cent out of facility from their employer and 16 per cent out of incentives.

Table 9.36: Opinion About the Duration of Stay

Sl. No.	*No. of days*	*No. of Respondents*	*% of Response*
1.	<3	12	7
2.	3-7	88	50
3.	7-15	65	37
4.	>15	10	6
	Total	**175**	**100**

Source: Random Survey.

The data in the table reveals that people prefer short term visit of 3 to 7 days (50 per cent), within 7 to 15 days (37 per cent) and more than 15 days only 6 per cent.

Table 9.37: Preference About Lodging Facility

Sl. No.	*Lodging facility*	*No. of Respondents*	*% of Response*
1.	Friends/Relatives	75	43
2.	Guest House	28	16
3.	Hotel	67	38
4.	Luxurious Hotel	5	3
	Total	**175**	**100**

Source: Random Survey.

On being asked where you would like to stay 43 per cent replied with friends/relatives, 38 per cent in hotels and 165 in guesthouses. The majority likes to stay with friends and relatives. This gives us to think that hotel industry in Rajasthan lack hospitality as a friend host.

Table 9.38: Best Age Group to Visit Tourist Spots

Sl. No.	*Age*	*No. of Respondents*	*% of Response*
1.	Student	35	20
2.	Young	52	30
3.	Matured age	44	25
4.	Old age	44	25
	Total	**175**	**100**

Source: Random Survey.

The table reveals that almost every part of life is the preferred to for tourism. This shows how charismatic tourism is for people, an eternal never ending thirst to know unknown by our human race. Really encouraging for boosting tourism.

Table 9.39: Rating of Government Role for Promotion of Tourism

Sl. No.	*Government Role*	*No. of Respondents*	*% of Response*
1.	Positive	28	16
2.	Supposition	89	51
3.	Informative	53	30
4.	Negative	5	3
	Total	**175**	**100**

Source: Random Survey.

The table reveals government role to promote tourism is rated as supportive (51 per cent) and informative (30 per cent).

Table 9.40 : Ranking of Financial and Economic Implication Factors

Sl. No.	*Factors*	*No. of Respondents*	*% of Response*
1.	Increase in standard of living	16	9
2.	Employment generation	28	16
3.	National/International recognition	19	11
4.	Expanse of literacy and education	21	12
5.	Increase in income	40	23
6.	Improvement in health and family welfare	12	7
7.	Eradication of social evils	7	4
8.	Advantages of cross cultural change	9	5
9.	Increase in Export/Foreign Exchange	16	9
10.	Increase in investment opportunities	7	4
	Total	**175**	**100**

Source: Random Survey.

The above table and the collection of the opinion from Public reveals that tourism industry is a gold mine in the economy of Rajasthan as it generates employment (16 per cent) gives recognition at national/international level (11 per cent), increase income (23 per cent) and expansion of literacy and education (12 per cent).

Respondents—Regulating Agencies (Tourism Department/R.T.D.C. and Other Government Deptts.)

Table 9.41: Agency Responsible for Promotion of Tourism

Sl. No.	*Agencies*	*No. of Respondents*	*% of Response*
1.	Central Government	8	32
2.	State Government	12	48
3.	Local autonomous bodies	3	12
4.	Body of association	2	8
	Total	**25**	**100**

Source: Field Survey.

The table reveals that chief responsibility lies on the State Government to promote tourism of course with the support of Central Government. This is true also, as the main gainer of the tourist inflow would be the Host State where tourists are attracted to visit. The opinion gathered also Seconds State Government at 48 per cent and Central Government at 32 per cent, besides local autonomous bodies at 12 per cent and bodies associated at 8 per cent.

Table 9.42: Most Benefited Class from Tourism

Sl. No.	*Class*	*No. of Respondents*	*% of Response*
1.	Poor people	6	24
2.	Middle class	8	32
3.	Rich class	5	20
4.	Government	6	24
	Total	**25**	**100**

Source: Field Survey.

The above table shows that middle, poor and rich classes and the government derive the benefits of tourism almost equally. This shows the socio-economic impact of tourism in society as well as at Government level and gives the message that as more we develop the facilities we fetch more benefits from tourism.

Table 9.43: Most Obstacle Element in Promotion of Tourism

Sl. No.	*Name of the Benefit*	*No. of Respondents*	*% of Response*
1.	Government Department and Policy	8	32
2.	System of promotion	10	40
3.	Negative attitude of promoting agency	3	12
4.	Political levels	4	16
	Total	**25**	**100**

Source: Field Survey.

The above table shows that government departments, their policies, system and the style of promoting on tourism are main obstacle here, the red-tapism is the only cause between policy formation and its implementation which it needs to be removed.

Table 9.44: Reason for Poor Growth Rate of Tourist Inflow in the Rajasthan

Sl. No.	*Reasons*	*No. of Respondents*	*% of Response*
1.	Poor infrastructure facilities	10	40
2.	Non-cooperation of engaged staff	4	16
3.	Poor publicity and advertisement	6	24
4.	Lacking Govt support/encouragement	5	20
	Total	**25**	**100**

Source: Field Survey.

The table reveals that poor infrastructural facilities, *i.e.* 40 per cent, besides poor publicity and advertisement lacking of Government support/encouragement and non-cooperation of engaged staff/ranging from 16 and to 25 per cent all are the main causes for poor tourism inflow growth rate in Rajasthan.

This requires all-round attention on the part of agencies engaged in the business of tourism promotion, besides infrastructural growth of facilities as a host.

Table 9.45: Opinion About Tourism Growth, If Privatised

Sl. No.	*Growth*	*No. of Respondents*	*% of Response*
1.	Increase very fast	5	20
2.	Increase fast	15	60
3.	Remain as usual	5	20
4.	Decrease	-	-
	Total	**25**	**100**

Source: Field Survey.

The table suggests that if every tourism activity is given to the private hands (*i.e.*, 60 per cent) the tourism traffic will increase fast.

Table 9.46: Comments About New Tourism Policy of Rajasthan

Sl. No.	*Government Policy*	*No. of Respondents*	*% of Response*
1.	Only formal	8	32
2.	Only informal	3	12
3.	Without much impact	6	24
4.	Have more impact	8	32
	Total	**25**	**100**

Source: Field Survey.

The table shows that the tourism policy framed by the Government from time to time has more impact but it remain only formal (both have 32 per cent equally). This suggestion that only formal declaration are framing of policy will not do, it requires implementation.

Table 9.47: Role of Government Participation

Sl. No.	*Government participation*	*No. of Respondents*	*% of Response*
1.	Regulator	8	32
2.	Supervisor	5	20
3.	Investor	3	12
4.	Promoter	9	36
	Total	**25**	**100**

Source: Field Survey.

The above table says that government participation should remain as promoter (36 per cent), regulator (32 per cent) and supervisor (25 per cent) and not as investor (7 per cent).

Table 9.48: Opinion About R.T.D.C. as a White Elephant in Tourism

Sl. No.	*Name of the benefit*	*No. of Respondents*	*% of Response*
1.	Yes	10	40
2.	No	12	48
3.	Can'tsay	3	12
	Total	**25**	**100**

Source: Field Survey.

An opinion that R.T.D.C. is proving as a white elephant in tourism was gathered and we have received a mixed Yes 40 per cent and No. 48 per cent which suggests that R.T.D.C. requires improvement in its working to eliminate 40 per cent Yes votes.

Table 9.49: Opinion About Poor Spending of Budget Allocation

Sl. No.	*Name of the benefit*	*No. of Respondents*	*% of Response*
1.	Yes	15	60
2.	No	8	32
3.	Can't say	2	8
	Total	25	100

Source: Field Survey.

The table reveals that even 10 per cent of budget allocation for development of tourism infrastructure is not spent by the Government (60 per cent). This attaches government attention.

Table 9.50: Ranking of Financial and Economic Implication Factors

Sl. No.	*Factors*	*No. of Respondents*	*% of Response*
1.	Increase in standard of living	3	12
2.	Employment generation	4	16
3.	National/International recognition	3	12
4.	Expanse of literacy and education	2	8
5.	Increase in income	4	16
6.	Improvement in health and family welfare	–	–
7.	Eradication of social evils	2	8
8.	Advantages of cross cultural change	2	8
9.	Increase in Export/Foreign Exchange	2	8
10.	Increase in investment opportunities	3	12
	Total	**25**	**100**

Source: Field Survey.

The above table and the collection of the opinion from Government Departments/R.T.D.C. and other State Departments reveal that tourism industry is a gold mine in the economy of Rajasthan as it increases the standard of living (12 per cent) generates employment (16 per cent) gives recognition at national/international level (12 per cent), increase income (16 per cent) and increases investment opportunities (12 per cent).

Results

The actual value of *P* is calculated as undertaking into consideration of field survey of tourist, service providers, public and regulating agencies as mentioned below:

Table 9.51: Calculation of Matrix for Financial and Economic Implications of Tourism in Rajasthan

No.	*Factors*	*Tourist*	*Public*	*Service Providers*	*Regulators*	*Ranking*	*No. 1*	*Matrix*	*Ranks*
		I	*II*	*III*	*IV*	*P* *I+II+III+IV*	*(T-P)*	*P/T-P*	
1.	Increase in standard of living	8	7	2	3	20	180	0.1111	IV
2.	Employment opportunity	15	12	5	4	36	164	0.2195	I
3.	National and international recognition	7	8	2	3	20	180	0.1111	IV
4.	Expansion of literacy and education	8	9	1	2	20	180	0.1111	IV
5.	Increase in income	13	17	6	4	40	160	0.2500	II
6.	Improvement in health and family welfare	6	5	–	–	11	189	0.0582	VI
7.	Eradication of social evils	4	3	1	2	10	190	0.0526	VII
8.	Advantages of cross culture change	2	4	2	2	10	190	0.0526	VII
9.	Increase in export/foreign exchange	8	7	4	2	21	179	0.1173	III
10	Increase in investment opportunity	4	3	2	3	12	188	0.0638	V
	Total	**75**	**75**	**25**	**25**	**200**	**1,800**	**1.1473**	

Above 3 factors of financial and economic activities have their ranking as under:

1. Increase in income
2. Employment generation
3. Increase in export/foreign exchange

It is inferred from the above table that the calculated value of '*P*' is more than 1. It ultimately led to accept the research hypothesis, which shows that there are significant relations between financial economic implications and tourism. But as we could see that there is very thin margin in the calculated value of *P* and standard value of *P* which needs corrective steps at the government/service providers and regulating agencies level.

Chapter X

CHANGING DIMENSIONS IN TOURISM INDUSTRY

The present chapter presents birds eye view of the study on Rajasthan. The study, which comprises seven chapters, begins from the conceptual level, *i.e.* the basis of tourism constituting the very foundation of the study. After a detailed discussion of tourism from the conceptual level it gradually reaches the most significant point the financial and economic implications of the tourism industry in Rajasthan.

An empirical study has been conducted, which was to a large extent a complete success. 400 respondents were selected on random sampling basis, as explained in Chapter No. 1 (Research Methodology). The respondents (Tourists, Service Providers, Public and Regulating Agencies) were very clear, assertive and factual. Some of the responses were not included in the analysis as they were incomplete. Selected 400 questionnaires were analysed in computer through Fox pro package. The main findings emanated from random survey is given hereunder:

Main Findings

Table 10.1: Travel Plan

Sl. No.	*Most Favoured Reply*	*Score %*	*Random Survey*
1.	Tourist prefer to travel in special groups	43	Tourists
2.	Believe more on friends advise	50	Tourists
3.	Pleasure is the reason to visit Rajasthan	43	Tourists
4.	Prefer short period visits	51	Tourists
5.	Best season Nov. to Dec.	30	Tourists
6.	Best season Oct. to Dec.	40	Service Providers

MANAGERIAL STRATEGIES TO IMPROVE TOURISM

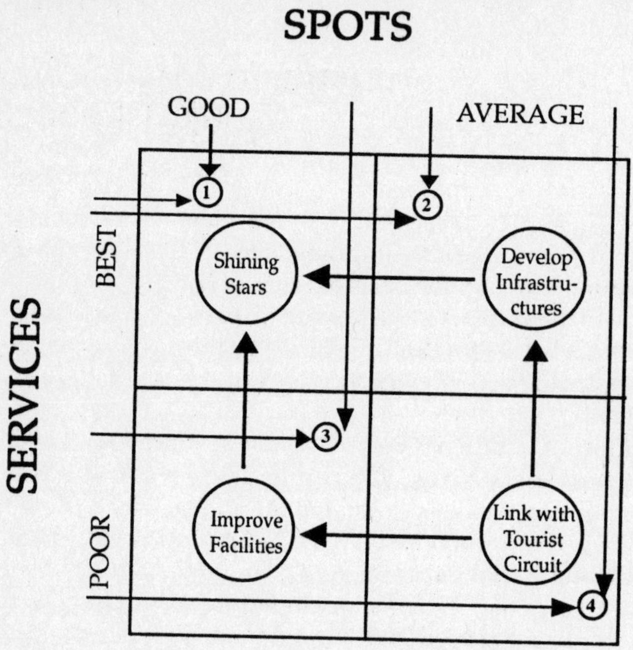

S. No.	*Position*	*Action/Strategies*
1.	Good Spots and Best Services	Shining Stars – Expand
2.	Average Spots and Best Services	Develop Infrastructure through Investments
3.	Good Spots and Poor Services	Improve Facilities through Incentives
4.	Poor Spots and Poor Services	Link with Tourist Circuit

Fig. 10.1

(Designed and Compiled by the Authors)

The above table reveals that majority of tourists preferred travelling in special groups, they visit Rajasthan on the advise of their friends/relatives for a short period and they consider season to visit Rajasthan from October to December. It is also revealed from the table that they are pleasure-seekers. This gives an idea for arranging package tours keeping in mind the comforts of travelling tourists. It is also revealed that how mouth to mouth publicity works, besides media and encourages the idea of more hospitality provision to the visiting tourists so that when they leave Rajasthan, they carry an everlasting memory of Rajasthan as a great host.

Table 10.2: Travel Facilities

Sl. No.	*Most Favoured Reply*	*Score %*	*Random Survey*
1.	No one choice is to see museum architecture and monuments	24	Tourists
2.	Bus service is the most convenient mode in Rajasthan	36	Tourists
3.	Would like to stay in moderate hotel	41	Tourists
4.	Average spending per trip Rs. 4,000	43	Tourists

It can be seen from the above table that tourist's main attractions are the museums, architecture and monuments and they prefer travelling through bus and stay in a moderate hotel. This suggests that we should pay more attention towards upkeep of Castles/Forts of the State, with all sorts of infrastructure. The arrangement of buses and the maintenance of roads are also needed and provision of moderate hotels/motels.

Table 10.3: Rating of Facilities

Sl. No.	*Most Favoured Reply*	*Score %*	*Random Survey*
1.	Travel facility is good	45	Tourists
2.	Boarding facility has been rated good	62	Tourists
3.	Midway and package tour facility of R.T.D.C. is good	40	Tourists
4.	R.T.D.C. got good rating	51	Tourists

The table reveals that arrangements made by R.T.D.C. in respect of travel, boarding, midway and package tours as GOOD rating by the tourists.

Table 10.4: Spending Preference

Sl. No.	*Most Favoured Reply*	*Score %*	*Random Survey*
1.	Would like to spend maximum on shopping	29	Tourists
2.	Purchasing preference is traditional items	32	Tourists

The table reveals that Service Providers have felt that mostly tourists spend on shopping and prefer purchasing traditional items.

Table 10.5: Experience of Visits

Sl. No.	*Most Favoured Reply*	*Score %*	*Random Survey*
1.	After having visit they found it as enjoyable	37	Tourists
2.	Would like to recommend to others	96	Tourists

The table reveals that tourists have enjoyed their visit and they will recommend it to others, as gathered from Service Providers.

Table 10.6: Benefits and Promotions

Sl. No.	*Most Favoured Reply*	*Score %*	*Random Survey*
1.	Middle class is the most benefited group from tourism	32	Regulating Agencies
2.	Lacking in systematic promotional campaign	40	Regulating Agencies

The survey reveals that Regulating Agencies have found that mostly benefited group is the middle class, however, systematic approach is lacking in promotional campaigns.

Table 10.7: Infrastructure and Budget Allocation

Sl. No.	*Most Favoured Reply*	*Score %*	*Random Survey*
1.	Poor infrastructure facility	40	Regulating Agencies
2.	Even 10 per cent budget is not being spent on infrastructure	60	Regulating Agencies

The survey reveals that Regulating Agencies feel that infrastructure facilities are poor and even 10 per cent of the budget allocation are not spent. This aspect needs attention from the Government.

Table 10.8: Opinion about Government Role and Policies

Sl. No.	*Most Favoured Reply*	*Score %*	*Random Survey*
1.	Privatisation of Government/Central facility including R.T.D.C. will increase tourist traffic	60	Regulating Agencies
2.	Is R.T.D.C. a white elephant? No	48	Regulating Agencies
3.	New Tourism Policy is a formal charter of recommendations	32	Regulating Agencies
4.	Government role should be like a regulator and promoter	36 & 32	Regulating Agencies

The survey reveals that Regulating Agencies feel that facilities arranged by State Government or Central Government, including by R.T.D.C. should be handed over to private hands, though R.T.D.C. is doing a good job and it is not a white elephant. It is also felt that policies declared by the Government are only formal and lacks implementation. The Government should only act as a Promoter and a Regulator.

Table 10.9: Potential Tourists

Sl. No.	*Most Favoured Reply*	*Score %*	*Random Survey*
1.	Awareness of tourists spots in Rajasthan	92	Public
2.	No. of places yet to be visited	57	Public

The survey reveals that public is aware of tourists spots in Rajasthan and several numbers of places are yet to be visited by them.

Table 10.10: Tenure and Source of Spending

Sl. No.	*Most Favoured Reply*	*Score %*	*Random Survey*
1.	Future plan to visit only after a year	52	Public
2.	Domestic savings is the main source of spending	56	Public

The survey from the public confirms that people spend their domestic savings on travel once in a year.

Table 10.11: Choice Preference of Potential Tourists

Sl. No.	*Most Favoured Reply*	*Score %*	*Random Survey*
1.	Period of stay 3-7 days	50	Public
2.	Choice for staying with friends and relatives	43	Public
3.	Would like to visit in young age	30	Public

The survey reveals that public prefers stay of only 3 to 7 days and their preferred choice is to stay with their friends and relatives. This gives message that hospitality is lacking somewhere in hotel industry.

Table 10.12: Details of Service Providers

Sl. No.	*Most Favoured Reply*	*Score %*	*Random Survey*
1.	Exclusively engaged in the tourist activity	48	Service Providers
2.	No. of employee employed from 10–12	32	Service Providers

The survey reveals that nearly 50 per cent of Service Providers are exclusively engaged in tourism activities with 10 to 12 number of employees.

Table 10.13: Investment and Marketing Strategies

Sl. No.	*Most Favoured Reply*	*Score %*	*Random Survey*
1.	Average investment Rs. 0.50 to 5.00 lakh	35	Service Providers
2.	Business is growing income-wise	36	Service Providers
3.	Expansion plan	48	Service Providers
4.	Fairs and festivals should be organised at tourist spots for promotion	40	Service Providers
5.	Services have improved because of globalisation/liberalisation	52	Service Providers

The survey reveals that Service Providers feel tourism industry is growing income-wise and is waiting for expansion. There is lot of scope for the growth of the industry due to globalisation and liberalisation. The fairs and festivals should be organised at tourist spots is also the view of Service Providers.

Recommendations

Rajasthan has emerged as a very popular Tourist State in last one decade, where in Seventies, the total number of domestic and foreign tourists was 20 lakh, it is now 79.97 lakh, out of which 6.23 lakh are foreign tourists, besides domestic tourists numbering 73.74 lakh. Because of world fame Golden Triangle, *i.e.*, Delhi-Agra-Jaipur, Jaipur has its special attention in world map. 60 per cent of foreigners visiting India, essentially travel golden triangle. Both these categories of tourists, spend Rs. 2,000 crore in Rajasthan. Rajasthan has established its name for its rich cultural and historical heritage, its colourful fairs and festivals and hospitable people. Excepting seashore and icy hillocks, every resource/attraction is available for all sorts of tourists here. Tourists' products of Rajasthan like Palace on Wheels, Heritage Hotels, Camel Safari, Pushkar Mela, Maru Festival, Game Sanctuaries etc. have gained international fame. In view of this, the Government of Rajasthan declared Tourism as an industry in 1989 to develop employment opportunities, especially in rural areas, to use its tourism resources in such a way that inland and foreign tourists do not miss visiting it, motivate private sector to develop infrastructure for tourism, to preserve enriched natural source, historical architecture and cultural heritage, specially historical monuments, to develop market for handicrafts and cottage industry of the state, to develop cultural neighbourhood by arranging fairs and festivals. For upliftment of social and economic level, especially in backward areas, through tourism industry, it has been decided by the state to make a Public Industry.

The present study entitled a study of financial and economic implication of tourism in Rajasthan has intensively studied, examined and analysed tourism in all its manifestations with regard to financial and economic implications. To evolve financial and economic implications, the study suggest following recommendations on the basis of findings:

- To make available new attractions in tourism like Environmental Tourism, Rural Tourism, Caravan Tourism, Heritage Walk, Development of Camel/Horse Safari, Boating in rivers and canals, to provide House Boats and Shikara facilities in lakes.
- Cultural institutions like Jawahar Kala Kendra at Jaipur should be linked with tourism.
- The Government should work as Promoter and arrange to provide infrastructure facilities.
- The Government should administer law and order, tourism police, rectification of complaints, frame rules and regulation for tourism industry.
- The Government should prepare a master plan on the basis of its districts and towns to avail external and central help.
- The Government should motivate private sector to invest so that basic infrastructure for tourism could be constructed and to promote/develop tourism through them.
- The Government should develop rural tourism so that employment opportunities are available in these areas.
- The Government should widely advertise tourism through media like Television, Print and Internet.
- The Government should coordinate between Handicrafts and its market.
- The Government should ensure security of tourists so that they are self-motivated to visit Rajasthan.

- Since Rajasthan is country's biggest State, it has extreme opportunities to develop tourism, therefore basic infrastructure like residential accommodation, roadways, airports, railways, local transport, means of communication and other facilities are essentially required to be developed.

Residential Accommodation

- Residential accommodation for tourists in different categories and number is the prime necessity. It is, therefore, essential to arrange accommodation from budget category to Five Star categories in abundance.
- The Government should motivate private sector to come forward for development of residential accommodation. In exceptional backward areas, where investment by private sector is not made, the Government itself should invest for residential accommodation.

Heritage Hotels

- Rajasthan has been the first state, among other states, to develop heritage hotels by renovating Old Havelis and Palaces into hotels. These hotels have become very popular amongst tourists.
- To preserve these old monuments, the Government should try to establish more heritage hotels in the state.

Camp/Environment Tourism

- Camping sites made available in Pushkar Mela, Maru Festival, Pashu Mela and Jhalawar Mela have become very popular.
- Efforts should be made to provide more camping sites by identifying new sites, especially for budget tourists during peak season.

Paying Guest Residence

- The Government should popularise Paying Guest

residence by identifying and registering those residences and families, which can provide sufficient comfort to tourists.

Transit Facilities

- The State, however, is spread over 3.42 lacs sq. km. in area, it lacks in fully developed air and rail facilities. Therefore, the maximum use is made of roads as mode of transport.
- It is therefore, essential to provide transit facilities for the comfortable journey of tourists. These should be provided at every distance of 100 to 125 kms. by the governments or private sector.

Development of Heritage Archaeological Properties

- The state has historical buildings/monuments in abundance, which are not looked after by Archaeological Department of the State. These buildings should be taken over and taken care of.
- These properties should be transferred to Tourism Department/R.T.D.C. for developing heritage hotels, tourism museums, tourist complexes, and tourists' resorts.

R.T.D.C.—To Work as Promoter

- For the development of infrastructure facilities for tourism, R.T.D.C. should work, as is being done by R.I.I.C.O. (Rajasthan Industrial Development and Investment Corporation) for development of industrial estates.
- R.T.D.C. should acquire land from the Government, develop it and establish hotels and work for projects related to tourism.

Devasthan Land

- Government should develop land owned by Devasthan

Department for using it as Yatri Niwas, Dharamsalas, and Tourism Complexes in coordination with Tourism Department, R.T.D.C. and Devasthan Department.

Joint Venture with Private Investors

- There is several numbers of valuable properties in different cities of Rajasthan, which are not being properly used nor they required for government use. These properties should be used as tourist facilities in joint venture with private investors and R.T.D.C.
- For managing the Government owned infrastructural facilities, private sector should be given priority.

Tourism as an Industry

- Since the Government has declared Tourism as an Industry, it should be given all sorts of facilities and relaxation as are being extended to other industries in the State.

Rail Transport

- Prominent places of Rajasthan are already on rail map and conversion of meter gauge to broad gauge has increased tourists rush. It should be the endeavour of the government to convert other rail lines to broad gauge.
- To make journey through rail more comfortable, there is necessity to arrange more comfortable tourist trains and for local sightseeing, R.T.D.C. should arrange buses.
- The Palace on Wheels has become very popular amongst foreigners and NRIs. A separate Palace on Wheels for budget tourists should also be arranged.

Road Transport

- Since Rajasthan lacks in sufficient air links and rail heads, road transport has become more important. The Government should explore for external help for promoting more road heads.

- Special attention should be given to recognised and approved AC Tourist Buses, Tourist Cars and specially designed Non AC Sightseeing buses to encourage them.
- R.T.D.C. should make arrangements along with private sectors for local sightseeing and travel to nearby places on national highways.
- The Government should ensure that standard fare is taken from inland and foreign tourists and arrange for pre-paid Taxis/Coaches and encourage Heritage Taxi operations.
- There is need for improvement of local transportation in various tourists places. For transportation of tourists, Car taxis should be encouraged and three wheelers should be bounded to ply their vehicle through meter reading so that tourist are not cheated with excess fare.

Air Travel

- The Government should encourage Air Taxi operators for air taxi and helicopter service in the State so that tourists can visit maximum number of places during their short stay.
- The State has air strips and helipads at various places. They should be maintained and air taxi operators should be encouraged to use them.
- The private sector should be encouraged to establish international airport in the State and the air taxi operators should be encouraged to operate their services as Feeder/ Regional Airlines.
- R.T.D.C. should promote air tourism with the help of air taxi operators by providing them ground handling facilities to start with air travel to tourist places.
- Jaipur airport should be converted into International Airport and Civil Aviation Ministry should be approached for permission of tourist charter flights.
- Arrangement of chartered flights for foreign tourists belonging to elite class be made.

Tourist Welcome Centres

- In view of incoming flow of inland and foreign tourists,

it is essential for establishing modernised tourist welcome centres at prominent places in the State like Mumbai, Bangalore, Kolkata and Chennai.

- These centres should work as a reservation centres for the hotels of R.T.D.C. and the hotels of private sector.
- These Centres should be fully computerised and information like package tours, paying guest facility, fairs, festivals etc. should also be given.
- Inter-state package tours should also be started in association with other Corporations and Railways.
- The Centres located in prominent places of Rajasthan should work round the clock.

Tourist Information and Advertisement Centres

- For wide publicity of Rajasthan, necessary tourism brochures, films, videos, etc. should be produced and printed.
- An extensive advertising policy should be framed and the concerned literature should be made available to all concerned with tourism activity to increase awareness about Rajasthan.
- The literature should be got prepared in other foreign languages also like French, German, Spanish, Arabian and English etc.
- With the help of tour operators and agents, links for promotion and marketing of tourism should be established in foreign countries also.

Expansion of Tourism Products

- Rajasthan has a rich heritage in handicraft, handmade and other products, which are purchased by tourists coming here.
- A market for such products should be developed/ arranged by R.T.D.C. so that the manufacturer can exhibit and sale its product.
- Shilpgram should be established at various tourist places.
- A Handicraft Museum should also be established.

Week-end Tourism

- Tourists from neighbouring States like Delhi and Gujarat visit Rajasthan on weekends.
- Keeping in view their necessities, package tours along with development of new places should be done to attract them more for their weekend spending.

Tourism and Wildlife

- Rajasthan has Forest Reserve places and National Parks like Sariska, Bharatpur, Ghana and Ranthambore. Other places, where wildlife exists should be developed for tourists interest.
- Conservation of flora and fauna of desert should be done as it attract tourists.

Guides

- Multilingual guides should be trained as they are very important for deployment in tourists places and circuits.
- A foreign language course should be arranged with the help of RITTMAN, other Universities and the Embassies of different countries in Delhi.

Inland Tourism

- Rajasthan attracts tourists from Gujarat and Bengal. There should be sufficient literature available in these languages. Package tours can be arranged from Ahmedabad and Kolkata for these tourists.
- Inter-State Package tours should be arranged keeping in view the basic needs of inland tourists visiting for pilgrimage.

Tourism

- Rajasthan is basically a desert place, however, it attracts inland and foreign tourists for trekking, horse riding, camel safari, polo and gold activities.

- Besides desert, the State has several lakes, where water sport can be developed like canoeing, boating etc.
- The river of Chambal and Indira Gandhi Canal can be used for boating and canal safari.
- Shikara Boats can be had from States like J&K and Kerala and they can be marketed as Palace on Waves in big lakes of the State.
- These activities will not only attract the tourists but will make them stay in the State for a longer period.

Coordination with Other States

- The R.T.D.C. should try to promote Package Tours in coordination with other State's Tourism Corporations of UP, West Bengal, MP, Gujarat, HP, Delhi etc.
- This coordination will introduce a new era of mutual tourism amongst these states.

HRD for Tourism Industry

- Tourism industry needs trained and skilled personnel at government and private sector levels.
- To meet the demand of trained personnel in Hotel Management and Foodcraft, the government should motivate private sector for establishing such centres.
- RITTMAN should come forward with specialised courses for all categories of personnel working for tourism.

Excise Duty for Liquor

- The present Excise Regulations should be simplified for obtaining Bar licences by the Hotels.
- Rajasthan has its own heritage liquor like Asha, Jagmohan, Kesar Kasturi, Chandrahas etc. and can be used as souvenir.

Tourism Awareness

- Since tourism has immense importance in daily life and

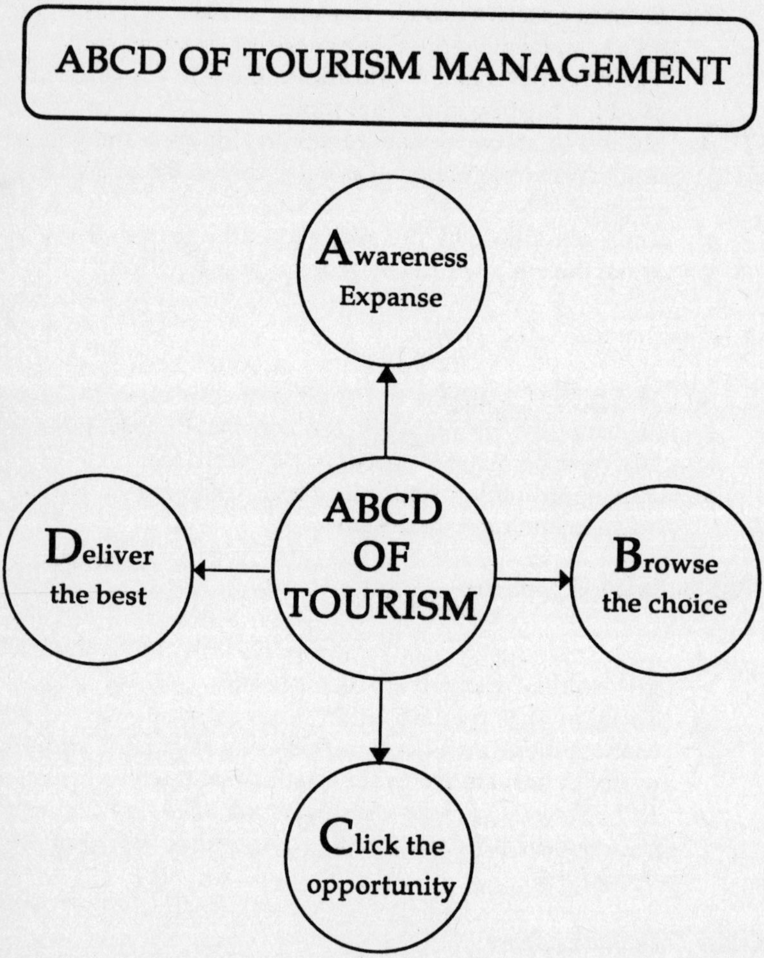

Fig. 10.2

(Designed and Compiled by the Authors)

it has become a tool for economic development all over the world, the government should come forward for tourism awareness amongst people, especially the new generation.

- A separate chapter for awareness towards tourism should be included in the study courses at school/college level.

Others

- The image of the Tourism in the State should be of international standard.
- Infrastructure like roads, accommodation and communication should be improved.
- More attractive areas should be developed to lessen the weight of local urban tourists.
- Environmental damage should be protected to maintain ecological balance.
- Promotional activities to be vigorously strengthened to woe more tourists, especially from Europe and America.
- Scope to be widened to increase the tourist stay in the State.
- To train and provide bilingual or multilingual guides to lift language barriers.
- Arrangement should be made to provide food and beverages of international standards besides local dishes.
- Food adultery should be checked to provide genuine and valid stuff.
- A perfect tourism culture should be cultivated so that tourists visiting the State escape burglary or pick-pocketing or snatching of their valuables.
- A courteous and inviting image has to be established through media to attract tourist.
- Tourist information centres should be well equipped with latest information of local and international interest.
- Heritage monuments to be renovated and refurbished with basic amenities.
- To promote sustainable as well as eco-tourism, new tourism destinations and need to be identified and promoted.
- High standards of hospitality should be maintained to earn name for the State in the world.
- Above all multi-media position approach, courteous hospitality and basic amenities are the need of hour for the State to attract tourist.

Other Suggestions

The conceptual framework of this study is now complete and if the following facts are taken into consideration, there will be considerable improvements in every context.

- Renovation and reactivation of the infrastructure.
- Declaration of tourism as a priority sector in the State Development Plans.
- Involving a consultant in preparing for the future tourism.
- Government Missions should be directed abroad to give a current picture.
- Steps should be taken to avoid any harassment and restrictions imposed on tourists.
- Management of tourist products and ensuring culture of tourism.
- Introduction of Eco-Tourism Culture.
- Providing for all categories of tourism accommodation facilities.
- Proper steps to ensure closer collaboration between local, regional and foreign tourist offices.
- Propagate the idea that tourism depends entirely on private-public collaboration.
- Declaration of Tourism Industry as an Export-Oriented Industry.
- Decentralisation of the R.T.D.C. in as far as policy framing is concerned.
- Setting up tourism training institution.
- Need for tourist sensitive police.
- Travel agents should be cautious of changes taking place.
- Ideal tourism structure in Rajasthan.
- Tourist police on the line of Traffic Police in Rajasthan to grab "LAPKA" MEN at the tourist spot.
- There is a need to refocus marketing strategy to effectively promote Rajasthan as a destination by Tourist Offices of Department of Tourism, all over India/abroad.
- We should not impose Visa restrictions, in reciprocation other countries doing so. It should be Visa-on-arrival.
- There is a need of an independent International Airport in the State for an easy access to Rajasthan.

- There should be uniformity in Hotel prices so that tourist does not feel cheated as tourism is an invisible export and if there are more tourists arrival, the hotel industry is automatically benefited.
- There should be one more Train, in line with PALACE ON WHEELS for Shekhawati Bikaner Region.
- The recent tragic incident of terrorist attack on America has shaken tourism industry all over the world, including India. This gives us to think that we should enhance/promote tourism amongst inland tourists through media.
- Tourism should be propagated as a tool for peace and dialogue among civilisations.
- Tourism department should open tourist offices in all major cities of the country for advertisement and marketing of tourism.
- Private sector plays major role in tourism industry of the State. The government should announce sufficient tax/interest relaxation/rebate and subsidy to promote the same.
- The industry of tourism should be linked with Doordarshan channels, handicrafts, ornamental gold and silver jewellery, readymade garments, tourist guide training, hotel management centre, besides hotel and restaurant businesses.
- There should be actual personification of 'PADHARO MHARE DESH' tradition so that outgoing tourists carry memorable impact of their stay in Rajasthan and canvass among their friends/relatives.
- Inland tourists are mainly attracted on low cost facilities, entertainment and food, whereas, foreign tourists come for leisure and pleasure and require fully modernised facilities, besides, security, peace and for the gain of knowledge. We should groom our facilities to meet their demand.
- Employees relating to Government lack in professional approach with flexibility of thought and behaviour. They should be trained and groomed to personify PADHARO MHARE DESH tradition of the State.

Last but not the least, we should not think that tourists are our customers, they are our Guests, hence, PADHARO MHARE

DESH (Welcome to our State) should be our PARIVESH. The suggestion contained in the present study will go a long run long way in giving boost to this industry and will pave the way for a better future of tourism in the state.

Implications

Tourists having better socio-economic status and attractions from State could mobilise more tourist therefore, regulating agencies should keep choice of these people in mind so that better linkage can be established.

The findings of the study will help the service providers to complete more efficiently in the liberalised era taking into consideration the choice of tourists and public.

In order to make the tourism more attractive and effective in serving the purpose of financial and economic growth. It is necessary to be made tourism as friendly home/users.

Suggestions for Future Research

- Similar study can be conducted in different district of circles of the state so that awareness can be increased.
- Further study can be undertaken regarding problems faced by tourists and service providers in the liberalised state economy.
- A comparative study may be undertaken financial and economic implication of other tourist rich states in India.

BIBLIOGRAPHY

BOOKS

Akhtar, Javed, *Tourism Management in India*, Ashish Publications, New Delhi, 1990.

Akshay Kumar, *Tourism Management*, Commonwealth Publishers, New Delhi, 1997.

Anand, M.M., *Tourism and Hotel Industry in India*: A Study in Management, Prentice Hall, New Delhi, 1976.

A.S. Chawla and G.S. Batra, *Tourism Management*, Deep & Deep Publication Pvt. Ltd., New Delhi, 2001.

Bala, Usha, *Tourism in India: Policy and Perspectives*, Arushi Publications, New Delhi, 1990.

Batra, K.L., *Problems and Prospects of Tourism*, Printwell Publishers, Jaipur, 1990.

Bhatia, *A.K., International Tourism: Fundamentals and Practices*, Sterling Publishers Private Limited, Delhi, 1983.

Bijendra, K. Punia, *Tourist Management: Problem and Prospectus*, Ashish Publishing House, New Delhi, 2001.

Bryden, John M., *Tourism and Development*, Cambridge University Press, London, 1973.

Bukart, A.J., *The Management of Tourism*, Heinemann, London, 1975

Bukart, A.J. and Medlik, S., *Tourism: Past, Present and Future*, Heinemann, London, 1976.

Charles, Kaiser and Helber Larry E., *Tourism Planning and Development*, CBI Publishing Company, Boston, Massachusetts, 1978

Chib, Somnath, *Essays on Tourism*, Cross Section, New Delhi, 1989.

Colley, G., *International Tourism Today*, Llodys Bank Review, London, 1967.

C.Y. Gee, Dexter J.L. Choy, *The Travel Industry*, The AVI Publishing Company, Westport, Connecticut, 1984.

Davis, H.D., *Potentials for Tourism of Developing Countries*, Finance and Development, London, 1968.

Dharmarajan, S. and Rabindra Seth, *Tourism in India Trends and Issues*, Harand Publications, New Delhi, 1994.

Gupta, Vijay K., *Tourism in India*, Gyan, New Delhi, 1987.

George, Young, *Tourism Blessing or Plight*, Harmondsworth Penguin Books Ltd., England, 1973.

G.S. Batra and R.C. Dangwal, *Tourism Promotion and Development*, Deep & Deep Publications Pvt. Ltd., New Delhi, 2001.

Jafari, J., *Role of Tourism in Social Economic Transferred of Development*, Counties, 1973.

Joana Morris, *The Encyclopaedia of Cooking*, The National Magazine Co. Ltd., New York, 1985.

Kaul, R.N., *Dynamics of Tourism*, Sterling Publishers Pvt. Ltd., Volume II and III, Delhi, 1985.

Krippendorf, J., *Marketing of Tourism*, Herbert Lagb, Bern., 1971.

Krishan K. Kamra, *Tourism, Theory, Planning and Practice*, Indus Publishing Co., New Delhi, 1997.

Lickorish, J.L. and Kershaw, A.G., *The Travel Trade*, Practice Press Ltd., London, 1958.

Lundberg, D., *The Tourist Business*, Cahners Books International Inc., Boston, 1974.

Mc.Intosh, R.W., *Tourism, Principles, Practices and Philosophies*, John Wiley, New York, 1986.

Medlik, S., *Profile of Hotel and Catering Industry*, Heinemann, London, 1972.

Michael, M.C., *Introduction to Travel and Tourism, An International Approach*, Van Nostrand Reinhold, New York, 1989.

Mill, Robert Christie, *Tourism, The International Business*, Prentice Hall, New Jersey, 1990

Mill, R.C., Morrisom, A.M., *The Tourism System, An Introductory Text*, Prentice Hall, New Jersey, 1985.

Negi, J.M.S., *Tourism and Travel Concepts and Principles*, Gitanjali Publishing House, New Delhi, 1982.

Nirmal Kumar, *Tourism and Economic Development*, ASH Publishing Corporation, New Delhi, 1996.

Norval, A.J., *The Tourist Industry, A National and International Survey*, Pitman, London, 1936.

Ogilive, F.W., *The Tourist Movement: An Economic Study*, Staples Press Ltd., London, 1980.

Peter Douglas, *Tourist Development, Longman*, London, 1981.

Peter Michael, *International Tourism*, Hutchinson, London, 1969.

Puri, G.K., *Travel and Tourism for All*, IIMS, New Delhi, 1986.

Raina, A.K., *Tourism Industry in Kashmir*, Shipra Publications, Delhi, 2002.

Raina, A.K. and Jain, Neelu, *Dynamics of Tourism Concepts, Philosophy Strategies*, Kanishka Publishers, Distributors, New Delhi, 2004.

Ram Acharya, *World Tourism,* National Publishing House, New Delhi, 1981.

Ram Acharya, *Tourism in India*, R.B.S.A. Publishers, Jaipur, 1977.

Robert T. Reilly, *Travel and Tourism* Merton House, TNT Publishers INC, 1980, Weaton, USA.

Robinson, H., *A Geography of Tourism*, Macdonald and Evans, London, 1976.

Seth Pran Nath, *Successful Tourism Planning and Management*, Cross Section Publications, New Delhi, 1978.

Sharma, K.C., *Tourism Policy Planning and Strategy*, Efficient Off Set Printers, New Delhi, 1996.

Sharma, Vivek, *Tourism in India*, Arihant Publications, Jaipur, 1991.

Singh, Ratandeep, *Tourism Today*, *Structure Marketing and Profile*, Volume II, Kanishka Publishers, Delhi, 1994.

Singh, T.V., *Tourism Industry in U.P.*, New Heights Publishers, Delhi, 1978.

Sinha, P.C., *Tourism Planning*, Anmol Publications Pvt. Ltd., 1998.

Sinha, R.K., *Tourism Strategies, Planning and Development*, Commonwealth Publishers, New Delhi, 1996.

Smith, Stephen, *Tourism Analysis*, *A Handbook,* Longman, London, 1989.

Wahab, S.E., *Tourism Management*, Tourism International Press, London, 1985.

Will, Stephen E. and Mountinho, B. Luizeds, *Tourism Marketing and Management Handbook*, Prentice Hall, London, 1985.

W.Mc. Intosh and S. Gupta, *Tourism Principles*, Practices and *Philosophies*, Grid Publishing Inc., Columbs, Ohio, 1980.

W.W. Hunter, *The India Empire: Its People, History and Product*, Smith Eden and Co., London, 1987.

REPORTS AND BULLETINS

Bhaba Institute of Management Sciences, Udaipur "Report on International Conference of Hotel and Tourism Management" held at Udaipur, 20-22 September, 1996.

Cheechi and Co., "Future of Tourism in Pacific and Far East" (Report Sponsored by U.S. Department of Commerce), Washington D.C., 1961.

Chib S.N., "Perspective on Tourism in India", Sardar Patel Memorial Lecture, PATA Chapter, New Delhi.

Ensiquez Antonic, "Inaugural Address" presented at International Conference on Youth Tourism held at New Delhi, 12-18 November, 1991.

Government of India, Department of Tourism, New Delhi, Hotel Review Survey Committee Report.

Government of India, Department of Tourism, New Delhi, Performance Appraisal (1996-1998)

Government of India, Lok Sabha Secretariat, New Delhi, Tourism Policy, 1985.

Government of India, Ministry of Tourism, New Delhi, Report on Economic Benefits of Tourism, 1987.

Government of India, Ministry of Tourism (Tourism Research and Statistical Unit), New Delhi, Report on Pattern of Tourism in India

Government of India, Ministry of Tourism, New Delhi, Report on Manpower Development—Needs of Various Sectors of Travel Industry (1990-95-2000), 1987.

Government of India, New Delhi, Annual Report, Pragati Prativaden and Various Other Reports of Department of Tourism, Ministry of Civil Aviation and Ministry of Information and Broadcasting.

Government of India, Planning Commission, New Delhi, Five Year Plans (I to X Plans).

Government of Rajasthan, Department of Tourism, Art and Culture, Jaipur, New Tourism Policy—2001.

Government of Rajasthan, Jaipur, "Proceeding of IRC 2000" (held at Jaipur, 23rd to 24th September, 2000).

Government of Rajasthan, Department of Tourism, Art and Culture, Jaipur, Annual Reports and Other Reports.

Government of Rajasthan, Department of Tourism, Art and

Culture, Jaipur, Report on 7th South Asia Travel Mart (held at Jaipur 4-7 December, 1999).

IIPO, New Delhi, Report of Indian Tourism Performance and Potentials (1991-1997).

Indian Institute of Travel and Tourism Management, New Delhi, Tourism as an Industry, 1989 (Monograph).

Institute of Economic and Market Research, New Delhi, Tourism in India's Perspective to 1990.

National Conference on Tourism, U.G.C. Sponsored, "Issues and Challenges Before the Tourism Industry"—Conference Proceeding at DAV College, Ajmer, 8-9 December, 2000.

National Council of Applied Economic Research, India, Cost Benefit Study of Tourism, Report 1975.

Indian Chapter Survey on Marketing and Tourism:

- Report on Indian International Tourism Mart, at Pune, 8-10 October, 2000.
- Report on India International Trade Fair, IITF, New Delhi, 14-27 November, 2000.
- Report on Travel and Tourism Fair (TTF 2001) at Mumbai, 17-19 February, 2001.
- Report on TTA Convention and Exhibition, held at Hong Kong, 1-3 September, 1999.
- Report on Tech Service Asia, 2000.
- Report on TTF 2000 held at Mumbai, 11-20 February, 2000.
- Report on 2nd Hospitality and Tourism Technology Show held at Singapore, 11-14 April, 2000.

EXCERPTS INTERVIEWS, SPEECHES, ADDRESSES

Ananth Kumar, Former Union Minister of Civil Aviation, interviewed by Nandita Vijay, published in *Express Travel and Tourism*, Mumbai, August 1-15, 1999.

Ashok Gehlot, Honourable Chief Minister of the State of Rajasthan, Inaugural Address at IRC Conclave, 2000, 23-24 September, 2000 at Jaipur.

Ashok Gehlot, Honourable Chief Minister of the State of Rajasthan, Inaugural Address at Hotel Tech. Exhibition, 17-19 December at Jaipur.

Badri Bajaj, Vice President of I.A.T.O., Address at SATTE 2000, 6-9 April, 2000, Jaipur.

Baijal Anil, Indian Airlines, Chairman and Managing Director, interviewed by Sangita P. Menon, published in *Times of India*, New Delhi, August 10, 1999.

Bezbaruah, M.P., Secretary of Tourism, Government of India, interviewed by Bhishm Mansukhani, published in *Express Travel and Tourism*, Mumbai, April 1-15, 2000.

Bezbaruah, M.P., Secretary of Tourism, Government of India, Welcome Address at SATTE 2000 held at Jaipur, 6-28 April, 2000.

Bina Kak, Honourable Minister of Tourism, Government of Rajasthan, interviewed by Monica Lathar, Published in *Rajasthan Atithi*, Jaipur, Volume 4, No. 1, Jan.-Feb., 1999.

Chandrika Shantilal, Assistant Director, Exhibition and Conventions, Singapore Tourism Board, interviewed by Seema Pillai, published in *Express Travel and Tourism*, Mumbai, Dec. 1-15, 1999.

Dr. C.L. Raina, Add. Professor of Indology at Florida International University, U.S.A. Interviewed by the Author on 31st December, 2003.

Federieo Mayor, Director General of UNESCO and Francisco Frangiolli, Joint Message on the occasion of 20th World Tourism Day.

Hans Wiedemann, Vice Chairman of Hotels of the World Group and General Manager of Le Motreav Palace Hotel, Switzerland, interviewed by Lekha J. Shankar, published in *Times of India, Delhi*, June 7, 1999.

Jornid Abdullah, Director General of Tourism, Malaysia, interviewed by Umesh Luthria, published in *Express Travel and Tourism*, Mumbai, August 1-15, 1999.

Kanti Poddar, Managing Director of the Travel Group Orient Express and Official Coordinator of the Khajuraho Millennium Committee, interviewed by Narayani Ganesh published in *Times of India*, New Delhi, 15th October, 1999.

Kaul Pt Janki Nath, Interview Conducted by Sandhya Kaul on Tourism Prospects of Rajasthan on 21st February, 2004 at 4/404, Malviya Nagar, Jaipur.

K.K. Mehera, President of the Federation of Hotel and Restaurant Association of India and Director of Oberoi Hotels, interviewed by Sangita P. Menon, published in *Times of India*, Delhi, 1st September, 1999.

Lalit K. Pawar, Honourable Secretary of Tourism, Government of Rajasthan, Inaugural Address at National Conference on Tourism, Dayanand College, Ajmer, 8-9 December, 2000.

Maharaja Gaj Singh, Former Ruler of Jodhpur and Chairman, Heritage Hotels Association of India, Address at SATTE 2000, Jaipur, 6-8 April, 2000.

Naresh Goyal, Chairman of Jet Airways, interviewed by Sangita P. Menon, published in *Times of India*, New Delhi, 18 August, 1999.

PATA Membership from India looks up as feels fall, Exclusive Round Table Discussion of prominent entities of Tourism Trade, compiled by Subhash Narayan, Raadia Mukadam and Jyoti Kaul, published in *Express Travel and Tourism*, Mumbai, May 1-15, 2000.

Pradip Madhavji (President TAAI), Yatin Dossa's (President T.A.R.), Santosh Shetty's (President FHRAI) views with regard to "Tourism Industry in the New Millennium" compiled by Raadia Mukadam, published in *Express Travel and Tourism*, Mumbai, 1-15 February, 2000.

Raina Dr. Chaman Lal, Interview conducted on Cultural Significance of Tourism at 2 KH 19, Shastri Nagar, Ajmer on 22 November, 2003.

Satish Kumawat, Chairman Hotel Association of Jaipur, Inaugural Address at Hotel Tech. Exhibition, 17-19 December at Jaipur.

Sen Gupta, Former Director General, Tourism, Government of India, at Seminar organised by I.A.T.O. "Tourism Challenges in the New Millennium 2000" at New Delhi, January, 2000.

Shane J. Hunt, Manager Marketing and Sales, Cristopher Frieean Communication Manager, Asia Pacific for Walt Disney, attraction interviewed by Navin Tairo, published in *Express Travel and Tourism*, Mumbai, 1-15 September, 2000.

Subhash Goyal, President of I.A.T.O., Address at 15th I.A.T.O. Annual Convention, Jaipur, 4-7 December, 2000.

Sharad Pawar, Honourable Minister of Civil Aviation, Government of India, Address at Seminar organised by I.A.T.O. "Tourism Challenges in the New Millennium 2000", New Delhi, January, 2000.

Sushil Gupta, M.D. Asian Hotels and Hyatt, New Delhi,

interviewed by Sangita M. Malhan, published in *Times of India*, New Delhi, July 28, 1999.

Uma Bharati, Former Minister of Tourism, Government of India, inaugural address at XV Annual Convention of I.A.T.O., Jaipur, 4-7 December, 2000.

V.A.P. Mahajan, Former Director of Tourism, Goa and MD of Goa Tourism Development Corporation, interviewed by Umesh Lutharia, published in *Express Travel and Tourism*, Mumbai, 1-15 July, 1999.

Vijay Pathran, Sales Manager, India Star Cruises, interviewed by Seema Pillai, published in *Express Travel and Tourism*, Mumbai, June 16-30, 1999.

PERIODICALS, JOURNALS, MAGAZINES AND NEWSPAPERS

- Annals of Tourism Research
- *Asia Travel Trade*—New Delhi and Malaysia
- *Asian Panorma*, New Delhi
- *Business world*—Special Supplements
- *Commerce*—Special Supplements
- *Cross-Section* Publications, New Delhi
- *Eastern Economist*—Special Supplements
- *Explore India*, New Delhi
- *Eve's Weekly*—Special Supplements
- *Express Travel and Tourism*—Special Supplements
- IGNOU's Study Material on Tourism
- *India Today*—Special Supplements
- *Indian Journal of Marketing*
- *Indian Journal of Tourism and Hotel Management*
- *Indian Journal of Tourism Management*
- *Intelligent Hotelier* : Andheri (East), Mumbai
- *International Journal of Hospitality Management*
- *International Journal of Management and Tourism*
- *Jet Wing*, Mumbai
- *Journal of Industry and Trade*
- *Outlook Traveller*, New Delhi
- *Rajasthan Atithi*
- *Rajasthan Sujas*
- *Safari*—India, New Delhi

- *Swagat*—Indian Airlines, New Delhi
- *TAAI Travel News*, A Journal of TAAI
- *The Economic Challenger*, Ajmer
- *The Economic Scene*
- *The Economic Times*—Special Supplements
- *The Financial Express*—Special Supplements
- *The Hindu*—Special supplements
- *The Hindustan Times*—Special supplements
- *The Indian Express*—Special supplements
- *The Nav Bharat Times*—Special supplements
- *The Rajasthan Patrika*—Special supplements
- *The Times of India*—Special supplements
- *Travel Mail*, New Delhi
- *Travel Links*, Ram Publication, New Delhi
- *Travel Research Journal*
- *Travel Talk*, New Delhi
- *Tourism Management*
- *Tourism Recreation Research*
- *Tourism and Wildlife*, New Delhi
- *U.S. Travel Data Centre Outlook for Travel and Tourism*, Washington
- *World of Travel and Tourism*, New Delhi
- *World Tourism Statistics*, W.T.O., Madrid
- *Yojana*, New Delhi

COMPACT DISK (AUDIO AND VIDEO)

- Glimpses of Rajasthan

WEB-SITES ON TOURISM

- www.123world.com/Tourism/
- www.heritageforfamilies.com/
- http://www.travelsolver.com
- mav.net/phil/tourism-shtml
- www.univ.edu/Tourism/wacky.html
- www.world-tourism.com/-10k
- www.theinfoguide.com/-15k

Index